VISUAL QUICKSTART GUIDE

POCKET PC

C. P. Collins and Tracy Brown

 Peachpit Press

Visual QuickStart Guide
Pocket PC: Visual QuickStart Guide
C. P. Collins and Tracy Brown

Peachpit Press
1249 Eighth Street
Berkeley, CA 94710
510/524-2178
800/283-9444
510/524-2221 (fax)

Find us on the World Wide Web at: http://www.peachpit.com
To report errors, please send a note to errata@peachpit.com

Peachpit Press is a division of Pearson Education

Editor: Karen Reichstein
Technical Editor: Jason Dunn
Production Coordinator: Becky Winter
Compositor: Jerry Ballew
Indexer: Joy Dean Lee
Cover Design: The Visual Group
Cover Production: George Mattingly

ISBN 0-321-19727-5

9 8 7 6 5 4 3 2 1

Printed and bound in the United States of America

For Grendel

Special Thanks to:

Karen Reichstein for her upbeat encourage-ment, laid back style, and downright fine handling of the whole project; Marjorie Baer and Nancy Ruenzel for continuing to believe in and support us; Mike Meehan for his persistence and good humor; Jason Dunn for his eagle eye and crucially helpful store of Pocket PC knowledge; and Becky Winter and Jerry Ballew for their terrific work in laying out the book.

The authors would like to acknowledge the helpful facilities and services provided by The Iowa City Public Library, The Java House, Avalon Networks, The Riviera Hotel and Casino, Area 51, The Little A 'Le' Inn, and the Sands Convention Center.

TABLE OF CONTENTS

TABLE OF CONTENTS

TABLE OF CONTENTS

TABLE OF CONTENTS

INTRODUCTION

Let's get some perspective here: A mere decade ago, a computer cost upwards of a thousand dollars. It was ugly and heavy. It whined, it crashed all the time, and it was extremely beige. Maybe there was a 40MB hard drive and 16MB of memory. The thing wheezed along, offering Windows 3.1 as the interface. Often it made you angry. (We're not talking to Mac people here—they found a more elegant path long ago.)

Today, for far less money, you can buy a faster, more powerful, and more reliable machine that you can hold in your hand. (Notice we didn't say "Palm.") This marvel, bearing all the heft of a tuna salad sandwich, hardly ever has a system problem. It can converse with other devices and the Internet through, in some cases, thin air. It's an address book, scheduler and calendar, word processor, email center, photo album, personal stereo system, Web browser, scratch pad, and you can waste all your time playing games on it. You can buy a plane ticket, read thousands of periodicals, or donate to charity with it. In some places, you can use it to vote. The computer revolution is succeeding.

But doggone it, these handheld devices are still machines, and we're impatient with machines— and probably always will be, no matter how smart they get. Think of a book.

A book is a perfect technology. It's portable, attractive, full of juicy thoughts, and it has more than 500 years of proven worth as a technique of communication. But any machine nowadays is a snapshot of a frantic technical culture—who knows where hand-held devices are going? And why have you bought one?

It's a tragic extravagance to spend $300 or more for a beeping, blinking day planner if you still keep calendars and illegible sticky notes all over your desk. You have to integrate it into your lifestyle, or it'll just lie there smirking and wasting potential. The thing to do is take control and find out how to utilize the amazing services your new handheld device is brimming over with. Focus on what you want done and master the way to do it. Then go on about your life.

How to use this book

The idea behind this book is to predict what most people will want to do with their Pocket PCs—don't you wish there was a better name for them?—and describe how to do those things in a way that's easy to follow, while illustrating the steps with hundreds of screen shots. The book covers all the essential Pocket PC software and settings, along with some pointers to third-party software and accessories. We've tried to use a friendly, informal tone throughout.

How to start? Use the index, the Table of Contents, or a "flip test" to find out how to do stuff—then stop reading and go to it.

What you should already know

All we assume here is that you have a Pocket PC that runs the Pocket PC 2003 operating system, or are about to buy one. No prior knowledge about them is required. We also assume that you own or have used a Windows computer and know how to work a mouse, click on menus, and so on. If not, you can just ignore us when we talk about computers.

Let us know what you're doing with your Pocket PC in an email to xochi@avalon.net.

Meet the Pocket PC

Before we get into how to run programs, adjust settings, and integrate the Pocket PC into your life, in this chapter we give you an overview of the device itself—its hardware, built-in software, and the potential for expanding its capabilities with add-on technologies.

When you first turn it on

Your device shipped with the battery partially charged, and you should charge it more before settling down to play with it. Plug the AC adapter cord into your device and into an outlet. (If your model will only charge in the cradle, charge it there, but don't connect the cradle to the computer yet.) Let it charge for at least half an hour. Four hours will fully charge it.

The temptation will be there to just turn it on and start messing around. The first thing that happens is that the machine will ask you to tap the screen to set it up. Follow the instructions to calibrate your taps and keep tapping Next to get through the tutorial. Then—like anyone would, coming out of suspended animation— the Pocket PC will want to know where it is. Follow the instructions for choosing your time zone and set the date and time by tapping on the date line under the Start button.

You'll also need to install the ActiveSync software on your computer *before* connecting the cradle to your computer.

A Look at the Hardware

Because there are so many different models, the exact makeup of the Pocket PC hardware—the physical device itself—varies somewhat. The device shown in **Figure 1.1** is an HP iPAQ 5500. It shows typical hardware features found on many Pocket PCs, plus a few extras built in.

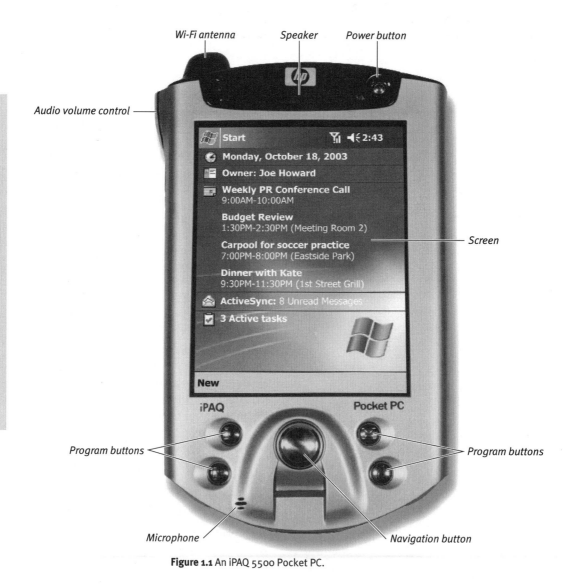

Figure 1.1 An iPAQ 5500 Pocket PC.

Figure 1.2 The stylus is what you use to tap the screen.

Getting used to a different screen

Notice that your computer screen is wider than it is tall—landscape orientation. The Pocket PC screen's portrait orientation—taller than it is wide—is made necessary by the shape of the human hand and the way it attaches to the arm. You couldn't hold the device securely if it the screen were sideways. Having a tall screen makes it hard to view Web sites—which are designed to be viewed on landscape screens. On the Pocket PC, you often end up scrolling left and right to read news articles, for example. Pocket Internet Explorer offers viewing options that can help ease this problem, and some "mobile" Web sites are formatted for easier viewing on Pocket PCs (see Chapter 12 for more the Pocket PC and the Web).

The screen

Most Pocket PCs have a color display screen that measures between 3.5 and 4.0 inches diagonally. The display is 320 pixels tall by 240 pixels wide (pixels are the individual points of light that create the display). That's not much room. In comparison, your PC's screen display is probably 800×600 pixels, if not $1{,}024 \times 768$—up to ten times the screen area of your Pocket PC. Nonetheless, the Pocket PC display is surprisingly bright and readable. The screen is touch-sensitive and responds to input you make through the stylus.

The stylus

The stylus is what you use to interact with your Pocket PC, from tapping on programs and files to writing emails. You should receive at least one stylus with your Pocket PC (**Figure 1.2**).

✔ Tips

■ As you can imagine, days, weeks, and years of tapping and dragging over anything with anything will cause wear. You can—and should—buy screen protectors while your screen is still unmarred. Screen protectors are thin, clear plastic sheets that stick to your screen to take the brunt of your stylus activity (see Appendix C).

■ Don't press too hard with the stylus. You'll quickly get a feel for how sensitively the screen responds.

■ Pocket PC manufacturers gravely warn against using anything other than the stylus to interact with the screen, but in a pinch, there's no harm in gently tapping with your fingernail. Don't ever use a pen or metal object, though.

A LOOK AT THE HARDWARE

The buttons

The Pocket PC has the following physical buttons on its face, as shown in **Figures 1.3** and **1.4**.

Figure 1.3 Press the power button to turn it on.

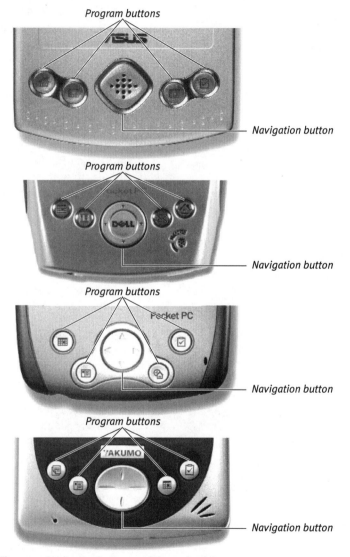

Figure 1.4 Application buttons and the navigation button vary in arrangement from model to model.

Power button. The one at the top is usually the power button. You turn your device on and off with this. Don't worry about shutting down your device prior to turning it off, or saving or closing applications beforehand. Unlike a regular computer, everything in a Pocket PC is always automatically saved and stored away safely. In fact, if you turn it off with programs running, when you turn it back on those programs will still be running, as if you'd never been away. In fact, you can't really turn the thing off at all! The power button puts the device in "suspend mode," where it's still running on minimum power. So, even when the device is "off" and you're not using it, it's still burning battery power.

Program buttons. Toward the bottom of the Pocket PC's face, the four small buttons are program buttons, or application buttons, and the middle one is a navigation button. The shapes and arrangements of these vary from model to model. Each program button is pre-set to launch applications, typically Calendar, Contacts, Inbox, and Notes.

Navigation button. This works kind of like a joystick. Pressing along its edges moves the screen around within a program. For example, pressing on the bottom of it scrolls down in most programs. Pressing the center of the navigation button selects an option that is highlighted—like double-clicking a file on your computer or tapping one on your Pocket PC.

✔ Tips

■ You can reprogram the application buttons to start whichever programs you want (see Chapter 2).

■ The program buttons also turn on the device when it's off and immediately start their associated applications. This can be quite handy—you can open your email by pressing one button, for example.

A LOOK AT THE HARDWARE

Indicator lights

Depending on the model, lights on the Pocket PC blink and gleam to give you clues about what's going on with it (**Figure 1.5**).

Power indicator. On an iPAQ, for example, this light flashes when the device is charging and shines steady orange when it's fully charged. It flashes green to remind you of an event you entered in Calendar.

Bluetooth indicator. If your device has Bluetooth, a Bluetooth indicator light flashes blue when you have Bluetooth turned on (see later in this chapter for more on Bluetooth).

Wi-Fi indicator. If your device has built-in Wi-Fi networking, a light probably flashes to indicate that it has connected to a wireless link (see later in this chapter for more on Wi-Fi).

Slots and ports

The Pocket PC connects to other hardware, such as your computer or an expansion card, through slots and ports. You'll find these along the top, bottom, or sides of the device. The types of slots and ports on different devices vary, and may include ones for CompactFlash, Secure Digital Input/Output, and PC card. These expansion possibilities can add quite a bit to your Pocket PC experience. We discuss them in a little more detail later in the chapter and in still more detail in Appendix C.

All Pocket PCs have a charging/communication port at the bottom, and some iPAQs have an expansion pack connector (**Figure 1.6**).

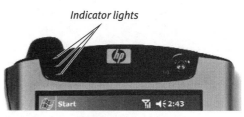

Indicator lights

Figure 1.5 Indicator lights tell you whether Bluetooth is on, Wi-Fi is connected, and whether your device is charging or fully charged.

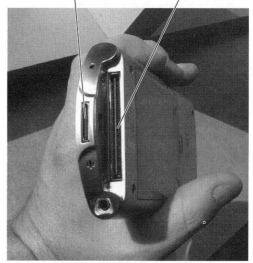

Expansion pack connector

Charging/communication port

Figure 1.6 The way to a Pocket PC's heart is through its charging/communication port and its expansion pack connector.

A LOOK AT THE HARDWARE

Figure 1.7 A tiny little microphone is all you need for dictation.

Charging/communication port. Some Pocket PCs have a dedicated charging port; others use the communication port to charge. The communication port is where your device connects to its cradle or cable in order to communicate with your computer and charge its battery via the cradle or cable's AC adapter.

Expansion pack connector. Here is where things get fancy. If your device has one of these, it means you can buy an expansion pack that will let you add all kinds of things, such as modems and other devices, by attaching expansion cards. See your documentation to see which expansion packs your device's manufacturer offers.

CompactFlash and SD slots. These are also for expansion cards (more on these later in this chapter).

✔ Tip

■ An entire industry has sprung up offering Pocket PC accessories, including modems, GPS systems, memory cards, digital cameras, radio receivers, and so on (see Appendix C).

Microphones and headphones

Many Pocket PCs have a tiny microphone built into them to allow you to record your voice for dictation—or reminders, notes to self, directions, or any other use you can think of. Its location on a device varies, but it looks something like **Figure 1.7**.

✔ Tips

■ You'll learn how to record audio in Chapters 7 and 8.

■ Most Pocket PCs also have a headphone jack where you can plug in to listen to music. A Pocket PC actually makes a perfectly decent MP3 player, even though its capacity to store lots of big files is limited. A memory card can greatly improve the situation—see Chapter 14 for more.

A LOOK AT THE HARDWARE

The speaker

It seems every machine nowadays needs to beep and squawk at you, and the Pocket PC is no exception. The location of the speaker varies from model to model (it will look similar to that shown in **Figure 1.1**). You control the volume in the software (see Chapter 2 for how).

✔ Tips

- Some devices have a physical volume control along one side, as shown in **Figure 1.8**. Check to see whether yours has one. If it does, it's much easier to use that instead of tapping around to adjust the volume setting.

- On devices that have a headphone jack, you can plug power-driven computer speakers into it and use your Pocket PC as a small MP3 desktop stereo.

The cradle

The cradle is where your device connects to and synchronizes files and data with your computer through the ActiveSync program (see Chapter 4 for more on ActiveSync). It's also where the device recharges its battery (**Figure 1.9**). You set the device down into the cradle until the cradle's connector snaps into the Pocket PC's charging or communication port. The cradle's AC adapter plugs into a wall outlet. You also connect the cradle's connector cable to the appropriate port in the back of your computer. Typically, this is a USB or a serial port.

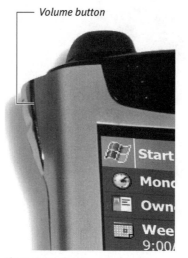

Volume button

Figure 1.8 Adjusting volume with a physical button is much more natural.

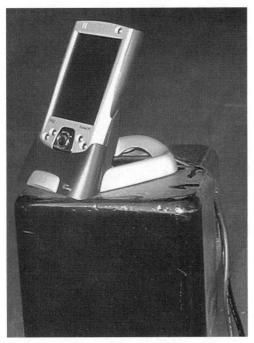

Figure 1.9 A happy machine resting in its cradle.

✔ Tips

- You can also charge most Pocket PCs by plugging the power cord directly into the device's charging port with an adapter included with your device.

- **Caution:** You have to do two things before you can connect your device and your computer with the cradle. First, you have to charge your device by plugging the AC adapter cord into a wall outlet and the device's charging port until you see the charging light blink on and off. Fully charging a battery typically takes four hours or so. Second, you have to install the ActiveSync software on your computer *before* you connect the cradle and put your device in it. Otherwise, it won't work. The ActiveSync software is on the CD-ROM that came with your device. See Chapter 4 for how to use ActiveSync.

- **Caution:** If your cradle has both a USB and a serial connector cable, only use one at a time (USB is faster). If you connect both at once, you'll confuse your computer.

- Some models of Pocket PC come with a cable instead of a cradle. It works the same. And any Pocket PC owner can buy an accessory cable to take on the road to avoid having to fit the awkwardly shaped cradle into a suitcase (see Appendix C).

A LOOK AT THE HARDWARE

The battery

A fully charged battery should give your Pocket PC anywhere from 4 to 16 hours of life before it needs recharging. Obviously, the more you use it—especially if you're engaging in energy-hungry activities like Wi-Fi Web surfing—the quicker you'll drain the battery.

✔ Tips

■ The best battery advice we have is to get in the habit of always putting the device back in its cradle at night (kiss it good-night if you like—who would know?) so that it's fully charged by morning.

■ Check your documentation to see if it's okay to plug the AC cord directly into your Pocket PC, bypassing the cradle entirely.

■ If you find yourself with a Pocket PC whose battery is low, and there's no spare electric outlet around, you can still charge its battery purely with energy from your computer (see Chapter 4 for how).

■ A few models allow you to replace a drained battery with a charged one. You'll need to buy the second battery from your model's manufacturer or a third-party vendor.

■ **Caution:** If you can and do replace the battery, swap it quickly. During the time when there is no battery in the device, the Pocket PC relies on a small backup battery to preserve everything that is stored in RAM memory—in other words, all your files and the programs you've installed. If you leave the battery out for too long—more than a few minutes—you'll lose everything in your Pocket PC except the programs it came with, and you'll have to reinstall what you lost. This is one reason to back up your Pocket PC regularly (see Chapter 4).

The difference between ROM and RAM memory

Your Pocket PC stores all its programs and data in one of two places: ROM or RAM.

ROM stands for Read-Only Memory. The programs that came with your device are stored in ROM. ROM is permanent—you can't destroy it through neglect.

RAM stands for Random Access Memory. All the files, documents, MP3s, and so on that you store in your device are normally stored in RAM. RAM is not permanent. If your battery dies completely, or if you perform a hard reset, you'll have to reinstall all the programs you've added to your device (see later in this chapter for more on hard and soft resets).

The good news is that after you restore power to the device, performing an ActiveSync connection with your computer restores all your files—your emails, contacts, documents, music, and so on—to the state they were in the last time you synchronized. Remember: all those files are stored on your computer as well as on your Pocket PC—that's what ActiveSync is for.

Flash ROM/File Store is a built-in way to store files in ROM. Many newer Pocket PCs come with this handy option. See Chapter 4 for more on using ActiveSync and backing up your device.

Resetting the Pocket PC

Occasionally, you may need to reset your Pocket PC. It may freeze up and not respond to your taps, for example. Or it may not turn on. Don't worry, it's probably not broken, but you do need to be careful at this point.

First, try turning it off and on with the power button. If that doesn't do anything, you have no choice but to reset. There are two types of reset, soft and hard, and you should try soft reset first.

Soft reset on the Pocket PC is like restarting your computer or pressing Ctrl+Alt+Delete. The device turns off and comes back on, but all the unsaved data it had going at the time is gone. Your programs and files will still be there if you perform a soft reset. To soft reset, press the tip of the stylus into the recessed reset button on your device for a few seconds until it springs back to life. If a soft reset doesn't fix your problem, you will have to do a hard reset.

Hard reset means sending your Pocket PC back to square one—the way it was when you first turned it on. Everything you ever did on it is gone and must be restored using ActiveSync.

The exact way to perform hard resets varies from model to model. It usually involves using the stylus to press the reset button while also pressing an additional program button or two. See your documentation for how to reset your device.

✔ Tips

- After you do a hard reset, your battery may be automatically disabled. If pressing the power button doesn't turn on your Pocket PC after you hard reset, put it in the cradle or otherwise connect it to AC power. Then press the reset button once more. It should power on then. If not, trying taking the battery out and putting it back in again.

- If your device still isn't working right after you try everything mentioned here, it's time to call your manufacturer's tech support number. You may have to send the poor thing back to the factory.

A Look at the Hardware

A Look at the Software

Pocket PCs with the Pocket PC 2003 operating system, also known as Windows Mobile 2003, typically come with the software shown in **Table 1-1**. Some manufacturers pre-install other programs, such as the iTask program manager that comes with the newer iPAQs, and not all models will have every one of these programs pre-installed (but they should be on the included CD-ROM).

✔ Tip

■ Explore the CD-ROM that came with your device. You'll probably find an assortment of bonus software goodies ready to install.

Table 1.1

Pocket PC 2003 Programs

PROGRAM	DESCRIPTION
Calculator	A calculator, like the one in Windows
Calendar	Make appointments and keep your schedule
Contacts	Like a Rolodex, synchronizes with Outlook's Contacts module
File Explorer	Manages your device's files like My Computer or Windows Explorer
Inbox	The Pocket PC email program, synchronizes with Outlook
Beam	Controls how your device uses its infrared port to beam files to other devices
Jawbreaker	An addictive visual game—easy to learn, hard to master
MSN Messenger	Lets you send Instant Messages
Microsoft Reader	Lets you read eBooks
Notes	The place to write notes, draw pictures, and record your voice
Pictures	Displays your digital photos and other JPG files
Pocket Excel	The Pocket PC version of MS Excel
Pocket Internet Explorer	For browsing the Web
Pocket Word	A word processor
Solitaire	Single-player card game
Tasks	Provides a to-do list
Text entry software	Offers four ways of entering text into your device via the stylus
Voice Recorder	Turns your Pocket PC into a digital dictation machine
Windows Media Player	Plays music and video

A Wide Range of Features

Not all Pocket PCs are created equal. Several companies make them, including HP, Dell, Toshiba, and Fujitsu. Some devices are bigger, faster, and have more memory than others. Some come with fancy stuff built in, such as Bluetooth and Wi-Fi transceivers, telephones, and digital cameras. Depending on how you think you'll use your device, you should have no problem finding just the right one for you. It would be hopeless to try and keep up with current models in a book like this—by the time it publishes, there will likely be many more models.

You should try and find the best deal on a Pocket PC that has all the features you want, without paying for features you don't think you'll need. The main thing you want is for your Pocket PC to run the current Microsoft Pocket PC OS (operating system), called Pocket PC 2003 by many Pocket PC manufacturers. Microsoft calls it Windows Mobile 2003—they're different names for the same thing.

Following are some of the features available in today's Pocket PCs. We discuss these in further detail in Chapter 10 and Appendix C.

A WIDE RANGE OF FEATURES

802.11b Wi-Fi

Wi-Fi stands for Wireless Fidelity. The 802.11b part of it is just the technical name of the particular wireless networking protocol it uses. Almost all wireless networks support 802.11b Wi-Fi, though you may occasionally encounter 802.11a and 802.11g. Wi-Fi capability means your Pocket PC can access wireless networks.

Some of the more expensive Pocket PCs come with Wi-Fi capability built into them. With others models, you can add Wi-Fi capability through add-on networking cards that plug into their expansion slots. Wi-Fi is probably the single coolest thing you can get for your Pocket PC. Wireless networks are proliferating everywhere. They work just like regular networks except that they communicate via radio waves instead of Ethernet or other types of cable. Depending on antenna strength and interference, such as trees, your Wi-Fi-enabled Pocket PC can pick up an Internet connection from a Wi-Fi network at a distance of anywhere from several feet to 100 yards or so.

Bluetooth

Bluetooth is the name of another wireless scheme. Its range is shorter—around 30 feet. Like Wi-Fi, Bluetooth can get your Pocket PC on the Internet. The way to do it is to partner your device with a Bluetooth-enabled cell phone or a Bluetooth-enabled computer that has Internet access. Bluetooth also allows two or more devices to easily connect to share files, contacts, business cards, and so on. Some Pocket PCs have Bluetooth built into them; with others, Bluetooth can be added via expansion cards. You can also find Bluetooth-enabled keyboards, mice, digital cameras, and camcorders.

Figure 1.10 The behemoth Hitachi NC1 is a full-featured Pocket PC and phone hybrid.

Figure 1.11 The Motorola MPx200 Smartphone is sleek-looking like a cell phone, but runs Windows Mobile software.

Pocket PC Phone Edition

This special version of the Pocket PC 2003 operating system is available on specialized Pocket PCs, such as the Hitachi NC1, that are also cell phones (**Figure 1.10**) offering full mobile phone capability and SMS (Short Message Service) text messaging. The technology of such "convergent" devices is still in its early stages, but surely this is the wave of the future.

Smartphone

Whereas a Pocket PC Phone Edition device is a Pocket PC that is also a cell phone, Smartphones, like the Motorola MPx200, are mobile phones that also function like Pocket PCs (**Figure 1.11**). They look like cell phones but have many features of Pocket PCs. You would probably prefer a Smartphone over a Pocket PC Phone Edition if you think you'd feel silly holding a Pocket PC up to your ear.

Digital phone card

A digital phone card is a CompactFlash card that lets you connect a Pocket PC to a data-capable cellular phone so you can use it to dial up an Internet connection. These typically come with a for-fee monthly dialup plan.

SD/SDIO

SDIO stands for Secure Digital Input/Output, a type of expansion slot built into most Pocket PCs. An SDIO slot accepts a postage stamp-sized SD (Secure Digital) card, which adds memory storage to your device. It will also accept SDIO peripherals, such as cameras and scanners.

A WIDE RANGE OF FEATURES

CompactFlash

Abbreviated CF, this is a bigger slot than SDIO that accepts memory cards and CF devices such as digital cameras, Ethernet cards, modems, GPS systems, and Wi-Fi and Ethernet networking cards. CF comes in two types, I and II, which differ in thickness. Some Pocket PCs require an expansion pack in order to accept CF add-ons.

PCMCIA (PC) cards

Developed for laptops, a PC card slot accepts add-ons such as digital cameras, modems, and network adapter cards. For some Pocket PCs, you can buy expansion packs that will allow them to accept PC cards. This can be really handy. For example, you can use the same PC card network adapter or modem for your laptop and your Pocket PC—just pull it out of one and stick it in the other. PC cards come in three types, according to thickness: I, II, and III.

MMC

MMC means MultiMediaCard. It is similar to an SD card and can store files for easy transfer between a Pocket PC and a computer.

Where to go from here

After you charge your Pocket PC and install the ActiveSync software onto your computer from the CD-ROM that came with your device, you're ready to ActiveSync if you like. ActiveSync establishes a connection between your computer and your Pocket PC and lets them share information about your device and files. ActiveSync is also how you install software on your device. Chapter 4 discusses ActiveSync in detail, including installing programs. If you're anxious to learn the basics of working with your Pocket PC, proceed to Chapter 2.

POCKET PC BASICS

With a Pocket PC, you can conceivably access all the information you need to do your job and run your life smoothly. Telephone numbers, email, your calendar and appointment schedule, to-do lists—even the Internet—are available to you in one compact device. But before you can use all these functions and features of the Pocket PC, you have to learn how to interact with it.

This chapter is an overview of the Pocket PC interface. Here, you will find out how to navigate your way to find and manage files and work with applications. You will also learn about beaming—sending information through thin air from your Pocket PC to another device—and customizing a few aspects to make your little machine better fit your needs and preferences.

✔ Tip

■ In this chapter, you will be using the "soft" (that is, onscreen) keyboard occasionally. If you find this to be an extremely slow and inefficient tool, fear not. In the next chapter, we cover the four different ways of entering text into your Pocket PC.

About the Today Screen

The Today screen (**Figure 2.1**) appears by default when you turn on your device and follow the set-up instructions. The Today screen is like a personal assistant: Each day, it tells you what appointments you have, whether you have new emails, and what tasks are on your to-do list. The Today screen is similar in function to Outlook Today in Microsoft Outlook 2000 and later. Note the prompt for owner information: Once you enter your information in your device, it appears here.

At the top of the Today screen, you see the Start button, volume control, clock, and a connectivity indicator (which you learn more about in Chapter 10). If you don't see your name on the Today screen, you haven't entered your owner information yet.

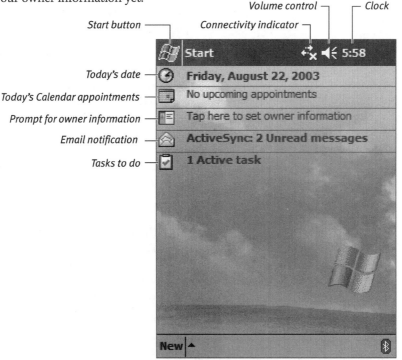

Figure 2.1 The Today screen lets you see all your important information—like tasks, unread emails, and upcoming appointments—all in one place.

Tap the 123 key to open the numeric keyboard

*Tap here to make the keyboard go away,
revealing a check box behind—tap it
again to bring back the keyboard*

Figure 2.2 When you first start up your Pocket PC, you're prompted to enter your owner information.

Figure 2.3 Tap this screen, and the Today screen appears.

To enter owner information:

1. Tap "Tap here to set owner information" if that is showing. Otherwise, tap Start > Settings > Owner Information to access the Owner Information screen.

2. Make sure the Identification tab at the bottom of the screen is selected, and then tap inside the Name area.

   The soft keyboard appears.

3. Use the keyboard (tap the letters with your stylus) to fill in the various fields (**Figure 2.2**).

   (Hint: tap Shift 2 to access the @ symbol for your email address.)

4. Tap the "Show information when device is turned on" check box if you want your owner information to appear when your Pocket PC is turned on.

5. Tap the Notes tab if you want to add any additional information, such as an alternative contact number or an offer of a reward if someone finds and returns your Pocket PC.

6. Tap OK in the upper right-hand corner of the screen and turn off your device.

   Because we selected the check box in step 4, the owner information now appears in the My Info screen (**Figure 2.3**).

✔ Tips

- Tapping any of the items on the Today screen launches the application associated with that item. For example, tapping the email notification item opens the Inbox email program.

- You can always change your mind. Make changes to your owner information anytime by tapping Start > Settings > Owner Information.

- See Chapter 6 to learn about making appointments and adding tasks to your Tasks list. For more on emailing, see Chapter 12.

ABOUT THE TODAY SCREEN

To remove items from the Today screen:

1. Tap Start > Settings.

   The Settings screen appears. (We discuss the Start menu shortly.)

2. Tap the Today icon on the Personal tab to access the Today screen settings options.

3. Tap the Items tab at the bottom of the screen.

   A list of items appears on the Today screen (**Figure 2.4**).

4. Uncheck the box next to any item you do *not* want to appear on the Today screen and tap OK in the top right-hand corner of the screen.

   The unchecked item disappears from the Today screen (**Figure 2.5**).

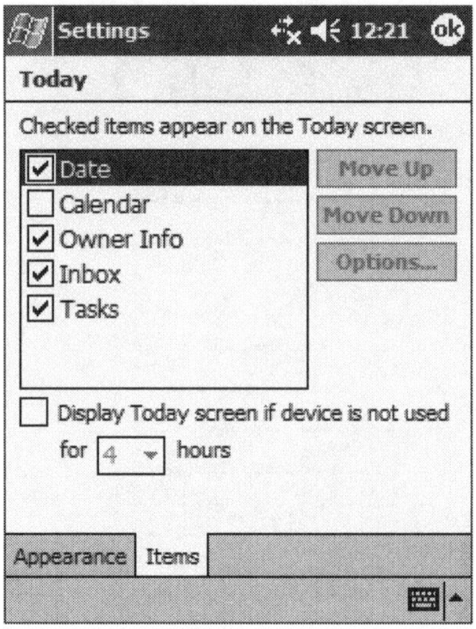

✔ Tip

■ You can choose to make the Today screen display after a certain number of hours. To set this option, check the box next to "Display Today screen if device is not used for ___ hours," and then choose the number of hours from the pull-down menu. This is just kind of a nice thing—without it, whichever program you were running when either you pressed the power button or the device went to sleep will still be showing. It's always nice to see the Today screen when you power up your device after a period of inactivity.

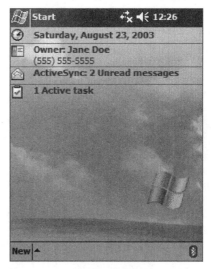

Figure 2.4 Deselect the check box to remove Calendar...

Figure 2.5 ... and the Calendar item disappears from the Today screen.

ABOUT THE TODAY SCREEN

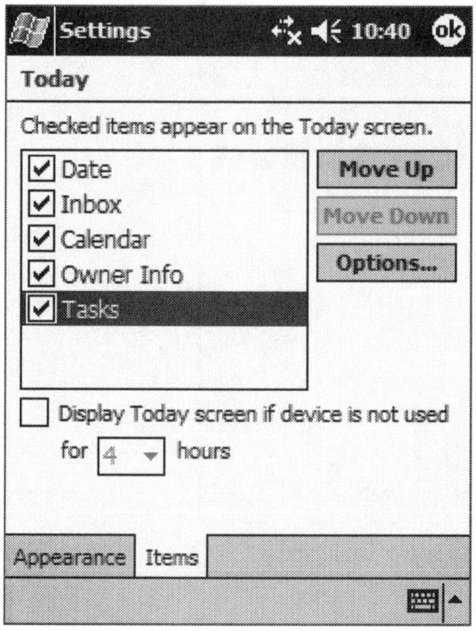

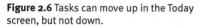

Figure 2.6 Tasks can move up in the Today screen, but not down.

Figure 2.7 The Tasks item is now first.

To change the order of items on the Today screen:

1. Follow steps 1–3 from the previous task, "To Remove items from the Today Screen."

2. Tap an item—but tap the word itself, such as Tasks, not the check box.

    There are three buttons to the right of the items list: Move Up, Move Down, and Options. The buttons that are available for the item you selected appear in bold (**Figure 2.6**).

3. Tap the Move Up button to make that item appear higher up in the Today screen, Move Down to make it go down in the list, or Options to see which options are available for the item.

4. Tap OK.

    The order of the Today screen items is changed (**Figure 2.7**).

✔ Tips

- As with Windows applications on your PC, options that are not available on the Pocket PC appear grayed out.

- The Calendar and Tasks items offer additional options. For Calendar, you can choose whether you want your next appointment, upcoming appointments, or all day events to display in the Today screen. For Tasks, you can select whether you want to see high priority tasks, tasks due today, or overdue tasks. For more on Calendar and Tasks, see Chapter 6.

ABOUT THE TODAY SCREEN

To change the background theme:

1. Tap Start > Settings > Today to open the Today Settings dialog box.

2. Select the Appearance tab.

   Depending on the make and model of your Pocket PC, you'll see at least two choices of themes: Windows Default (shown in Figure 2.1) and Spiral should be among them.

3. Select Spiral and tap OK (**Figure 2.8**).

   Your background theme changes to Spiral when you return to the Today page (**Figure 2.9**).

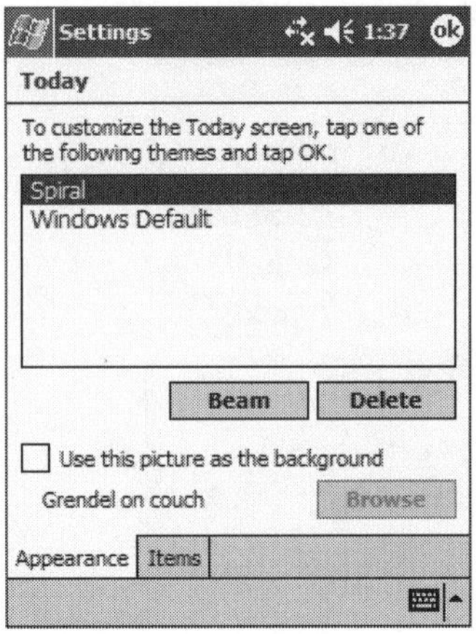

✔ Tips

- You can find more themes online at www.pocketpcthemes.com and www.pocketthemes.com or by searching your favorite search engine or Pocket PC software site for "Pocket PC Today themes." Also, check the CD-ROM that came with your device to see if additional themes are available on it.

- For the truly hardcore, there are animated themes. Solution's Animated Today (www.gigabytesol.com) makes it possible to have swimming fish or a hypnotic lava lamp for your theme.

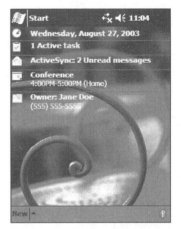

Figure 2.8 Select a new Today background theme.

Figure 2.9 With this new theme, the Today screen spirals out of control.

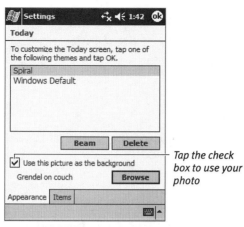

Tap the check
box to use your
photo

Figure 2.10 If you're not happy with the default background options, you can use one of your own photos as the Today background theme.

Name ▲	Folder
dock g	
grendel on couch	
grendel, tracy on porch...	

Figure 2.11 Choose from the photos stored on your Pocket PC.

Figure 2.12 In this example, we've used a picture of our dog, Grendel, as the background image. Be sure your photo, unlike this one, enables you to read your Today items. Here, we should have chosen the Windows Default theme.

To use a photograph as the background theme:

1. Tap Start > Settings > Today to open the Today Settings screen.

2. Check the "Use this picture as the background" box in (**Figure 2.10**).

3. Tap Browse to view a list of your Picture Files.

(If you haven't put any photos in your Pocket PC yet, see Chapter 15 to learn how.)

4. Tap the filename of the image you want (**Figure 2.11**).

You are returned to the Settings page. The name of the photograph file now appears under the check box.

5. Tap OK, and your photograph appears as your Today page theme (**Figure 2.12**).

✔ Tips

■ The Spiral theme displays white text in the Today screen, so use it for dark images. The Windows Default them, with its black text, is best used with light images.

■ See the sections later in this chapter on setting the clock and regional settings.

ABOUT THE TODAY SCREEN

23

Using the Start Button and Start Menu

The Start button is the gateway to your applications. Tapping the Start button drops down the Start menu. Both the Start button and menu are pretty much the same as their Windows PC counterparts, with a few differences. Most notably, the Start button is located in the top left-hand corner of the screen, rather than the bottom left-hand corner.

Also, the Start button on your Pocket PC is not used to shut down your device, as is the case with a computer. And the Start menu lists fewer applications than that on a computer—due to space constraints on your teeny, tiny screen—but the shortcut icons compensate nicely for this.

Opening programs with the Start button

The Start button is, of course, where you *start* programs—you just tap it and then tap the name of the program you want to run.

If the icon for the program you want is not shown on the row of recently used programs or in the drop-down list, tap Programs and select it from there—the program may have created a subfolder.

Use the scrollbar on the right-hand side of the Programs screen to view all the programs. Simply press and hold on the scrollbar button to drag it up and down.

When you open a new program, the Start button will still show on the screen, but the word "Start" will change to the name of the program. Tapping the Start button changes the program name back to "Start," and the Start menu is displayed.

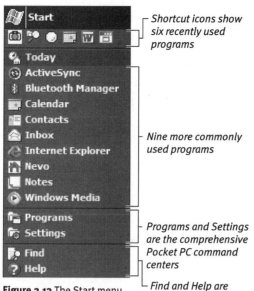

- *Shortcut icons show six recently used programs*
- *Nine more commonly used programs*
- *Programs and Settings are the comprehensive Pocket PC command centers*
- *Find and Help are always available*

Figure 2.13 The Start menu leads to just about everything in your Pocket PC.

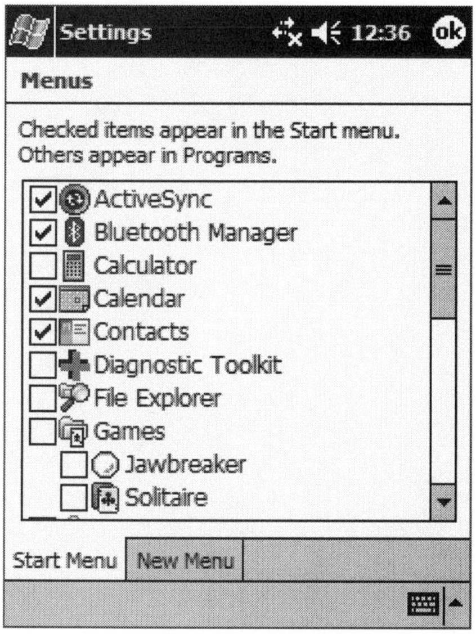

Figure 2.14 Choose which programs you want to appear on the Start menu.

To navigate Start menu options:

◆ The top section of the Start menu displays up to six shortcut icons, each representing an application you have recently used (**Figure 2.13**).

Tapping an icon automatically opens the particular application.

◆ The next section down includes up to nine of your commonly used applications.

◆ The next section, Programs and Settings, lets you access all the programs and settings on your device. We discuss these in detail later in this chapter.

◆ The bottom section of the Start menu contains Find, which lets you search for files on your Pocket PC, and Help, which launches the handy Help program.

✔ Tips

■ You're not stuck with the Start menu as it is. See the section on customizing it later in this chapter.

■ See the section on Help later in this chapter.

To customize the Start button:

1. Tap Start > Settings > Personal tab > Menus to open the Menus screen.

2. Tap to check the boxes next to the programs you want to display in the Start menu (**Figure 2.14**).

3. Tap OK. The programs you selected appear in the Start menu

✔ Tips

■ Deselect programs by unchecking them.

■ You can only select up to nine programs— naturally, you'll want to select the ones you use or plan to use the most.

USING THE START BUTTON AND START MENU

Using Menus

The menus in Pocket PC applications work pretty much as they do in Windows applications on your computer. Differences include the number and location of menus, how you access them, and the number of options available in each menu.

The menu bar you are used to seeing at the top of your computer's screen is found at the bottom of the Pocket PC's. Why? Not a clue. In keeping with the tininess of everything, there are fewer menus, and fewer choices within each menu.

When you right-click filenames and certain other items in Windows, a pop-up menu appears offering various options associated with the item. These options often include saving, sending via email, and copying and pasting. The Pocket PC also offers pop-up menus—but with no mouse, getting them to appear works a little differently.

To access program menus:

1. Start a program on your Pocket PC and notice the menu at the bottom of the screen (**Figure 2.15**).

2. Tap a menu to see its options (**Figure 2.16**).

3. Tap the menu command you want.

✔ Tips

■ Grayed-out options are not available.

■ The choice of menu commands will vary from program to program.

Figure 2.15 The Pocket Word menu bar shows a typical range of menu icons.

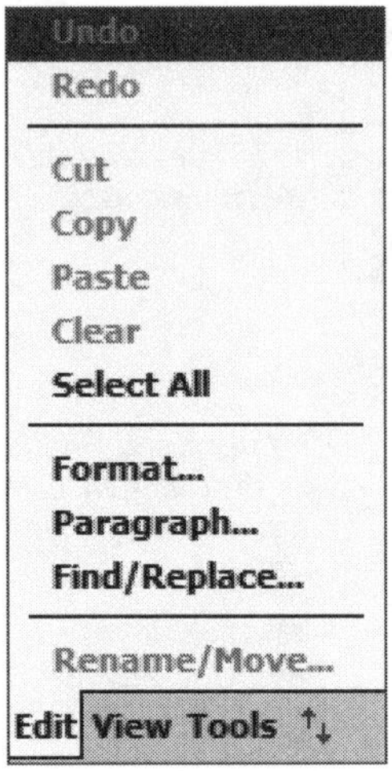

Figure 2.16 Tap Edit to access the Edit menu.

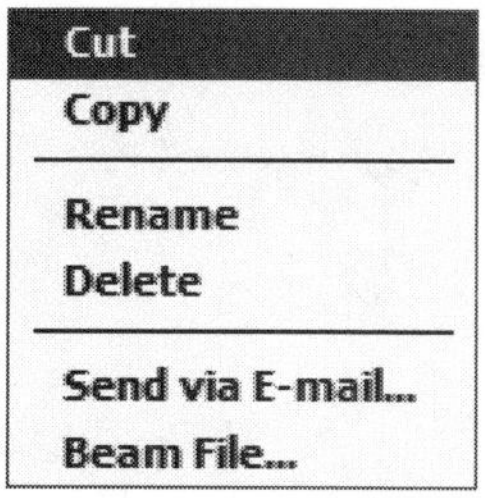

| Cut |
| Copy |
| Rename |
| Delete |
| Send via E-mail... |
| Beam File... |

Figure 2.17 A pop-up menu appears when you press and hold filenames and icons.

To access pop-up menus:

1. Tap Start > Programs > File Explorer to launch the File Explorer program.

2. Press and hold your stylus on a filename until you see a ring of colored dots appear around the tip of the stylus, followed by a pop-up menu.

3. Tap the option you want from the pop-up menu (**Figure 2.17**).

✔ Tips

■ File Explorer is the Pocket PC equivalent of My Computer or Windows Explorer. Tap a folder to access its files. We discuss File Explorer in more detail later in this chapter.

■ To find other timesaving pop-up menus, try pressing and holding on any item you see.

USING MENUS

Using Program Buttons

It's easy to forget about the program buttons—the physical buttons on the face of your Pocket PC—but they can be quite handy. They're the fastest and easiest way to launch programs. Your Pocket PC comes with programs already assigned to each button, but you can reprogram the buttons to start other programs that you use more frequently.

To reprogram program buttons:

1. Tap Start > Settings > Buttons to open the Buttons screen (**Figure 2.18**).

   Make sure the Program Buttons tab is selected.

2. In the list of Buttons, tap the button you want to reprogram.

3. Tap the "Button assignment" drop-down list and scroll to find the program you want to assign to that button (**Figure 2.19**).

4. When you find the program, tap it.

5. Tap OK.

   The button is now reprogrammed.

✔ Tips

■ Tap the Up/Down Control tab on the Buttons screen to access the Up/Down Control screen (**Figure 2.20**). Here, you can change the speed at which you scroll through the list of applications. The first option—"Delay before first repeat"—controls how quickly scrolling starts after you tap. The second option—"Repeat rate"—adjusts how fast the scrollbar moves.

■ The third tab at the bottom of the Buttons Settings page, Lock, brings you to the Lock screen where you can choose to disable the program buttons when your device is in Standby mode. Your device goes into Standby mode when it's been inactive for a certain period of time.

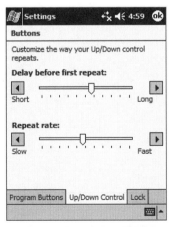

Figure 2.18 The Buttons screen shows what programs your program buttons are currently set to.

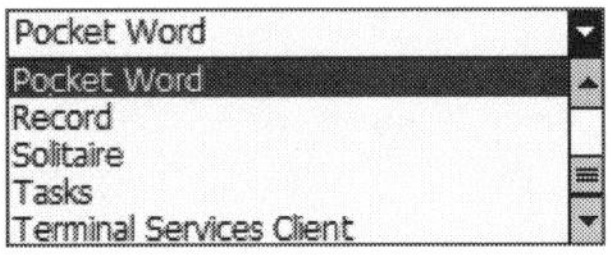

Figure 2.19 If you find yourself using an application frequently, you can assign it to a program button, which lets you launch the application instantly without having to navigate through menus.

Figure 2.20 Adjust your scrolling speed with Up/Down Control.

Figure 2.21 Choose from the list of topics in the general Help menu.

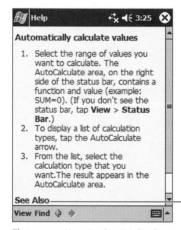

Tap See Also for more Help

Figure 2.22 Your Pocket PC displays the answer to your question—we hope.

Getting Help

Your Pocket PC comes equipped with a well-organized and easy-to-navigate Help system. As with the table of contents in a book, topics are arranged from broad to more specific, so you can tap your way through various selections until you've narrowed it down to the topic you seek.

To use the Help menu:

1. Tap Start > Help.

   The Help screen opens (**Figure 2.21**).

2. Scroll through the options to find the topic you need help with, and then tap that topic.

   You'll see subtopics of the broader topic you chose in the previous screen.

   If you're working in an application when you tap Start > Help, the device automatically narrows down Help to that topic. If that isn't what you want, tap the View menu and choose "All Installed Help" to open the main Help Contents screen.

3. Tap a subtopic to select it.

4. Continue narrowing your search by tapping subtopics, until you come to the screen that addresses your actual question (**Figure 2.22**).

5. Read the direction/explanation, and then tap the ⊗ button in the top right-hand corner when you're through.

✔ Tips

- Unlike close buttons in Windows, tapping the ⊗ button closes the window, but it does *not* close the application itself. So, it is actually a minimize button. See the section on closing applications later in this chapter.

continues on next page

GETTING HELP

- If you find you've navigated to an answer to the wrong question, tap the left-hand arrow in the menu bar to back up to broader topics.

- If you need further help with related topics, tap one of the "See Also" suggestions at the bottom of the final Help page in your search.

- See Appendix B for information on finding Pocket PC help online.

To use Help within a program:

1. Open a program, such as Pocket Word (**Figure 2.23**).

2. Tap Start > Help to open the Help menu.

3. From the list of Word-specific Help topics, tap a subtopic.

4. Continue tapping subtopics from the screens that appear until you have narrowed your search to a specific topic and receive a specific answer.

5. Follow the instructions you are given and tap the ⊗ button in the top right-hand corner to close the Help window.

Figure 2.23 Individual applications, like Pocket Word, automatically narrow down Help to topics pertinent to them.

Managing Files

You manage files on your Pocket PC in more or less the same way as you do on your computer. Your files are stored in folders that are viewable in File Explorer, which is similar to how files are stored and arranged in Windows. Files can be stored in subfolders (for example, My Pictures, Personal, or any folder you create), which helps organize them. You can open files, save files, and rename, copy, and paste them. And on your Pocket PC, you can even beam them to another handheld device—something most computers still cannot do.

To open a file:

1. Tap Start > Programs > File Explorer. The File Explorer screen appears (**Figure 2.24**).

2. Tap the filename you want to open. The application associated with the file launches and opens the file.

continues on next page

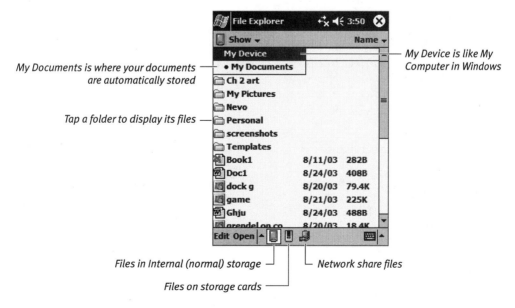

My Documents is where your documents are automatically stored

My Device is like My Computer in Windows

Tap a folder to display its files

Files in Internal (normal) storage

Files on storage cards

Network share files

Figure 2.24 File Explorer lets you access all your files.

✔ Tips

- Files and folders in File Explorer are stored somewhere within the root folder called My Device. My Device is similar to My Computer in Windows. It includes files and folders that your systems needs, such as program files. All of your documents are stored in the subfolder called My Documents.

- At the bottom of the File Explorer screen are three icons. 🔲 shows normal storage—files that are stored in RAM on your Pocket PC. 🔲 displays the files that are stored on storage cards, if any are installed. Some Pocket PCs, such as the newer iPAQs, allow you to use the device's ROM to permanently store programs and files (see Chapter 1 for more on ROM and RAM). 🔲 shows you a list of files available as files available on a network, called Network Share files (see Chapter 10 for more).

- By default, files and folders are sorted alphabetically by name (folders are listed before files, so folders and files are alphabetized separately). You can also sort by date, file size, or file type. Tap the Sort By drop-down list on the toolbar (**Figure 2.25**). (The word "Name" appears instead of "Sort By" if it's currently set to sort by name.) Then choose how you want to sort files.

- You can also manage your files from your desktop or laptop PC (see Chapter 4).

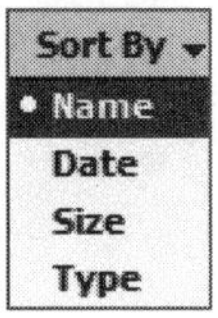

Figure 2.25 Select how you'd like your files and folders sorted.

To create a new folder:

1. Tap Start > Programs > File Explorer to launch File Explorer.

2. Tap Edit on the menu bar.

3. Tap New Folder.

4. Use the soft (onscreen) keyboard to name the folder.

Enter the name of the file   Go button

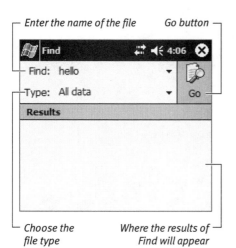

Choose the   Where the results of
file type   Find will appear

Figure 2.26 Use the Find function to search for a specific file.

Figure 2.27 Choose your file type.

To find a file:

◆ Open folders in File Explorer until you find what you need.

or

1. Tap Start > Find.

The Find screen appears.

2. Tap on the line next to Find and use the keyboard to enter the name of the file you seek (**Figure 2.26**).

3. Tap the down arrow next to Type to open the drop-down menu of applications.

4. Select the appropriate application for the file you seek (**Figure 2.27**).

If you don't know (or care) which application opens your file, choose All data.

5. Tap Go.

The results of the search appear in the Results section of the screen.

6. Tap the file in the Results section to open it.

The application associated with the file launches automatically.

✔ Tip

■ For a more sophisticated search, tap "Advanced…" at the bottom of your screen. This will bring you to the Advanced Options screen, which tells you how you can further specify your search.

MANAGING FILES

33

To rename a file:

1. Press and hold your stylus on the file you want to rename until you see a ring of colored dots followed by a pop-up menu.

2. Tap Rename (**Figure 2.28**) from the pop-up menu.

   The filename is highlighted and a flashing cursor appears at the end.

3. Insert the new filename over the existing one by typing the new name with the keyboard (or use your preferred text insertion method).

   or

   Tap in the space to the right of the flashing cursor, and then type to add to the filename or move the cursor to a new insertion point and edit the filename as necessary (**Figure 2.29**).

4. Tap elsewhere on the screen, and the new filename is saved (**Figure 2.30**).

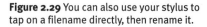

Figure 2.28 Tap Rename to rename a file.

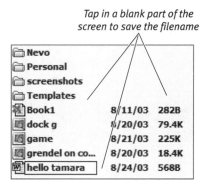

Figure 2.29 You can also use your stylus to tap on a filename directly, then rename it.

Tap in a blank part of the screen to save the filename

Figure 2.30 The new filename is saved.

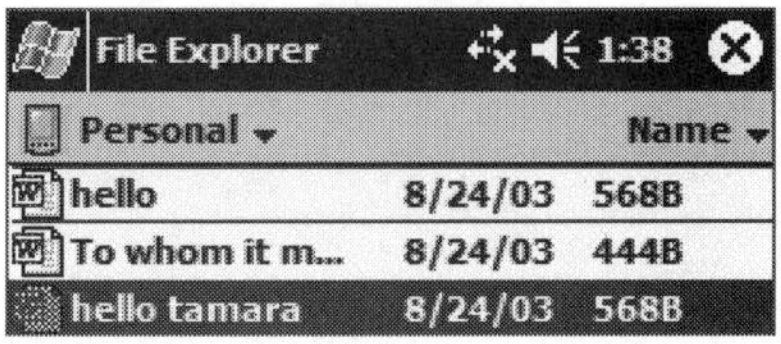

	File Explorer	⁺ᵡ ◀€ 1:38	✖
🖳	Personal ▾		Name ▾
📧	hello	8/24/03	568B
📧	To whom it m...	8/24/03	444B
📧	hello tamara	8/24/03	568B

Figure 2.31 Paste a file in a new location using the familiar Paste function.

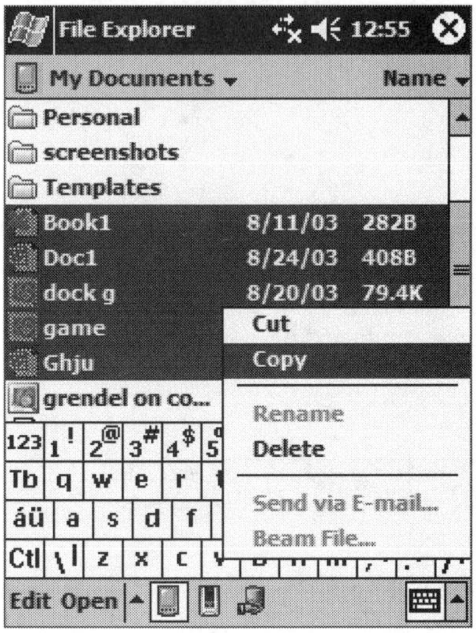

	File Explorer	⁺ᵡ ◀€ 12:55	✖
🖳	My Documents ▾		Name ▾
📁	Personal		
📁	screenshots		
📁	Templates		
📄	Book1	8/11/03	282B
📄	Doc1	8/24/03	408B
📄	dock g	8/20/03	79.4K
📄	game		Cut
📄	Ghju		Copy
📄	grendel on co...		
			Rename
			Delete
			Send via E-mail...
			Beam File...

123 1! 2@ 3# 4$ 5
Tb q w e r t
áü a s d f
Ctl \| z x c v
Edit Open

Figure 2.32 You can copy several files at once.

Refresh
View All Files

Paste
Paste Shortcut
New Folder

Figure 2.33 Selecting Paste Shortcut allows you to paste a shortcut to a file.

To copy a file:

1. Press and hold on the file you want to copy until you see a ring of colored dots followed by a pop-up menu.

2. Tap Copy on the pop-up menu.

3. Navigate to the folder or location where you want to save the copy of the file.

4. Press and hold the stylus on a blank section of the screen—away from all other files and icons—until a pop-up menu appears.

5. Select Paste from the pop-up menu, and the copied file is pasted in the new location (**Figure 2.31**).

✔ Tips

■ You can copy more than one file at a time, as you can using the Shift key in Windows. Simply press your stylus on the first file and drag down to select the files you want to copy. Then hold the stylus there until you see the pop-up menu. Select Copy, and all the selected files are copied (**Figure 2.32**). You can select nonconsecutive files by tapping Ctrl on the soft keyboard and then tapping files to select them. When you are finished selecting files, press and hold on any of the highlighted files to get the pop-up menu.

■ If you want to paste a shortcut to a folder or document, select Paste Shortcut instead of Paste (**Figure 2.33**).

MANAGING FILES

To delete a file:

1. Press and hold on the file you want to delete until you see a ring of colored dots followed by a pop-up menu.

2. Tap Delete in the pop-up menu.

✔ Tip

■ Make sure you mean it when you delete a file on your Pocket PC. There is no Recycle Bin—if you delete something, it's gone. However, it may still be on your computer, in which case you can restore it to your Pocket PC (see Chapter 4). But first make a copy of the file and place it in a different folder than the synchronized one—otherwise, ActiveSync assumes you want to delete it from your computer, too.

To create a new file:

◆ Tap New at the bottom of the Today screen and tap the type of file you'd like to create (**Figure 2.34**).

   or

◆ If you already have a file open, tap New in the menu bar of the program you're working in—Pocket Word, for example (**Figure 2.35**).

   You are asked whether you'd like to save the file you had been working in. Tap Yes, No, Cancel, or Save As.... See the next section "To save a file" for more on saving files.

✔ Tip

■ Each time you open an application, such as Word or Excel, you automatically create a new file.

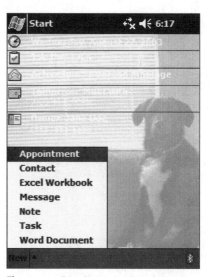

Figure 2.34 Creating a new Appointment for the Calendar program from the Today screen.

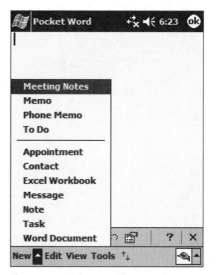

Figure 2.35 Pocket Word lets you choose what kind of document to create.

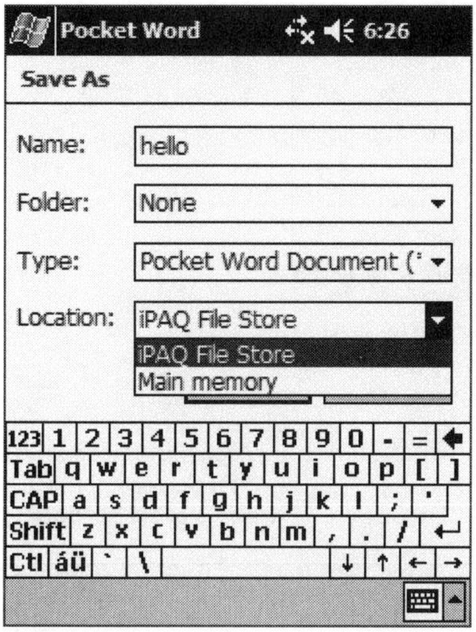

Figure 2.36 If you have a Pocket PC that has a user-accessible Flash-ROM area, you can save a document to ROM, where it'll be protected from accidental deletion or hard resets.

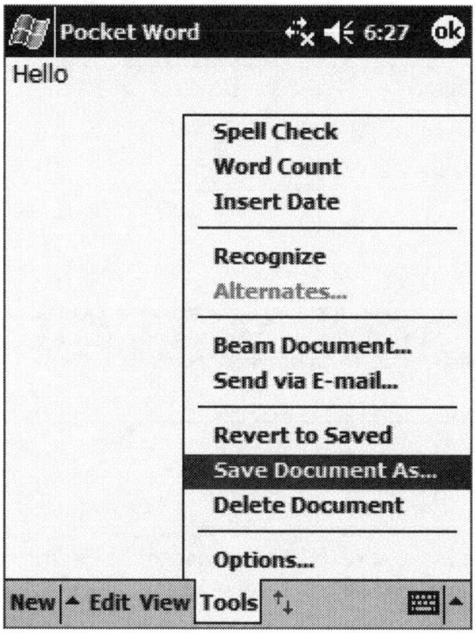

Figure 2.37 To save a file with a specific filename, tap the Save Document As... menu command.

To save a file:

◆ Files are saved automatically when you tap ⊗ in any application.

✔ Tips

■ If you are using an iPAQ and want to save something to ROM—meaning save it to a place where it won't be deleted even if you have to do a hard reset—tap Tools > Save As..., and select iPAQ File Store in the Location drop-down menu (**Figure 2.36**).

■ To save a file with a specific filename or in a specific folder, tap Tools and select Save As.... In Word, it will read, "Save Document As...," and in Excel it will read, "Save Workbook As..." (**Figure 2.37**).

■ When you create a new document while already working on a document in the same application, you are prompted to save your work on the document you are currently working on.

MANAGING FILES

Beaming

Beaming is one of the Pocket PC's most convenient and most *Star Trek*-like features. Beaming is a fast, easy way to share information—documents, emails, contacts—by simply pointing the infrared ports of two devices at each other and tapping a button. The infrared port is located at the top of your device.

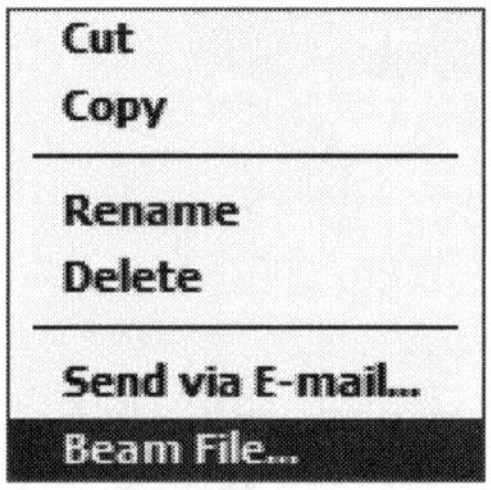

To beam a file:

1. Tap Start > Programs > File Explorer. The File Explorer screen appears.

2. Press and hold the tip of your stylus on the file you want to beam.

3. From the pop-up menu that appears, tap Beam File (**Figure 2.38**).

4. Point the top of your device toward the top of the device to which you want to beam your file.

   Your Pocket PC begins searching for an infrared port (**Figure 2.39**). When it finds one, it sends the beam (**Figure 2.40**).

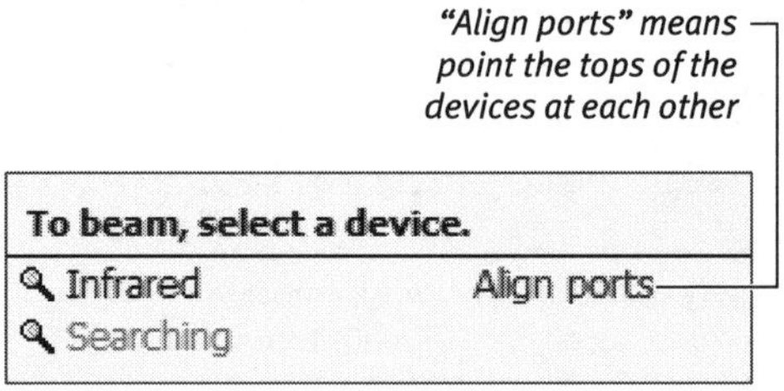

✔ Tips

- Beaming can be a little touchy, as the signal is rather weak (beaming only works within a few feet). If your beaming attempts fail, try moving the two devices closer.

- Pocket PC 2003 devices are set to receive beams by default, though you have to tap Yes to actually accept them. To double-check your setting (**Figure 2.41**), tap Start > Settings > Connections tab and tap the Beam icon.

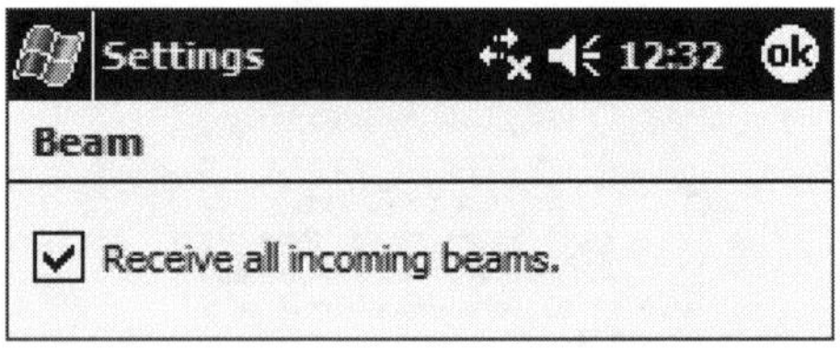

| Cut |
| Copy |
| Rename |
| Delete |
| Send via E-mail... |
| Beam File... |

Figure 2.38 Tap Beam File on the pop-up menu.

"Align ports" means point the tops of the devices at each other

To beam, select a device.
🔍 Infrared   Align ports
🔍 Searching

Figure 2.39 The Pocket PC is looking for a device to beam to.

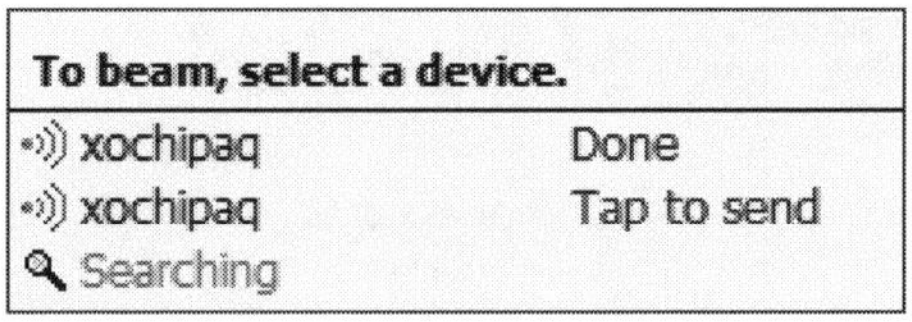

To beam, select a device.
•)) xochipaq   Done
•)) xochipaq   Tap to send
🔍 Searching

Figure 2.40 Beam complete!

Settings   12:32 ok
Beam
☑ Receive all incoming beams.

Figure 2.41 Make sure this box is checked, or your Pocket PC won't be able to receive beams.

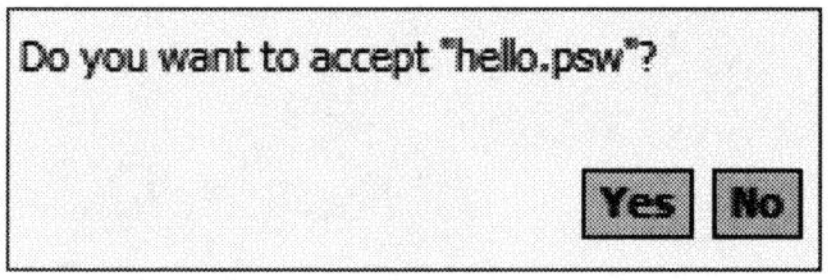

Do you want to accept "hello.psw"?

Yes No

Figure 2.42 Your Pocket PC asks whether you want to receive the beam.

- With the Pocket PC 2003 operating system, Palm devices and Pocket PCs can beam each other. You can also beam between a Pocket PC and any mobile phone that supports OBEX, a standard used by most phones, as well as Palm-based PDAs.

To receive a beam:

1. Point the top of your device (the infrared port) at the top of the device that is trying to beam you.

   A dialog box appears on your Pocket PC screen, asking whether you want to accept the beamed file (**Figure 2.42**).

2. Tap Yes to accept the file.

✔ Tip

- When you receive a beam, the beamed item is usually automatically saved in your My Documents folder. Beamed contacts are automatically available to use in your Contacts program.

BEAMING

Using Applications

You can get a lot out of your Pocket PC by using what you already know about PC applications. You work with Pocket PC applications in much the same way as you do with those running on your computer. You open them, close them, minimize them, and switch between them.

To open an application:

◆ Tap the Start button and tap the application you want to open from the list.

or

1. If you don't see the program you want, tap Start > Programs to access the Programs screen.

2. Tap the icon of the application you want to open.

   Note that there are three tabs of applications.

   or

1. Tap New at the bottom of the Today screen.

2. Select the type of application file you want to create (**Figure 2.43**).

To close an application:

1. Tap Start > Settings > System tab > Memory.

   The Memory screen opens.

2. Tap the Running Programs tab to view a list of running applications.

3. Tap the application you want to close (**Figure 2.44**), and then tap the Stop button.

   Repeat to close additional programs.

4. Tap OK when you have selected all the applications you want to close.

   or

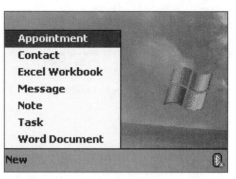

Figure 2.43 When you create a document with the New icon, the program for that document is automatically launched.

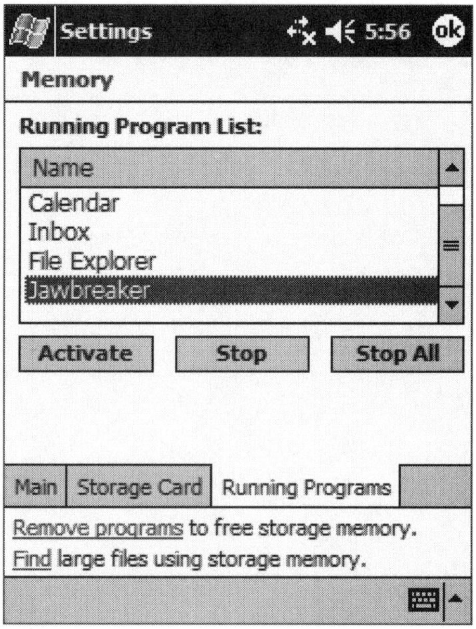

Figure 2.44 The addictive game Jawbreaker must be stopped!

USING APPLICATIONS

Figure 2.45 You can also close a program via iTask (iPAQ only).

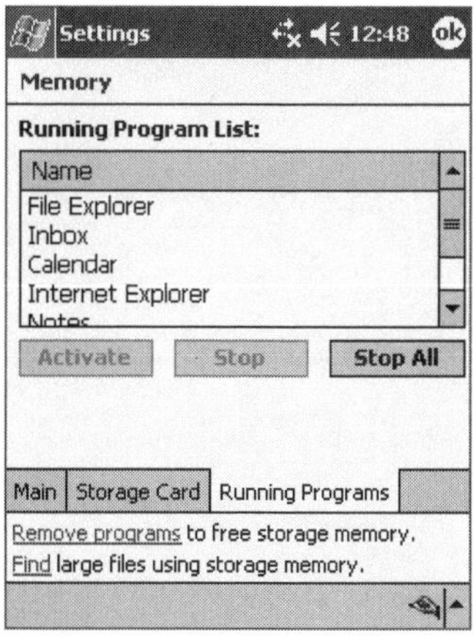

Figure 2.46 Use the Stop All button to quit all running applications.

The iPAQ's iTask

iPAQ users have a useful application called iTask, which you can use to launch applications as well as manage applications already in use.

 You can launch iTask in two ways: by tapping Start > Settings > iTask, or by pushing the 🖉 iTask button on the face of your iPAQ.

1. If you have an iPAQ, push the 🖉 iTask button.

2. In the iTask Task Manager, press and hold on the program you wish to close.

3. From the pop-up menu that appears (**Figure 2.45**), tap Close This Task.

✔ Tips

■ You can also use the soft keyboard to tap Ctrl+Q to quit some applications.

■ The ⊗ button in the top right-hand corner of applications looks like a close button, but in fact is just a minimize button. When you tap it the program disappears, but doesn't stop running.

To close all applications:

1. Tap Start > Settings > Systems Tab > Memory to open the Memory screen.

2. To view a list of running applications, tap the Running Programs tab.

3. Tap Stop All to close all running applications (**Figure 2.46**).

4. Tap OK.

 or

1. If you have an iPAQ, push the 🖉 iTask button on the face of your Pocket PC.

2. In the iTask Task Manager, press and hold on any program.

3. From the pop-up menu that appears, tap Close All Tasks.

To minimize an application:

◆ Tap the ⊗ button in the top right-hand corner of any running application to minimize it.

USING APPLICATIONS

To switch between applications:

◆ Tap the minimize button for each application until the one you want appears.

or

◆ Tap Start > Programs and select the application you want to work in.

or

1. If you have an iPAQ, push the iTask button on the face of your iPAQ.

2. From the list of running programs that appears in the iTask Task Manager, tap the program you want to switch to.

✔ Tips

■ See Chapter 4 for information on installing and removing applications.

■ There are third-party Pocket PC programs you can download that make it easier to see and control what applications are running. See Appendix A for more information on these.

Adjusting Other Basic Settings

The early stages of getting to know a new electronic device can be like starting a new courtship: there is only joy in having found compatibility, and you don't want to change a thing. Right now, you may not be able to think of anything that would make your Pocket PC better, but in time you may find yourself saying, "I love all that my Pocket PC has to communicate to me, but why must it do it so *loudly*?" And unlike in the dating world, you *can* change your Pocket PC—and you won't even offend it.

This section covers some general settings you can adjust to further customize your Pocket PC. Any settings not addressed in this section have been already covered in this chapter or will be in a relevant section elsewhere in the book.

To set the volume of notification sounds:

1. Tap Start > Settings > Personal tab > Sounds and Notifications (**Figure 2.47**) to open the Sounds & Notifications screen.

2. Tap your stylus at a point on the System volume slider (**Figure 2.48**). Tap to the left for quieter volume, and tap to the right for louder volume.

   or

   Press and hold your stylus on the volume slider and drag it left or right.

✔ Tips

- There are only six volume levels available, and they are indicated by the small vertical lines under the System volume bar. But you must tap the volume bar rather than these lines to adjust the volume.

- All the settings options are found in one of three tabs on the Settings page: the Personal tab (options that relate to your preferences); the System tab (settings to do with your device); and Connection (beaming and Internet settings).

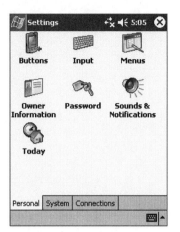

Figure 2.47 The Sounds and Notifications settings are in the Personal tab.

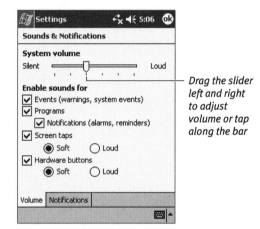

Drag the slider left and right to adjust volume or tap along the bar

Figure 2.48 Move the slider left for silence and right for top volume.

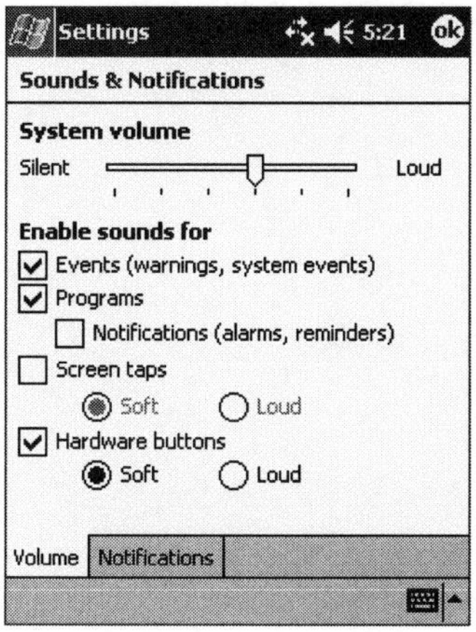

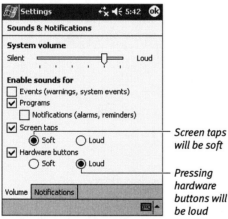

Figure 2.49 These choices mean there will sounds for Events, Programs, and hardware (program) buttons being pushed, but silence for screen taps and Notifications.

Figure 2.50 Select the Loud or Soft button to choose a loud or soft sound when tapping the screen or pressing a hardware, or program, button.

Screen taps will be soft

Pressing hardware buttons will be loud

To turn sounds on and off:

1. Tap Start > Settings > Personal tab > Sounds and Notifications to open the Sounds & Notifications screen.

2. In the "Enable sounds for" area, check or uncheck boxes to determine which events or activities you would like to be accompanied by a sound (**Figure 2.49**).

To adjust Pocket PC system sounds:

1. Tap Start > Settings > Sounds & Notifications to open the Sounds & Notifications screen.

2. Under "Enable sounds for," be sure the box next to "Screen taps" and "Hardware buttons" is checked.

3. Select the Soft radio button for a soft sound

   or

   Tap the Loud radio button for a loud sound (**Figure 2.50**).

✔ Tip

- When you tap Soft, you will actually hear the loud sound (because before you select Soft, you are in loud mode), and vice versa. But the adjustment changes once the settings are set.

ADJUSTING OTHER BASIC SETTINGS

To adjust regional settings:

1. Tap Start > Settings > System tab > Regional Settings (**Figure 2.51**). The Regional Settings screen appears.

2. Select the Region tab and scroll down the drop-down list to select your region and language (**Figure 2.52**).

3. Tap OK.

✔ Tips

■ When you select a region and language, check the Appearance samples and make sure that the currency, time, and date appear as you want them to.

■ You can adjust the way numbers, currency, time, and dates appear in your device by tapping the tab associated with that item and selecting the way you want the item to look. For example, to change the currency symbol from that of the American dollar to that of the Euro, tap the Currency tab and select Euro as the currency.

To set the clock to where you live:

1. Tap on the date item on the Today screen.

  or

  Tap Start > Settings > System > Clock to access the Clock Settings screen (**Figure 2.53**).

2. Tap the Home radio button.

3. Choose the appropriate time zone from the drop-down menu to the right of the Home clock and tap OK.

✔ Tip

■ The Pocket PC automatically sets the time to match your computer's clock every time you ActiveSync. Still, you can also adjust the time and date by hand by tapping the down arrows next to them in Clock Settings.

Figure 2.51 Regional Settings are located in the System tab.

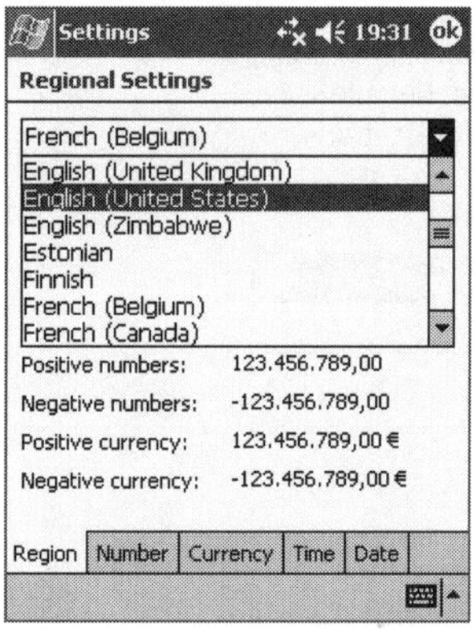

Figure 2.52 Select your language and region from the drop-down menu.

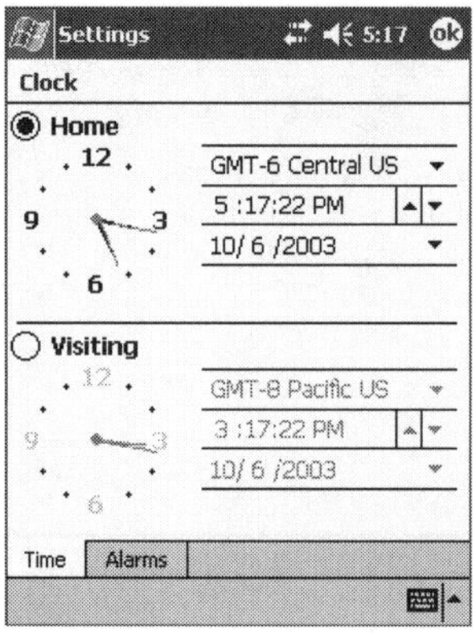

Figure 2.53 The Clock Settings screen is where you set the date and time.

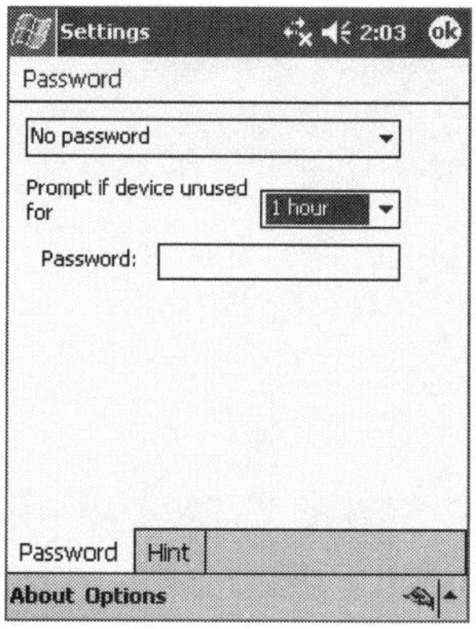

Figure 2.54 Choosing how long is long enough to require a password.

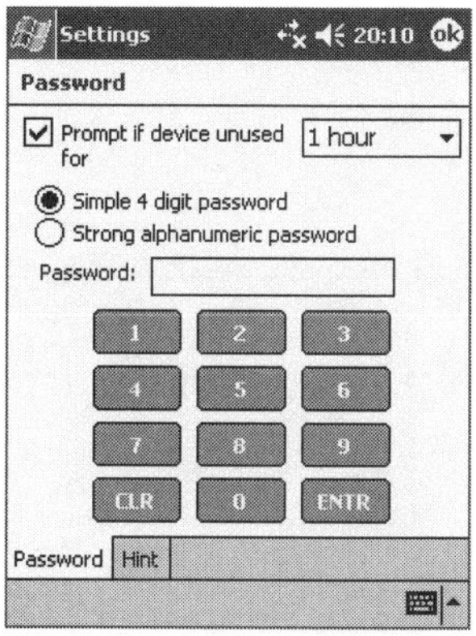

Figure 2.55 Enter your four-digit password when prompted by tapping the number pad with your stylus.

Making the clock analog

If you press and hold your stylus on the time display at the top of the Today screen, a pop-up menu appears. Here you can choose to make the clock appear like an old-time analog clock instead of a digital clock showing numerals. Be warned, however—it's so tiny as to be nearly unreadable.

To set the clock for travel:

1. In the Clock Settings screen, tap the Visiting radio button.

2. Choose the appropriate time zone from the drop-down menu to the right of the Visiting clock and tap OK.

✔ Tip

■ The Visiting clock feature is for travel. Its purpose is to let you maintain your Home time while switching temporarily to Visiting. However, it means all your appointments will change because the program assumes you made the appointments for local time. To avoid the whole issue, just travel the old-fashioned way: change the clock on your Home time and don't bother with Visiting time.

To password-protect your Pocket PC:

1. Tap Start > Settings > Password to open the Password tab of the Passwords Settings screen.

   The default is no password.

2. Check the box next to "Prompt if device is unused for."

3. From the drop-down menu to the right of this box, select how long you'd like your device to be shut off before it requests a password when turned back on (**Figure 2.54**).

4. Tap the "Simple 4 digit password" radio button if you want to set a password of four numbers.

   or

   Tap the "Strong alphanumeric password" to set a more complex password that includes numbers and letters.

5. Insert your four-digit password using the number pad that appears (**Figure 2.55**).

   or

continues on next page

ADJUSTING OTHER BASIC SETTINGS

Insert your alphanumeric password using the keyboard that appears (**Figure 2.56**).

6. Tap the Hint tab to enter a hint that may help you if you think you may one day forget your password.

7. Tap OK to set the password.

When prompted, after the inactive period you set in step 3, you will have to enter the password in order to use your device.

✔ Tip

■ **Caution:** If you set your device to use a password and then forget that password, there will be no recourse but to do a hard reset of your device, which means losing everything you ever entered in your device—although you will be able to restore it to the state it was in the last time you synchronized.

Figure 2.56 Use the keyboard to enter your alphanumeric password when prompted.

Biometric security on the iPAQ

Some iPAQs offer, depending on your point of view, the vaguely creepy or excitingly novel method of using your fingerprint as a password. To use biometric security, you have to "enroll" your fingerprint.

If your iPAQ has the biometric security feature, in the Passwords screen you will see additional fingerprint drop-down options. Choosing one of the fingerprint options prompts your device to ask you to begin "fingerprint training."

Tap Yes to begin fingerprint training. You will be shown a demo and then the Training screen will appear, in which you run your index finger several times down the biometric reader at the bottom of your device. The device determines whether your attempts are successful, as

 shown here.

Once your fingerprint is successfully enrolled, when your password is set to use your fingerprint, the device becomes accessible only after your finger is swiped across the reader.

This futuristic feature may sound neat, but it seems to us to be overkill, unless you truly have valuable secrets on your device. Still, your device would become unusable (without a hard reset) if your fingers were damaged. That's why it's a good idea to select the "Fingerprint OR PIN option" or "Fingerprint OR Password" option. That way, you can always access the device by entering the PIN or password.

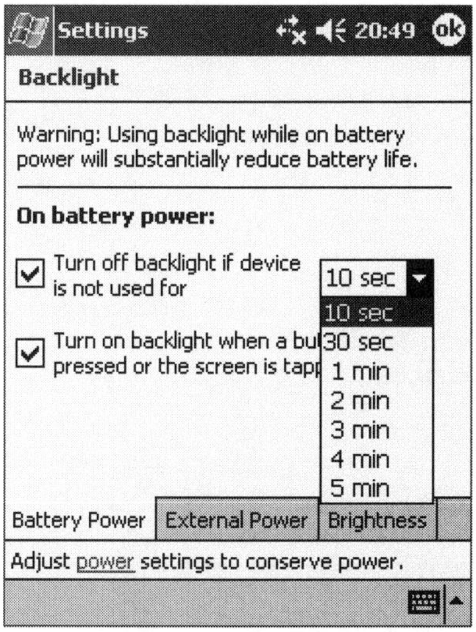

Figure 2.57 Select how much time you want to go by before your backlight shuts off when running your Pocket PC on battery power.

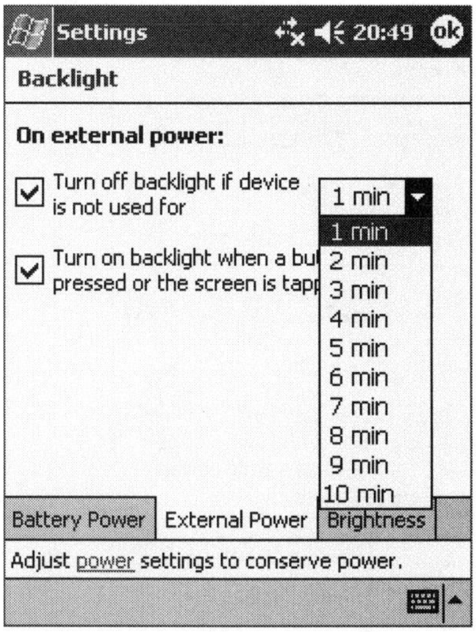

Figure 2.58 Select how much time you want to go by before your backlight shuts off when running your Pocket PC on external power.

To adjust Backlight settings:

1. Tap Start > Settings > System tab > Backlight to open the Backlight Settings screen.

2. Tap the Battery power tab at the bottom of the screen.

3. Tap the checkbox next to "Turn off backlight if device is not used for" and then select a period of time from the drop-down menu to the right (**Figure 2.57**).

4. Tap the checkbox next to "Turn on backlight when a button is pressed or the screen is tapped" to set the backlight to turn on when these activities occur.

✔ Tips

■ To make the same settings for when your device is being powered not by battery but by an external source, tap the External Power tab and repeat the steps (**Figure 2.58**).

■ Backlighting eats battery life. A good rule of thumb is to adjust your backlight settings to show the backlight for the least amount of time that you find acceptable.

■ In the Brightness tab, you can adjust how bright your backlight appears when your device is running on battery and external power.

ADJUSTING OTHER BASIC SETTINGS

To conserve battery power:

1. Tap Start > Settings > System tab > Power > Advanced tab.

2. Check the box next to "Turn off device if not used for" and select a period of time from the drop-down menu to the right to establish how long your Pocket PC is idle before it shuts itself off.

✔ Tips

■ You can set a different time limit for when your device is powered by battery or by an external source.

■ Change allotment or check how much standby time you have left in the Standby tab of the Power Settings screen (**Figure 2.59**).

■ Tap the Main tab to check how much battery power and backup battery power you have remaining (**Figure 2.60**).

■ Turning off the notification sounds and lights is another way to conserve your battery power.

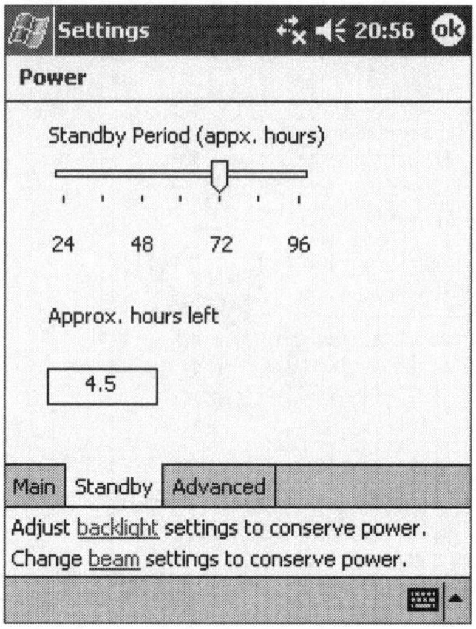

Figure 2.59 See how much standby time you have left in the Standby tab.

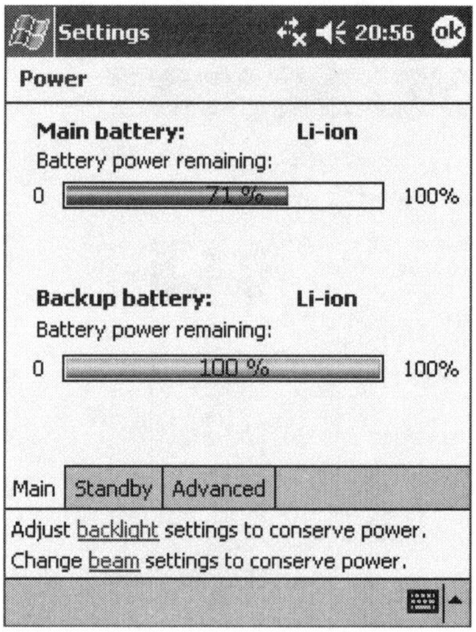

Figure 2.60 Check how much power you have in the Main tab.

ENTERING TEXT

When you first start using your Pocket PC, the built-in "soft" (onscreen) keyboard is the default way to enter text. By tapping little keys to enter letters and numbers, assuming you can type on a real keyboard, you can muddle along with it. But the Pocket PC's soft keyboard is kind of like training wheels. It gets you up and going, and it does work without requiring anything fancy, but it's too slow for some tasks, such as composing emails. It's really not the best long-term solution for efficiently entering text, though it's good to use when you want to be absolutely accurate, such as entering user names and passwords.

The other way to enter text is handwriting—drawing the letters and numbers directly on the screen. Getting machines to recognize human handwriting has long been a goal of personal computing. With the Pocket PC, that goal has come close to being achieved, though with some quirks and inconveniences.

The Pocket PC has four types of built-in text input:

- ◆ The soft keyboard
- ◆ Transcriber
- ◆ Block Recognizer
- ◆ Letter Recognizer

✔ Tips

- ■ There's yet another way to enter text: By doing the typing on your computer and using ActiveSync. See Chapter 4 for details.

- ■ For our examples in this chapter, we work with the Notes program, but text entry works the same in any program that will let you enter text. Tap Start > Notes and tap New on the menu bar to create a new Notes document.

Typing with the Soft Keyboard

The Pocket PC soft keyboard may seem intuitive at first, but it is in fact probably the least efficient text input method, mostly because of its tiny size. Using it to type anything longer than a user name, password, filename, or very short note is like eating a bowl of rice with a pair of tweezers. What's nice about the keyboard is its accuracy and the fact that you don't have to worry about whether the device can understand your handwriting—simply tap your stylus on the onscreen keys and insert your text one letter (one tap) at a time.

To enter text with the soft keyboard:

1. Create or open a document (**Figure 3.1**).

2. Tap the up arrow in the text input icon at the bottom right-hand corner of the screen and select Keyboard (**Figure 3.2**).

   (If the text input icon already looks like a little keyboard, you can just tap the keyboard part of the icon. If it looks like or 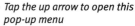, then at some point you changed your text input method—tap the up arrow.)

   The soft keyboard appears, ready for you to use.

3. Type your text by tapping the keys (**Figure 3.3**).

Figure 3.1 A new, blank Note.

Tap the up arrow to open this pop-up menu

Figure 3.2 Choose Keyboard as the text input method.

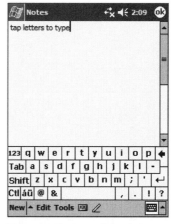

Figure 3.3 Kinda small, but it *is* a keyboard.

TYPING WITH THE SOFT KEYBOARD

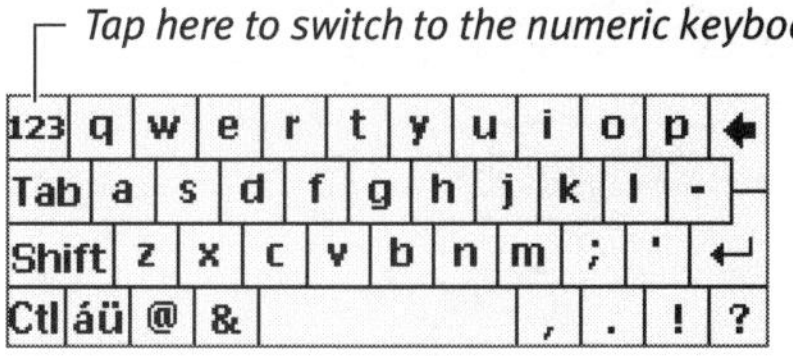

Tap here to switch to the numeric keyboard

Figure 3.4 To type numbers, tap the 123 key.

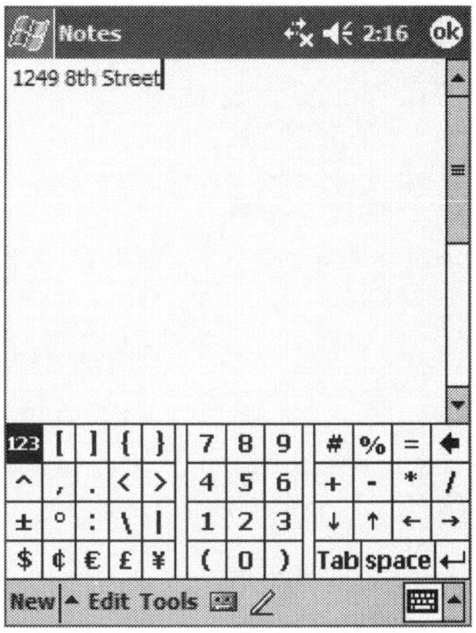

Figure 3.5 The numeric keyboard.

External keyboards

It is also possible to attach your Pocket PC to an external keyboard (see Appendix C for more information on these). An external keyboard allows you to type in the traditional way—with your hands. External keyboards are one of the most popular Pocket PC accessories. If you plan to enter a lot of text into your device, you should probably think about buying an external keyboard. That said, for most everyday Pocket PC purposes, it does sort of defeat the purpose of a handheld device. Even if you opt to buy an external keyboard for those times when you can set your device and keyboard on a desk or table, for all the other times you should become proficient in at least one of the alternative text-input methods.

✔ Tips

- At any time, you can make the keyboard go away by tapping the keyboard part of the ⌨️.

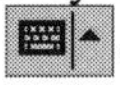

- To position the cursor, tap in the text where you want it to go.

- To select text to edit, just drag the stylus in any direction through the text you want to select. You can also double-tap (tap twice in quick succession) to select a whole word and triple-tap (tap thrice in quick succession) to select a whole paragraph.

To access the numeric keyboard:

1. Tap the 123 key at the top left-hand corner of the keyboard (**Figure 3.4**).

2. Tap to enter numbers from the numeric keyboard that appears (**Figure 3.5**).

✔ Tips

- Tap the 123 key again to return to the standard keyboard.

- The soft keyboard—have we mentioned this?—is extremely tiny (though you can make the keys bigger—see next section). If your taps regularly don't produce the letters or numbers you think they should, you should probably realign your screen. Tap Start > Settings > System tab > Screen, tap Align Screen, and follow the instructions.

TYPING WITH THE SOFT KEYBOARD

To access the numeric keys and large keys on the soft keyboard:

1. Tap the up arrow in the ⌨▲ text input icon and select Options to open the Input Settings screen (**Figure 3.6**). Make sure the Input Method tab is selected.

2. Tap the "Small keys" radio button to switch to a keyboard with smaller keys that includes numeric keys (**Figure 3.7**).

   or

   Leave the "Large keys" radio button selected and check the box next to "Use gestures for the following keys and remove them from the keyboard" (**Figure 3.8**).

   This frees up enough space for the numeric characters to appear on the keyboard while still showing larger keys (**Figure 3.9**).

3. Tap OK.

✔ Tips

■ Note that there is still a numeric 123 key in the keyboard shown in Figure 3.9. Tapping this brings up a fuller numeric keyboard with more keys—such as Tab, spacebar, and backspace—even though the numeric characters are already accessible on the keyboard.

■ Gestures are the Pocket PC's handwriting shortcuts to the keyboard's functional keys. They are normally used with the other three text input methods. We discuss gestures in detail later in this chapter.

■ We find that the default keyboard setting of large keys without gestures is the best combination, because it strikes a balance between increased visibility and maximizing the number of keys shown.

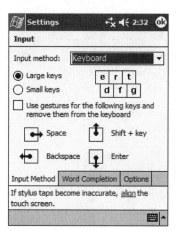

Figure 3.6 Navigate to the Input Settings dialog to tweak your keyboard settings.

```
123 1 2 3 4 5 6 7 8 9 0 - = ⌫
Tab q w e r t y u i o p [ ]
CAP a s d f g h j k l ; '
Shift z x c v b n m , . / ↵
Ctl áü ` \              ↓ ↑ ← →
```

Figure 3.7 Tapping the "Small keys" radio button makes the keys even smaller, but you now have letters and numbers on one keyboard.

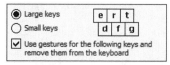

Figure 3.8 Removing a few keys from the "Large-key" keyboard...

```
123 1! 2@ 3# 4$ 5% 6^ 7& 8* 9( 0) - _
Tb q  w  e  r  t  y  u  i  o  p  = +
áü a  s  d  f  g  h  j  k  l  ; : ' "
Ctl \| z  x  c  v  b  n  m  ,< .> /?
```

Figure 3.9 ...results in numbers also appearing in the keyboard.

Figure 3.10 The keyboard in uppercase mode.

Figure 3.11 Even in uppercase, nothing on such a small screen really seems menacing.

To enter a single uppercase character:

1. Tap the **Shift** key on the soft keyboard once to display the uppercase characters (**Figure 3.10**) for only the next letter you type.

2. Tap the uppercase character you want to use.

   The keyboard automatically returns to lowercase mode.

To enter continuous uppercase characters:

1. Double-tap the **Shift** key on the soft keyboard to engage the familiar Caps Lock function.

2. Tap the uppercase characters you want to use.

   The keyboard remains in uppercase mode (**Figure 3.11**) until you tap **Shift** once more.

Special characters

To enter special characters—during those occasions when you need to ask a question in Spanish (¿) or spell something such as déjà vu or Mötley Crüe—tap the **áü** key on the keyboard. This brings up a special character keyboard containing the most commonly used special characters.

TYPING WITH THE SOFT KEYBOARD

To use word completion:

1. Begin typing a word using the soft keyboard.

   We'll start typing *pocket pc* as an example.

2. After you enter the second letter, notice that a little word completion box appears on top of the keyboard (**Figure 3.12**).

3. Tap the word in the word completion box if the word is what you were going to type.

   If the word in the box is not the word you wanted, go on and tap the next letter in your word. The boxed word changes with each new letter you type as the Pocket PC tries to narrow down and guess the word you want.

4. Continue typing until the word you want appears in the word completion box (**Figure 3.13**), and then tap the word you're trying to enter.

   The word appears as if you'd typed the whole thing.

5. If the word you were typing never appears in the word completion box, you are out of luck and must type the whole word.

✔ Tip

- You can customize word completion by tapping the up arrow in the ▦◣ text input icon and tapping Options. Tap the Word Completion tab to access word completion options (**Figure 3.14**), where you can check or uncheck boxes to make word completion behave more like you want it to. To turn it off, uncheck the box next to "Suggest words while entering text."

The word completion box

Figure 3.12 The Pocket PC thinks we might want to type the word *possible*.

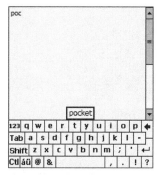

Figure 3.13 After three letters, it guesses our word.

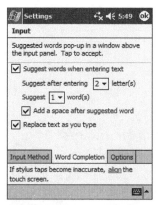

Figure 3.14 The word completion options in Input Settings let you customize the Word Completion feature—or turn it off altogether.

TYPING WITH THE SOFT KEYBOARD

Figure 3.15 We have now activated Transcriber. Use Transcriber mode whenever you want to enter text directly onto the screen in your own handwriting.

Figure 3.16 In Transcriber, the screen is your oyster, letting you write wherever (and however) you want.

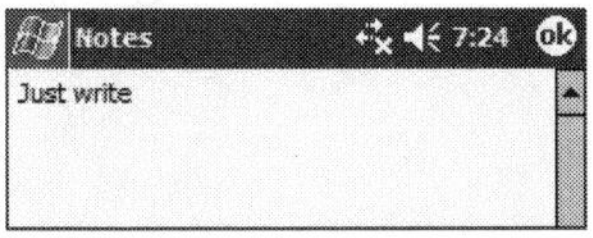

Figure 3.17 Transcriber recognizes your handwriting and converts it to text.

Writing Text with Transcriber

Wouldn't it be nice if the Pocket PC could recognize your own handwriting the way it is, even when you mix up cursive and printed characters, and if it would let you write anywhere on the screen? Well, it can and it does. What you're looking for is Transcriber, the most sophisticated, fun, and—if you work at it—the fastest way to enter text into your Pocket PC.

To enter text by writing with Transcriber:

1. Create or open a document.

2. Tap the up arrow in the text input icon at the bottom right-hand corner of the screen and tap Transcriber.

A Transcriber Intro screen appears.

3. Read the Intro screen and then tap OK.

The Transcriber menu and icon bars open beneath the document (**Figure 3.15**).

4. Write a few words anywhere on the screen (**Figure 3.16**).

After a second or so, your words are recognized (or not) and entered as text in your program (**Figure 3.17**).

✔ Tips

- Don't write too small. The bigger you write, the better you will be understood.

- Don't worry if a sentence you write wraps onto several lines. Transcriber will interpret your new lines as spaces in the same line.

- Be mindful when tapping around in Transcriber. It might think you mean to write instead of, say, tap a filename. If it does, wait until it registers its mistake and try again—a single tap on your item. Or tap the up arrow, choose Keyboard, and then do it again.

- With Transcriber, practice makes perfect—but training really helps.

WRITING TEXT WITH TRANSCRIBER

To train Transcriber to better understand your handwriting:

1. Tap the ⍺ icon on the Transcriber icon bar.

   The Letter Shapes screen appears (**Figure 3.18**).

2. Tap the letter, number, or character along the bottom of the screen that you want to train Transcriber to better recognize (**Figure 3.19**).

   The chosen character shapes appear at the top of the screen.

3. Tap a letter shape to make it show you how Transcriber expects this shape to be drawn.

4. Choose the Often radio button if the way the character drew itself is how you often draw the character.

5. Choose Rarely if you can imagine yourself ever drawing the character that way.

6. Choose Never if you never draw it that way. Disregarding letter shapes you never or rarely draw frees up Transcriber to discern your writing more quickly and accurately.

7. Repeat the process for every character you want Transcriber to recognize better.

✔ Tip

■ As mentioned earlier, Transcriber calls your handwriting "ink." The term refers to your handwritten words. The conversion between handwriting and text is called "recognition." Ink is a sort of halfway house between drawing and typing that enables the Pocket PC to attempt to recognize your characters.

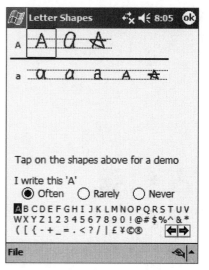

Figure 3.18 The Letter Shapes screen is where you "train" Transcriber to better recognize your handwriting.

Tap a character here to select it for training

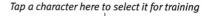

Figure 3.19 Select the character you want Transcriber to work on.

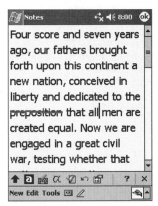

Figure 3.20 In Transcriber mode, draw a line through a word to select it.

Figure 3.21 You can also press and hold and then drag the stylus to select text.

Figure 3.22 Write to replace the selected text.

To edit text with Transcriber:

1. Create a document and enter some text or open a document containing text.

   Make sure you're in Transcriber mode (tap ![icon] if you don't see the Transcriber icon bar).

2. Double-tap to select a word or triple-tap to select a paragraph.

   or

   Draw a line through the text you want to select (**Figure 3.20**) and wait a second or two until Transcriber highlights the text.

   or

   Hold the tip of the stylus for about half a second at the beginning of the text you want to select and then drag through the rest of the text (**Figure 3.21**) to highlight it.

3. Once the text is highlighted, write what you want to replace the highlighted material (**Figure 3.22**).

   Transcriber replaces the highlighted text with what you wrote.

   or

   Press and hold on the selected text until the pop-up menu appears. When it does, choose Cut, Copy, Paste, or Clear (Clear means delete).

✔ Tip

- Selecting text with Transcriber is delicate—if you wait too long before dragging the stylus, a pop-up menu begins to appear, and you have to try again. It takes practice to get a feel for selecting text in Transcriber.

To edit text with Quick Correct without selecting text:

1. Create a document and enter some text or open a document containing text.

   Make sure you're in Transcriber mode (tap if you don't see the Transcriber icon bar).

2. Tap to place the cursor where you want to add characters or correct text.

3. Draw the ⇅ gesture (**Figure 3.23**). The Transcriber keyboard appears (**Figure 3.24**).

4. Use the keyboard to add characters or correct text.

✔ Tips

■ The ⇅ gesture is faster than hunting down and tapping the tiny on the icon bar. Getting in the habit of using it will save you time.

■ The Transcriber keyboard is great for things such as periods, hyphens, backspaces, and so on—characters that Transcriber can easily misinterpret.

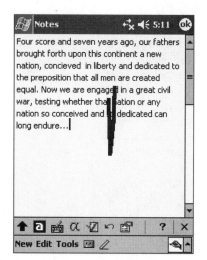

Figure 3.23 Use the Quick Correct gesture to make a correction.

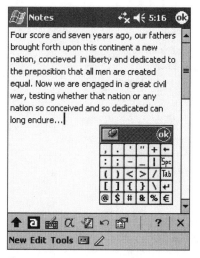

Figure 3.24 Transcriber's Quick Correct keyboard appears.

Transcriber gestures

Transcriber gestures are special written shapes that mean certain things to Transcriber. You write them in ink, just like you write your letters and numbers. ("Ink" is just Microsoft's term for your handwriting.) If you can be bothered to learn even a few gestures, your Pocket PC experience will be much more pleasant and satisfying. Transcriber recognizes the following gestures:

The **correction** gesture calls up the Correction window. Draw it like a check mark.

The **space** gesture inserts a space, like tapping the spacebar. Draw down and then to the right as least twice as far as down.

Use the **backspace** gesture to delete what came before. Draw right to left.

The **copy** gesture copies selected text to the clipboard, ready to paste somewhere else. Draw a line left to right and then back on the same line.

The **cut** gesture cuts selected text and enters it in the clipboard, ready to paste somewhere else. Draw a line right to left and then back on the same line.

Use the **paste** gesture to paste text from the clipboard to wherever the cursor is. Draw a line up at an angle and down again.

Use the **undo** gesture to undo whatever you just wrote, letter by letter. Draw a line up and down.

The **enter** gesture inserts a carriage return, like the Enter key on a keyboard. Draw a line down and then to the left at least twice as long as down.

The **quick correct** gesture opens the Alternates menu if text is selected or the Transcriber keyboard if no text is selected. Draw a line down, then up.

The **case change** gesture makes selected text uppercase if it's lowercase, and vice versa. Draw a line up.

Use the **tab** gesture to insert a tab, just like the Tab key on a keyboard. Draw a line up and over to the right at least twice as long as up.

WRITING TEXT WITH TRANSCRIBER

The Transcriber icon bar

Tap this to change the angle at which you write. You write perpendicular to the arrow's orientation. If you think you'd prefer writing sideways on the screen, try tapping the arrow to face left or right and turning your Pocket PC 90 degrees.

Tap to toggle among lowercase, uppercase, and numbers. The default is lowercase mode. In uppercase mode, Transcriber enters all uppercase letters, even if you write them as lower-case. In numbers mode, Transcriber forgets about letters altogether and interprets everything you write as numerical characters.

Tap this to make the Transcriber keyboard appear, which you can use to tap characters that are hard to remember or recognize.

Tap this to launch the Letter Shapes screen appear, where you can train your device to better comprehend your chicken scratches.

Tap this to open the Correction window.

Tap this to undo mistakes.

Tap this open Transcriber Options.

Tap this to start Transcriber Help. This icon seems to be the only way to access Transcriber Help, by the way. The General Help topics don't include Transcriber.

Tap this to turn off Transcriber, and tap to turn it on again.

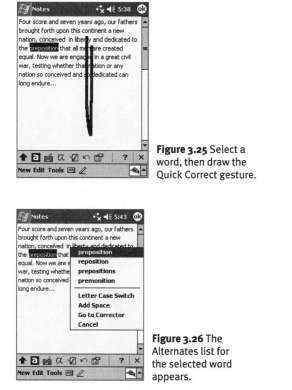

Figure 3.25 Select a word, then draw the Quick Correct gesture.

Figure 3.26 The Alternates list for the selected word appears.

To edit selected text with Quick Correct:

1. Create a document and enter some text or open a document containing text.

   Make sure you're in Transcriber mode (tap ✎▲ if you don't see the Transcriber icon bar).

2. Select the text you want to correct and draw the ↓‖↑ gesture (**Figure 3.25**). The Alternates list appears (**Figure 3.26**).

3. If one of the words in the Alternates list is what you want, simply tap it.

   To change the case of your selection, tap "Letter Case Switch."

   To add a space before the selection, tap "Add Space."

   To open the selected text in the Correction window, tap "Go to Corrector."

   If you don't see an option you want, tap Cancel.

The Correction window

Transcriber's Correction window is supposed to be a good and easy way to make corrections in your text, but in practice we find it to be fairly pointless. To open the Correction window, select some text and tap the ✎ icon or draw the ⟋ gesture. Your text appears in a window like this:

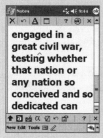

Here you can cut the selected text or undo your previous action—the same things you can do more easily by learning two gestures. The only new function available in the Correction window that's not available in regular old Transcriber is the option of underlining misspelled words in the selection—but for spelling, the Alternates list is better. For that matter, so is Pocket Word's spell check function.

Don't confuse the Correction window with Quick Correct, which we find more useful. With selected text, Quick Correct automatically brings up a list of alternate words for your questionable spellings *and* offers the Correction window as another option if you want it.

To change Transcriber options:

1. In the Transcriber icon bar, tap 🖼 to open the Transcriber Options screen (**Figure 3.27**).

2. On the General tab, choose from one or more of the following options:

   Tap to add or delete check boxes in the first three options: sound, intro screen, and icon bar.

   In the Inking area, tap Color to change the color of your ink to one of nine colors (**Figure 3.28**).

   Also in the Inking area, tap the up and down arrows to fatten or thin the width of your ink. The default is 3, and you can go as thin as 1 or as fat as 20.

3. On the Recognizer tab, choose from one or more of the following options:

   Tap the "Add space after" check box to control whether Transcriber adds a space after each word (which is handy).

   Tap to add a check to the "Separate letters mode" check box if you never write in cursive. If you only print your words, this option speeds up Transcriber's recognition brain by only focusing on recognizing disconnected, printed letters.

   In the "Speed of Recognition vs. Quality" area, choose your compromise between how fast you want Transcriber to recognize your writing and how well. If you think it takes too long, drag the bar left to make it faster. If you're impatiently waiting for it to understand you, drag it right to make it work harder.

   In the "Recognition start time" area, drag the slider left to have Transcriber begin trying to recognize your ink faster after you stop, and right to give you more time to finish writing on the screen.

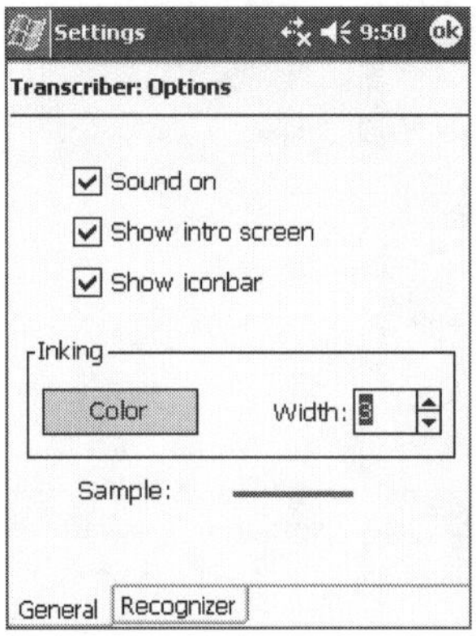

Figure 3.27 The Transcriber Options General tab lets you adjust Transcriber's ink color, sound, and icon preferences.

Figure 3.28 Pick an ink color. The default color is light blue—be sure to pick one that shows up bright and clear to you.

Transcriber's calculator

Transcriber has a built-in calculator that can solve simple addition, subtraction, multiplication, and division. Just write the beginning of your operation and end it with an equals sign:

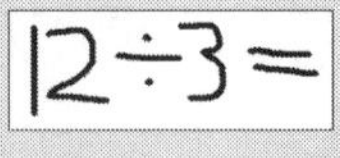

Transcriber automatically enters the answer when it recognizes the text:

Entering Text with Block Recognizer and Letter Recognizer

With Transcriber, the idea is to get the machine to recognize natural human input—handwriting, with all its flaws. With Block Recognizer and Letter Recognizer, the idea is conform that human input to match what the machine expects. These two input methods use an on-screen special area called an input panel, where you are expected to write. You cannot write just anywhere on the screen as you can with Transcriber.

Block Recognizer is based on characters that resemble uppercase letters of the alphabet. Letter Recognizer seems to be an attempt to make a lowercase version of Graffiti, the machine-friendly set of characters used by Palm handheld devices. Letter Recognizer is kind of a cross between Transcriber and Block Recognizer. On the whole, we prefer Block Recognizer to Letter Recognizer for its more simplified input panel.

✔ Tips

- Block Recognizer uses Graffiti, so if you're coming to the Pocket PC from the Palm world and have gotten used to writing in Graffiti, Block Recognizer will be a welcome friend.

- The only difference in the input panels is that the Block Recognizer's is divided into two halves—one on the left for letters and one on the right for numbers—whereas Letter Recognizer splits the letter part into uppercase and lowercase. Why? Search us.

BLOCK AND LETTER RECOGNIZER

To use Block Recognizer:

1. Create or open a document.

2. Tap the up arrow in the  text input icon at the bottom right-hand corner of the screen and tap Block Recognizer (**Figure 3.29**).

   The input panel appears (**Figure 3.30**).

3. Write letters in the left (abc) and numbers in the right (123) parts of the input panel.

✔ Tips

■ To shift to uppercase letters, draw a line straight up the abc panel and then write the same block letter shape. For continuous uppercase, draw two lines up in quick succession. To shift back to lowercase, draw one line up again.

■ You can write punctuation and symbols in either half of the input panel, but you have to tap it first. When you tap, the abc or 123 will turn into a circle (**Figure 3.31**), meaning you can write your punctuation. Or tap the  button in the input panel toolbar to the panel's right to call up a special character keyboard.

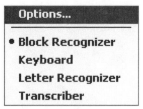

Figure 3.29 Select the Block Recognizer option.

Write letters here   Write numbers here

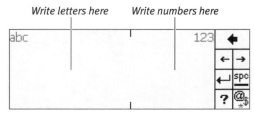

Figure 3.30 Block Recognizer's input panel.

Tap here to make the circle appear, which tells you it's okay to enter punctuation

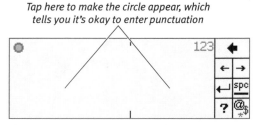

Figure 3.31 Tap to enter punctuation or symbols.

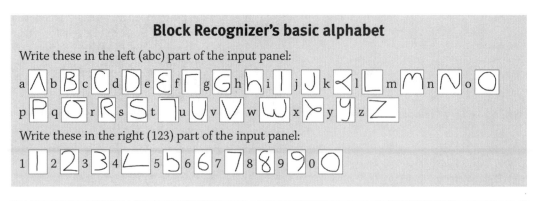

Block Recognizer's basic alphabet

Write these in the left (abc) part of the input panel:

Write these in the right (123) part of the input panel:

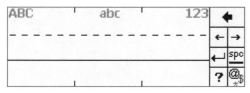

Figure 3.32 The Letter Recognizer's input panel has three parts for capital letters, lowercase, and numbers.

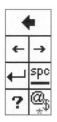

Figure 3.33 The Recognizer icon bar is a helpful collection of icons that let you enter common characters with a tap.

To enter text with Letter Recognizer:

1. Create or open a document.

2. Tap the up arrow in the ▦|▲ text input icon at the bottom right-hand corner of the screen and tap Letter Recognizer. The input panel appears (**Figure 3.32**).

3. Write letters and numbers in the appropriate parts of the input panel.

   Write lowercase letters in the abc part, and numbers in the 123 part. With Letter Recognizer, you always write lowercase letters—for uppercase letters, write lowercase letters in the ABC third of the panel.

   Write punctuation and symbols in the 123 part of the input panel. Or tap the 🄰 button in the input panel toolbar to the panel's right to call up a special character keyboard.

To use the Recognizer icon bar:

◆ Open either Block Recognizer or Letter Recognizer. Notice the icon bar to the right of the input panel (**Figure 3.33**).

   Tap the ◆ icon to backspace.

   Tap the ←|→ icons to move the cursor one space to the left or right.

   Tap the ↵ icon to conclude a paragraph and move down one line.

   Tap the spc icon to enter the space character (like a spacebar).

   Tap the **?** icon for Block and Letter Recognizer Help.

   Tap the 🄰 icon to access Block and Recognizer Help.

✔ Tip

■ The **?** icon leads to demos of how to use the Recognizers and change their options.

BLOCK AND LETTER RECOGNIZER

CONNECTING TO YOUR COMPUTER

Your Pocket PC is really an extension of your computer. All your stuff is on your computer, and your computer is very likely to remain the center of your information system. If your computer is the sun, your Pocket PC is the moon—it needs the sun for it to shine. The art of moving files, data, and programs between your computer and your device involves a program called ActiveSync.

With ActiveSync, you can make sure that email you send on your device also shows up in the Sent Mail folder on your computer's Outlook program, and that a change you make on your Outlook calendar is also updated on your device. (Outlook is Microsoft Office's email and contact-management program. It's also what your computer syncs up with for the Pocket PC's Calendar, Contacts, Inbox, Notes, and Tasks data.)

There are a few ways to use ActiveSync. The usual way is to use your cradle or cable to connect your device to your computer. There are other ways that can be more convenient, but they involve special connections such as infrared, Bluetooth, and network cards that you may not currently have.

ActiveSync is how you install and remove programs for your Pocket PC. It also lets you manage your device's folders and files from your computer, often faster than manipulating them on your device.

Synchronizing Your Device with ActiveSync

Installing and using ActiveSync is pretty straightforward—and you *must* install it if you want your device and computer to talk to each other (you only have to do so once). Putting the device in the cradle—the usual way of running ActiveSync—also charges it when the cradle's AC adapter is plugged in. If you have an iPAQ, you can also charge your Pocket PC without an outlet if one isn't handy (if you don't have an iPAQ, there is a way for you to do this, too—see sidebar, page 78).

To install ActiveSync:

1. Close all running programs.

   Make sure you do *not* connect your Pocket PC to the computer at this time.

2. Insert the CD-ROM that came with your device into the computer's CD-ROM drive.

   The installation program begins.

   (If it doesn't, go to My Computer, right-click the CD-ROM drive's icon, and choose AutoPlay. If it still doesn't start, look in the CD-ROM's folders for a file called SETUP and double-click it.)

3. Click Start Here and follow the onscreen instructions to begin the installation.

   Each manufacturer gets to customize the installation program (which is actually Internet Explorer) with a logo and picture of its device. **Figure 4.1** shows the Getting Started screen for a Dell Axim.

4. Choose whether to install Outlook before installing ActiveSync (**Figure 4.2**) by clicking Install Outlook [version] or Install ActiveSync 3.7.

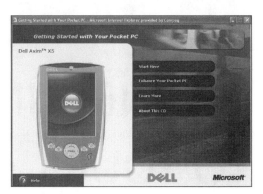

Figure 4.1 A typical ActiveSync installation opening screen.

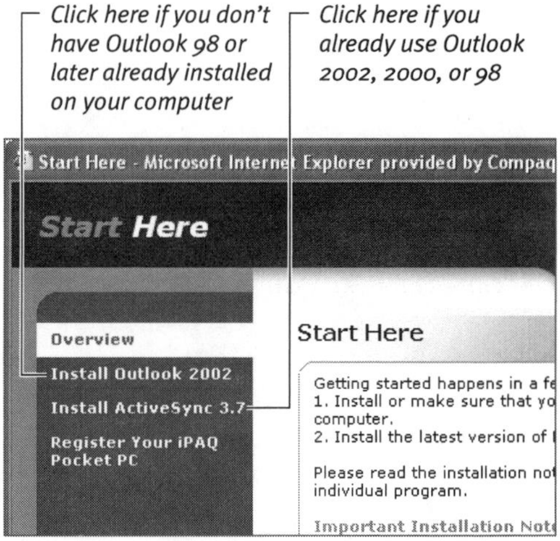

⌐ Click here if you don't   ⌐ Click here if you
have Outlook 98 or   already use Outlook
later already installed   2002, 2000, or 98
on your computer

Figure 4.2 To install Outlook 2002 or not to install Outlook 2002—that is the question.

Click here to proceed with the installation

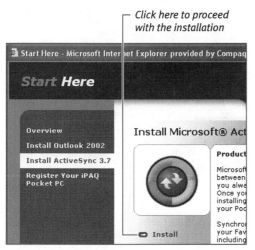

Figure 4.3 Once you've chosen which version of Outlook to install, you can click to install ActiveSync.

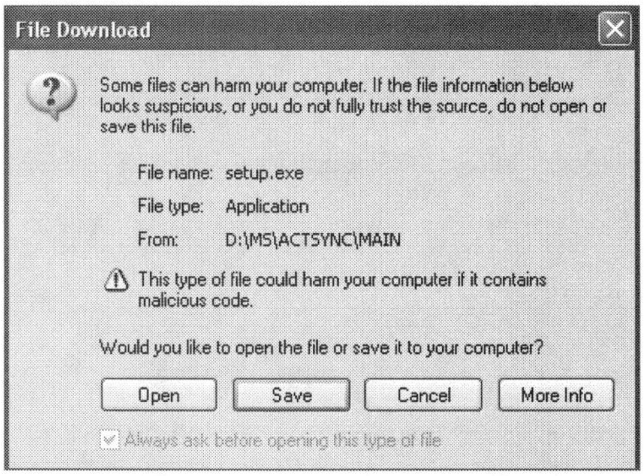

Figure 4.4 Click Open to continue installing from the CD-ROM.

If you already use Outlook 2002, 2000, or 98, you don't have to install Outlook 2002. ActiveSync works with all those versions. To skip installing Outlook, click Install ActiveSync 3.7 and go on to step 5.

If you don't have Microsoft Outlook installed—and note that Outlook Express does *not* work with ActiveSync—you should click Install Outlook 2002 to install/upgrade Outlook and then move on to step 5 after it's installed.

5. In the Install ActiveSync screen, click Install (**Figure 4.3**).

6. Choose Open if a dialog box appears asking you to open the file or save it to your computer (**Figure 4.4**).

7. In the Set Up ActiveSync dialog box that appears, click Next.

8. Click Next to accept the default folder location of ActiveSync.

If you want to install ActiveSync in a different folder, click Change, browse for the location you want, and then click OK.

Eventually, the Get Connected dialog box appears (**Figure 4.5**).

9. Plug in the cradle's or cable's AC adapter to a wall outlet.

continues on next page

![Get Connected dialog box]

Figure 4.5 When you see this, you can connect your cradle or cable.

10. Connect the cradle's or cable's USB adapter into a USB port on the back of your computer.

If your cable has two adapters, as with some iPAQs, use the USB one—the one that looks like one thin slot. If you don't have a USB port on your computer, you'll have to use the serial adapter—it's slower, but at least it works.

11. Connect your Pocket PC to your cable or set it gently into the cradle, being careful that the connectors meet up and it slides snugly into place.

If you used the USB cable, you don't need to click Next—just wait. If you used the serial cable, click Next.

The Set Up a Partnership dialog box appears (**Figure 4.6**). If it fails to appear, look for a New Partnership icon in the task bar along the bottom of your screen and click it.

12. Choose between a Standard Partnership and a Guest Partnership and click Next.

If you're setting up ActiveSync on your own computer, choose Standard Partnership. This ensures that all your Pocket PC's data can be synchronized with Outlook on your computer.

If it's not your computer and you just want to copy files between the machines or install a Pocket PC program, choose Guest Partnership. This limits the communication between the machines.

The "Specify how to synchronize data" dialog box appears (**Figure 4.7**).

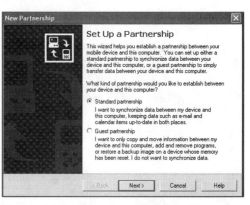

Figure 4.6 Pick whether you want full service (Standard) or just the basics (Guest).

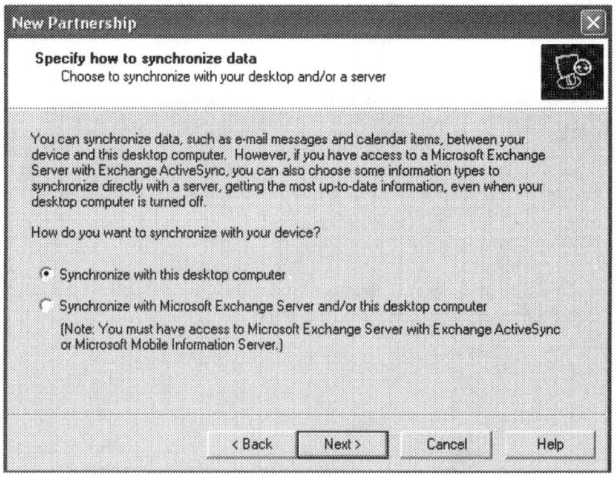

Figure 4.7 Unless your IS person at work instructs you to synchronize with a Microsoft Exchange Server, click "Synchronize with this desktop computer."

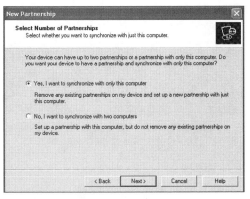

Figure 4.8 Here is where you choose whether to have your email synchronize with this machine.

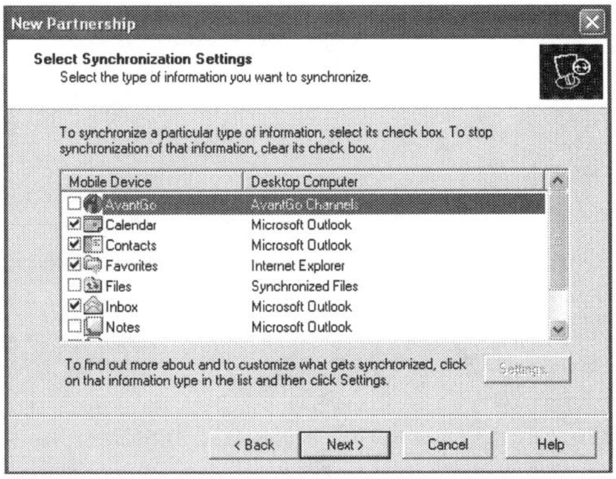

Figure 4.9 Picking what kinds of information will get synchronized.

Figure 4.10 Click Finish to complete setup and exit the Wizard.

13. Choose between synchronizing with the computer or a Microsoft Exchange Server and click Next.

Most likely, you want to synchronize data with your computer. However, if your workplace runs a Microsoft Exchange Server that supports ActiveSync, you may be required to synchronize with the server. Ask your office's tech support how to proceed if you think this might be the case.

The Select Number of Partnerships dialog box appears (**Figure 4.8**).

14. Choose between synchronizing with just this computer or with this computer and another computer and click Next.

This option is really about email, as both choices allow your other data to synchronize. You can only synchronize your email with one computer. If you choose Yes, then your email will be synchronized between your device and your computer. Choosing No means your email will not be synchronized.

If you plan to ActiveSync with computers at home and work, choose Yes during this setup for the computer with which you want to sync your email, and choose No for the other one.

The Select Synchronization Settings dialog box appears (**Figure 4.9**).

15. Click checkboxes to select or deselect the types of data you want to synchronize and click Next.

You can easily change these choices later in ActiveSync Options.

The Setup Complete dialog box appears (**Figure 4.10**).

16. Click Finish.

ActiveSync opens, and synchronization begins—if you chose a Standard Partnership. If you're set up as a Guest, you can see what files are on the device by clicking the Explore icon in ActiveSync.

To synchronize using a cable or cradle:

1. Connect the cradle or cable to your computer.

   Make sure your computer is on and that ActiveSync has been installed and is active. The 🔵 ActiveSync icon should be visible in the notification area of the Windows task bar (**Figure 4.11**). If you don't see the icon, ActiveSync might still be running. Sometimes icons in the taskbar hide if they haven't been used in a while. Click the 🔘 arrow to show icons that are hiding.

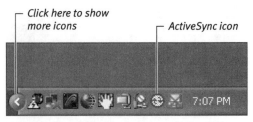

Click here to show more icons

ActiveSync icon

Figure 4.11 The ActiveSync icon appears in the taskbar's notification area when ActiveSync is running.

Pros and cons of different types of ActiveSync

When you're at home, it's probably easiest to keep your cradle on your desk and plugged into the wall and your computer. That way, to ActiveSync you just put the device in the cradle and ActiveSync can start automatically.

But when you're on the road or at work, it can become a hassle to pack, lug around, and keep connecting and disconnecting a cradle. One solution is to buy another cradle and keep that at work.

If your laptop is what you want to ActiveSync with, and it has an infrared port, you don't need to buy anything else—dispense with the cradle and synchronize via the infrared port. Infrared synchronization is slow, however.

A fancier way—if your device has Bluetooth capability (either built-in or via an expansion card)—is to purchase a Bluetooth adapter for your laptop or for the computer you'll be using (you can get one for $30 or so; see Appendix C for more on Bluetooth and other accessories). With Bluetooth, you can dispense with the cradle and ActiveSync through thin air. And it's mighty fast.

Still another way to go cradleless is to ActiveSync via Wi-Fi—if your device has Wi-Fi capability and the computer you want to ActiveSync with is also connected to a Wi-Fi network. Wi-Fi synchronization is also fast. This chapter explains how to do all these things.

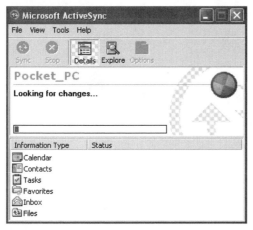

Figure 4.12 ActiveSync is underway.

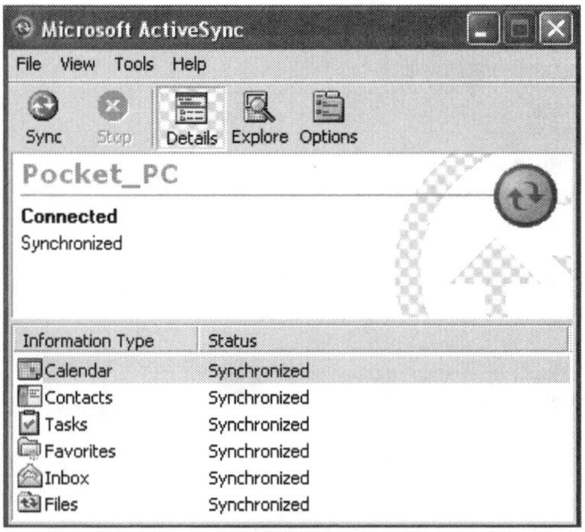

Figure 4.13 ActiveSync finishes synchronizing, ensuring that emails, files, and documents on your device and computer are kept up-to-date.

2. Set your Pocket PC in the cradle or connect it to the ActiveSync cable.

It doesn't matter whether it's on or not. Connecting it will turn it on.

ActiveSync automatically begins (**Figure 4.12**).

Wait until ActiveSync finishes synchronizing your machines—it takes a minute or two (**Figure 4.13**).

✔ Tip

■ You can change how often your device synchronizes by clicking Tools > Options > Schedule tab in ActiveSync on your computer. Your choices are Continuously (synchronize whenever anything changes), On Connection (synchronize only once each time you reconnect), and Manually (only synchronize when you click or tap the Sync icon). Choosing Continuously means you rarely have to think about ActiveSync.

To synchronize using an infrared port:

1. Make sure your computer has an infrared port.

   Some laptops have infrared ports, but very few desktop systems do. To see whether your laptop has an infrared port, click Start > Control Panel > System > Hardware tab > Device Manager and double-click the Ports item.

2. Point your Pocket PC's infrared port (along the top of the device) at your laptop's infrared port.

   They cannot be more than a few feet apart.

3. On your Pocket PC, tap Start > ActiveSync to display the ActiveSync screen (**Figure 4.14**).

4. Tap Tools > Connect via IR (**Figure 4.15**).

   A Connect To dialog box appears (**Figure 4.16**).

5. When you're connected, tap Sync in the ActiveSync screen (**Figure 4.17**).

   ActiveSync begins.

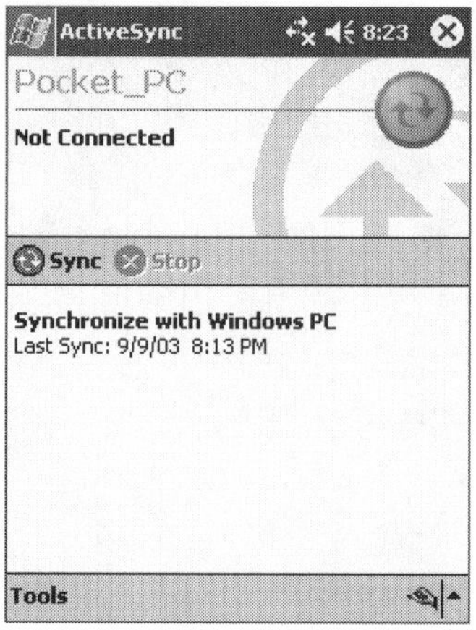

Figure 4.14 The Pocket PC's ActiveSync screen.

Figure 4.15 If both your computer and your Pocket PC have infrared ports, you can synchronize without wires or cables. From the Tools menu, choose Connect via IR.

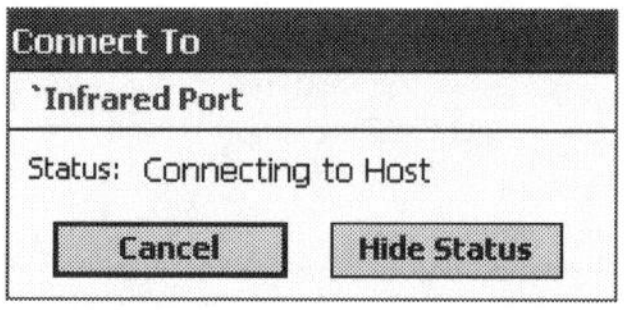

Figure 4.16 The device attempts to contact the laptop.

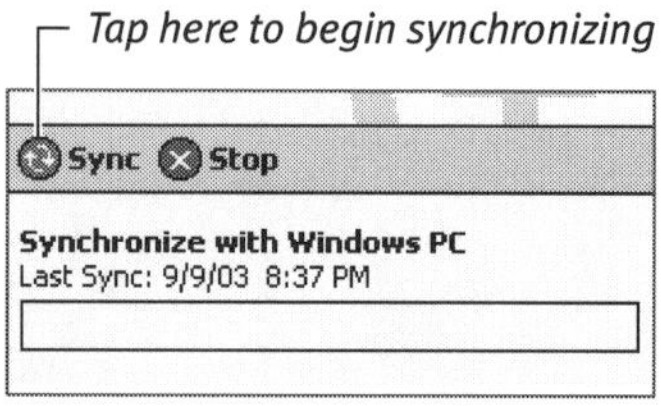

Figure 4.17 Initiate synchronization from the device by tapping Sync.

Figure 4.18 Bluetooth Manager is where you set up a Bluetooth ActiveSync session.

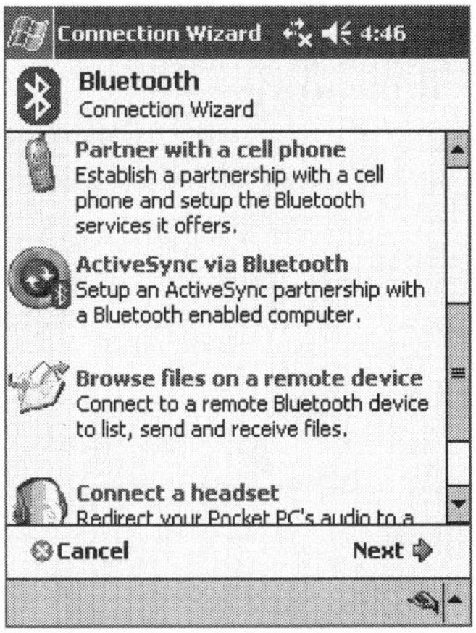

Figure 4.19 Tap ActiveSync via Bluetooth to start Step 1 of the Bluetooth Connection Wizard.

To synchronize using Bluetooth:

1. Make sure both your computer and Pocket PC have Bluetooth installed and enabled.

   (Each brand of Pocket PC manages Bluetooth differently. These steps are for the Bluetooth Manager found on models in the iPAQ 5500 series. See Chapter 10 for more on Bluetooth.)

2. Tap Start > Bluetooth Manager.

   The Bluetooth Manager screen appears (**Figure 4.18**).

3. Tap New > Connect!.

   The Bluetooth Connection Wizard starts.

4. Scroll down to find the ActiveSync via Bluetooth option (**Figure 4.19**), tap it, and then tap Next.

   The Step 1 screen appears.

5. Find out which COM port on your computer will be accepting the incoming Serial Port Profiles from the Pocket PC and tap Next.

   This information should be available in your computer's Bluetooth software help or manual.

   The Step 2 screen appears.

continues on next page

6. In ActiveSync on your computer, click File > Connections Settings.

Connection Settings appears. Select the COM port from step 5 in the drop-down list (**Figure 4.20**) and click OK.

7. On your device, tap Next.

A shortcut creation screen appears, showing the network name of your computer.

8. Tap Finish.

A shortcut is created in Bluetooth My Shortcuts (**Figure 4.21**), named the same as your computer's network name.

9. If ActiveSync doesn't begin synchronizing automatically, tap the new shortcut.

ActiveSync begins working its magic—through thin Bluetooth air.

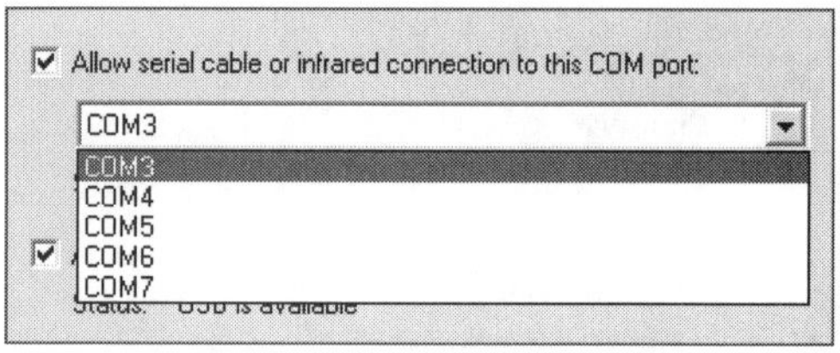

Figure 4.20 You must choose the right COM port—if it doesn't work, come back here and try a different one.

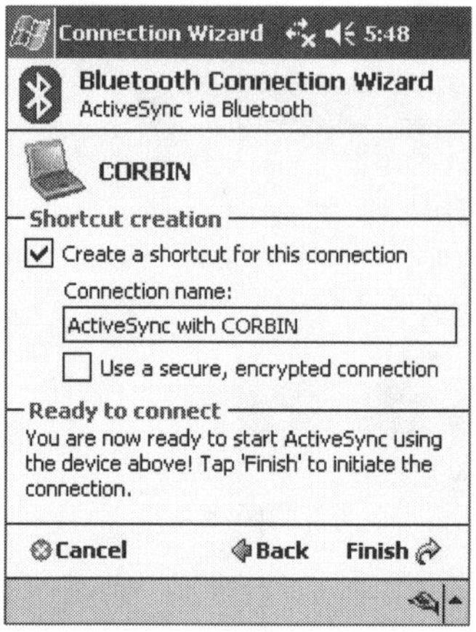

Figure 4.21 Now you'll have a shortcut and can forget all this setup stuff.

Charging your device without an outlet

The following information is for the iPAQ's 5000 series. For all other Pocket PCs, you can do the same thing by purchasing a miniSync cable from Boxwave (www.boxwave.com) or Pocket PC Techs (www.ppctechs.com).

Whether you charge your Pocket PC in its cradle or by connecting it to an AC adapter, you still usually need a wall outlet to juice up. If you're in a pinch though, you can charge it straight from your computer using the cradle or simply a USB or serial cable. Tap Start > Settings > System tab > Power, and then tap the USB Charging tab to bring up the USB Charging Selection. Tap to enable the Use USB Charging option.

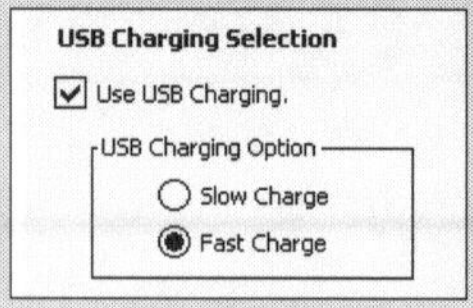

Choose Fast Charge if it is available as a choice (some ports cannot handle fast charging—if yours can, use it).

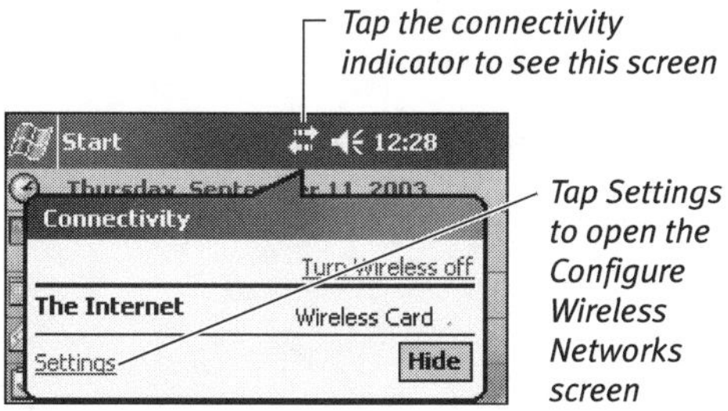

Tap the connectivity indicator to see this screen

Tap Settings to open the Configure Wireless Networks screen

Figure 4.22 The Connectivity drop-down balloon.

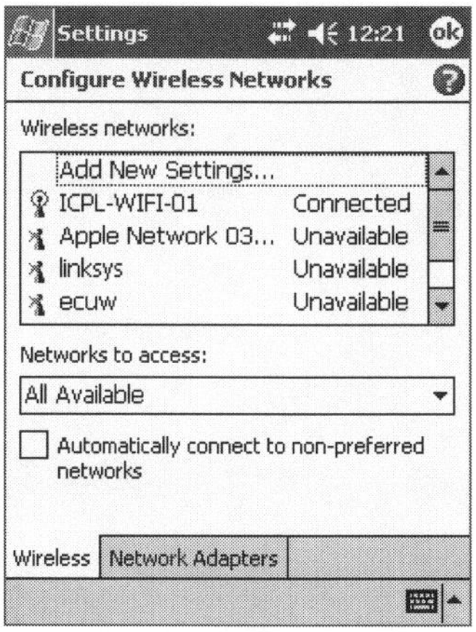

Figure 4.23 The Configure Wireless Networks screen is your Pocket PC's network command center.

To synchronize using an Ethernet network connection:

1. Follow the instructions given earlier in the section "To install ActiveSync."

2. Make sure you have a network card that is compatible with and set up for your device.

Unless your device came with built-in Wi-Fi, a network card—typically a CompactFlash or PC card—is required to connect your device to a network for synchronization. The card can either be a traditional Ethernet card, to which you connect the CAT5 Ethernet cable, or a wireless card. (See Chapter 10 for more on networking with the Pocket PC.)

You may need to contact your network administrator to set up your device for ActiveSync over Ethernet.

3. With ActiveSync running on your computer, remove your Pocket PC from its cradle or disconnect it from the cable.

4. Insert your network card into the Pocket PC and perform any setup tasks to connect your device to the network.

Tapping the connectivity indicator at the top of the screen produces a Connectivity drop-down "balloon," shown in **Figure 4.22,** letting you know if you're connected. Tapping Settings in the balloon opens the Configure Wireless Networks screen (**Figure 4.23**), where you can see which network you're connected to. You have to select the network that your computer with ActiveSync is on (see the first Tip for more on this).

5. Once your device is connected to the network, tap Start > ActiveSync and tap the Sync button in the ActiveSync screen. ActiveSync begins.

continues on next page

SYNCHRONIZING YOUR DEVICE WITH ACTIVESYNC

✔ Tips

- In many cases, ActiveSync can't "see" the desktop computer it needs to synchronize with unless the "My network card connects to:" item in the Configure Network Adapters screen (Start > Settings > Connections tab > Connections > Advanced tab > Network Card > Network Adapters tab) is set to Work rather than to Internet. It depends on how the local network is set up. If the ActiveSync process doesn't work with the network card set to Internet, try changing it to Work and try again. (See Chapter 10 for more on connecting your Pocket PC to networks.)

- If your Pocket PC has Wi-Fi built in, you don't have to buy a network card. Just install ActiveSync as described in the "To install ActiveSync" section, set up your Wi-Fi connection as discussed in Chapter 10, and then tap Start > ActiveSync > Sync button.

Connecting to a Mac

You would think that Macintosh users, used to instinctively snubbing Microsoft products, would simply use a Palm organizer instead of a Pocket PC—after all, the Palm was built on the old Motorola CPU. But no, these artsy iconoclasts manage to confound expectations even on this point. There are indeed ways to connect a Mac to a Pocket PC. Two good products are available to do just that: the cleverly named Missing Sync (www.markspace.com) and Pocket Mac (www.pocketmac.net).

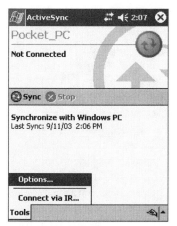

Figure 4.24 Select ActiveSync Options.

Figure 4.25 Select PC remote synchronization options.

To synchronize using a modem connection to an Exchange server:

1. Follow the instructions given in the section "To install ActiveSync."

2. Set up your modem to work with your device (see Chapter 10 for more).

3. Obtain the appropriate server information from your network administrator, such as phone number, login name, and password.

4. Tap Start > ActiveSync to open the ActiveSync screen.

5. Tap Tools > Options (**Figure 4.24**) to open the PC Synchronization screen (**Figure 4.25**).

6. Tap the PC tab if it is not already selected.

7. Tap to select your PC from the "Use this PC:" drop-down list and tap OK.

8. Set up a work connection on your device (see Chapter 10).

9. In the ActiveSync screen, tap Sync to begin ActiveSync.

✔ Tip

■ Synchronizing in this fashion is for enterprise users, not home users—you can't just dial into your home computer and synchronize. It's up to the network administrator to decide how corporate users will sync remotely. It also varies by versions of Microsoft Exchange.

Installing Programs

It's normally simple and straightforward to install new software on your Pocket PC. You install programs through your computer while your Pocket PC is connected. There are two main ways to install software: from a CD-ROM or from a Web site. The CD-ROM that came with your device is usually a good place to start looking for additional programs to install.

To install a Pocket PC program from a CD-ROM:

1. Connect your device to your computer.

2. Insert the CD-ROM into the computer's CD-ROM drive.

3. If a setup program automatically begins, follow its instructions to install the software (**Figure 4.26**).

   or

   If the CD-ROM just sits there, Click Start > My Computer > D: drive (or whatever your CD-ROM drive is called) and look for files called Setup or Install. Double-click them until the setup program starts and then follow the onscreen instructions.

Keeping an eye on memory

The more programs you add to your Pocket PC, the more of them you tend to run. And because tapping the ⊗ in the upper right-hand corner of a program's screen minimizes but doesn't actually close a program, before you know it you may run out of memory. To avoid this, you have to stop programs when they start getting out of hand. To stop them, tap Start > Settings > System tab > Memory > Running Programs tab. From the list choose the programs you want to halt and tap Stop—or tap Stop All.

There is at least one third-party task manager that turns the X into a real X—it actually closes the application when you tap the X. It's called Pocket Plus and can be found at www.spbsoftwarehouse.com.

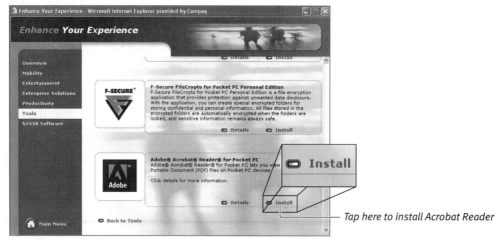

Figure 4.26 Choose a Pocket PC program from a CD-ROM's setup screen.

INSTALLING PROGRAMS

Figure 4.27 Click Open to continue or Save to store the installation file on your hard drive.

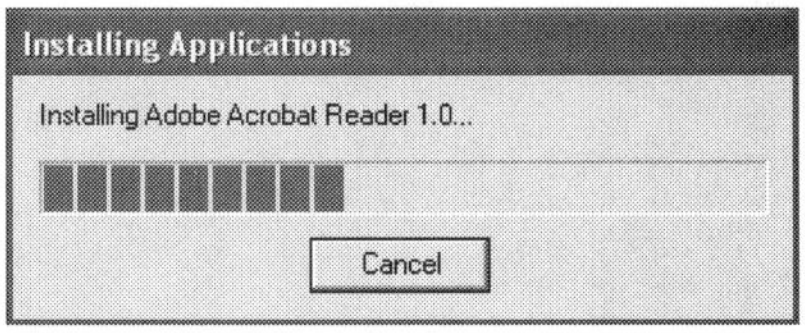

Figure 4.28 The installation is proceeding.

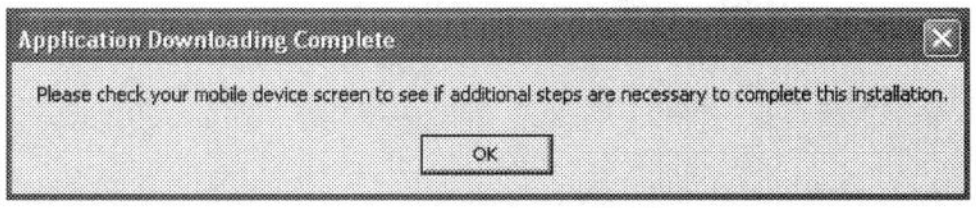

Figure 4.29 Some programs require some action to be taken on the device before installation can finish.

Figure 4.30 Your Pocket PC tells you how the installation is going.

4. If you see a dialog box like that shown in **Figure 4.27**, click Open to install.

You're not really downloading here—some install programs just use Internet Explorer as their interface.

5. Your computer screen displays the progress of the installation (**Figure 4.28**).

6. If a dialog box like **Figure 4.29** appears, asking you to check your device for additional steps, do so and then click OK.

7. Your Pocket PC will display the installation's progress, too (**Figure 4.30**).

8. Click Finish, if necessary.

9. Tap Start > Programs to see the Pocket PC program's icon on your device (**Figure 4.31**).

Tap the program's icon to start it.

Some programs require you to soft reset your device.

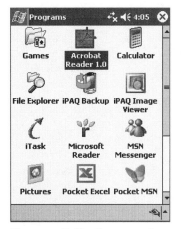

Figure 4.31 Voilà—the program's icon is automatically placed in Programs.

INSTALLING PROGRAMS

To install a Pocket PC program from the Internet:

1. Connect your device to your computer.

2. Connect your computer to the Internet.

3. In your Web browser on your computer, go to your favorite Pocket PC software site, such as www.handango.com, www.pocketgear.com, or www.pocketpc.com, and find a program (**Figure 4.32**).

   (See Appendix A for more sites to download programs from.)

4. Click Download or whatever link on the Web page prompts downloading.

5. When you see the Open or Save dialog box (**Figure 4.33**), click Open to continue installing now.

   You can also click Save if you want to download the program to your computer and install it later.

6. Follow the instructions beginning with step 5 in the preceding section "To install a Pocket PC program from a CD-ROM."

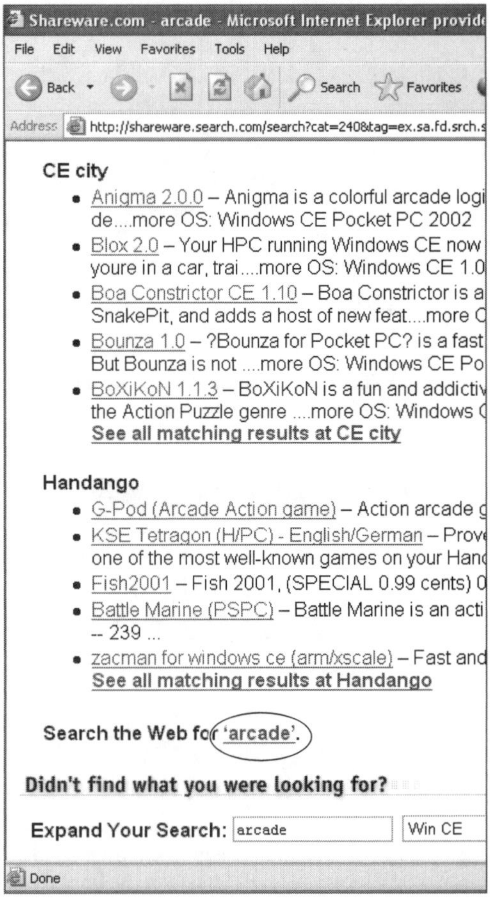

Figure 4.32 Searching www.shareware.com for Win CE programs and the word "arcade" turned up this page of links to several software sites.

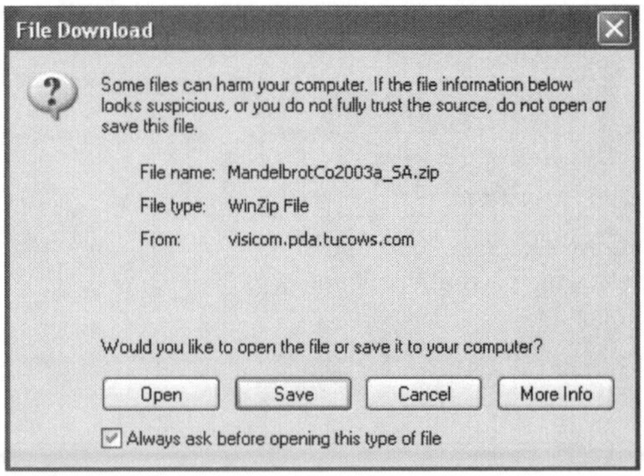

Figure 4.33 Click Open to continue installing.

✔ Tips

- There are excellent freeware, shareware, and commercial Pocket PC programs. Try a freeware program first to see if you like it before spending money on Pocket PC software.

- Some sites allow you to install directly with your Pocket PC browser. Go to www.handango.com using your Pocket PC, and you'll be re-directed to a mobile site that allows you to download free trials and even purchase full versions of the software, all using *only* your Pocket PC.

- Make sure you're downloading a program that is designed for the Pocket PC. Regular Windows programs won't work on your device. You want programs that are for Windows Mobile 2003 (Pocket PC 2003), ideally, but you can also install programs for Pocket PC 2002 and 2000. Any software site will offer this information for the programs it offers.

- If you save a program from the Internet to your computer instead of installing it, you can install it later by clicking Tools > Add/Remove Programs in ActiveSync.

INSTALLING PROGRAMS

Removing Programs

There are many reasons to remove programs from your Pocket PC. You may find that you never use certain programs, and they're just taking up precious memory in your device. Or you may install a better program and have no use for the has-been. You can remove programs with or without ActiveSync. It's easier and faster to do it just using your Pocket PC (and if you're away from your computer, it's the only way).

To remove a program using your Pocket PC:

1. On your device, tap Start > Settings > System tab > Remove Programs to bring up the Remove Programs screen (**Figure 4.34**).

2. Tap the program you want to remove to highlight it and tap Remove.

3. Tap Yes if you're sure you want to remove it.

4. Repeat steps 2 and 3 to remove more programs.

5. Tap OK after you've removed what you want.

Figure 4.34 Removing a program using the Pocket PC alone.

Microsoft ActiveSync
File View Tools Help
Options...
Resolve Items...
Backup/Restore...
Add/Remove Programs...
Import Database Tables...
Export Database Tables...
Sync
Connecte
3 items not
Information Type Status
Calendar Synchronized
Contacts Synchronized
Tasks Synchronized
Favorites Synchronized
Inbox Synchronized
Files 3 items not synchronized

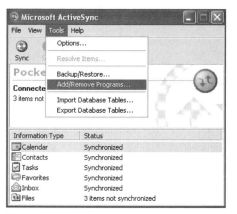

Figure 4.35 Preparing to remove a program using ActiveSync on the computer.

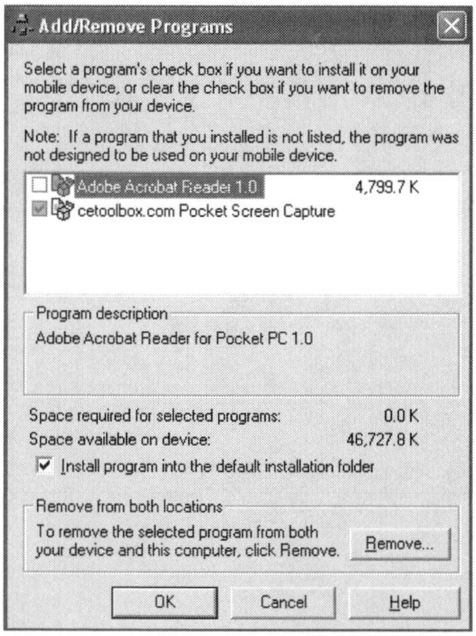
Add/Remove Programs
Select a program's check box if you want to install it on your mobile device, or clear the check box if you want to remove the program from your device.
Note: If a program that you installed is not listed, the program was not designed to be used on your mobile device.
Adobe Acrobat Reader 1.0 4,799.7 K
cetoolbox.com Pocket Screen Capture
Program description
Adobe Acrobat Reader for Pocket PC 1.0
Space required for selected programs: 0.0 K
Space available on device: 46,727.8 K
Install program into the default installation folder
Remove from both locations
To remove the selected program from both your device and this computer, click Remove.
Remove...
OK
Cancel
Help

Figure 4.36 Choosing which check boxes to clear in order to remove one or more programs.

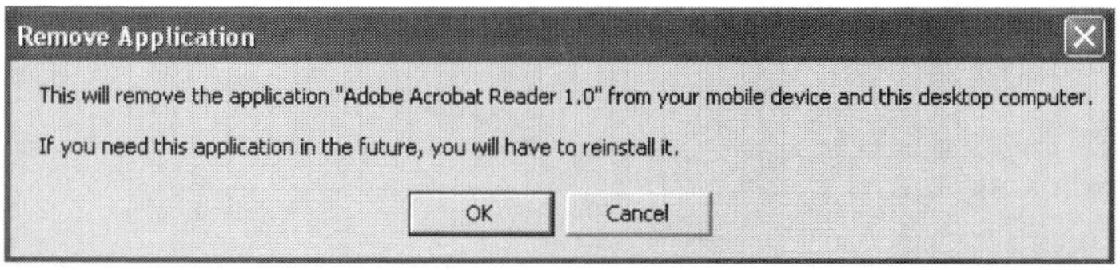
Remove Application
This will remove the application "Adobe Acrobat Reader 1.0" from your mobile device and this desktop computer.
If you need this application in the future, you will have to reinstall it.
OK
Cancel

Figure 4.37 You get one last chance to change your mind about removing a program from both places.

To remove a program using ActiveSync:

1. Connect your Pocket PC to your computer.
2. In ActiveSync on your computer, click Tools > Add/Remove Programs (**Figure 4.35**).

   The Add/Remove Programs dialog box appears (**Figure 4.36**).
3. Click to remove the check mark from any program you want to remove from your Pocket PC only.

   If you want to remove it from your computer as well, click the Remove button.

   A Remove Application warning appears (**Figure 4.37**).
4. Click OK. Your program is removed.

Managing Pocket PC Files from Your PC

"Managing" files means—what? Giving them a performance review every six months? No, it's Microsoft's term for cutting, copying, pasting, creating, deleting, and moving files. The Pocket PC program File Explorer lets you manage your files on your device, but let's be honest—it's not nearly as easy or powerful as My Computer in Windows. Luckily, ActiveSync lets you use My Computer to manage your Pocket PC's files remotely.

To manage Pocket PC files using ActiveSync:

1. Connect your Pocket PC to your computer.

2. In ActiveSync on your computer, click the Explore icon.

   The Mobile Device Screen appears (**Figure 4.38**)—this is really your Pocket PC's My Documents folder.

   From here you can do everything you normally do in My Computer, and everything you do automatically happens on your Pocket PC. You can:

   ▲ Open a folder by double-clicking it.

   ▲ Create a folder by right-clicking and choosing New > Folder from the pop-up menu.

   ▲ Cut, Copy, Paste, and Delete folders and files by right-clicking them and clicking the choices in the pop-up window.

   ▲ Move files and folders by dragging them from place to place.

   ▲ Rename a folder or file by clicking it, waiting a second, clicking again to highlight it, and then typing over it.

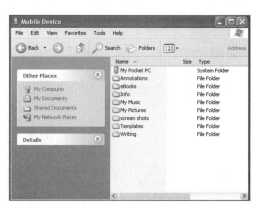

Figure 4.38 The Mobile Device screen on the computer is—literally—your Pocket PC's folders viewed on the PC.

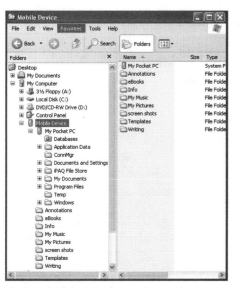

Figure 4.39 The oft-forgotten Windows Explorer makes managing files even easier.

✔ Tips

■ To get even fancier, right-click the My Device icon and click Explore in the pop-up menu that appears. This opens the My Device Screen in Windows Explorer, the even handier, partitioned-screen version of My Computer (**Figure 4.39**). Now you can drag files and folders back and forth without cutting and pasting.

■ You can also access the My Device screen by double-clicking the My Device icon in My Computer.

■ The name Pocket_PC My Documents is just the default name for your Pocket PC's My Documents folder. You can change the name by changing the name of your device. Tap Start > Settings > System tab > About > Device ID tab and entering a new name for the device.

Backing up and Restoring

Because one day every hard drive will in fact die, we all know we should back up our computers more often than we do. Same goes for the Pocket PC. But isn't that what ActiveSync is for? Not quite. ActiveSync makes it easy to ensure the preservation of your Outlook data—Contacts, Notes, Inbox, Schedule, Tasks—but that's all. A true back-up makes an "image" of your entire device, protecting programs and settings and other non-Outlook data and storing everything all on your computer so that should the unspeakable happen you can restore everything with no problem. Alternatively, you can back up your Pocket PC to a storage card instead of to your computer.

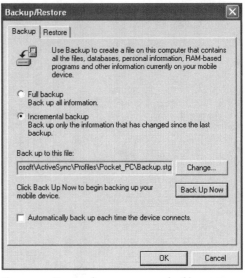

Figure 4.40 Here is where you manage backing up your Pocket PC to your computer.

To back up your Pocket PC to your computer:

1. Connect your Pocket PC to your computer.

2. In ActiveSync on the computer, click Tools > Backup/Restore.

    The Backup/Restore dialog box appears (**Figure 4.40**).

3. In the Backup tab, choose between a full backup and an incremental backup by clicking the corresponding radio button. Incremental is usually good enough.

4. If you want, change where to place the storage (.stg) file, which contains your Pocket PC's data, by clicking the Change button.

Getting files onto your Pocket PC

When you opt to synchronize your files by checking the Files checkbox under Tools > Options in ActiveSync on your computer, a folder shortcut is created on your desktop called Pocket_PC My Documents. (The folder is actually a subfolder of your computer's My Documents folder.) Every file you put in the Pocket_PC My Documents folder on your computer is automatically copied to your Pocket PC's My Documents folder during Active-Sync. Likewise, files anywhere in your device's My Documents folder are copied to your computer's Pocket_PC My Documents folder.

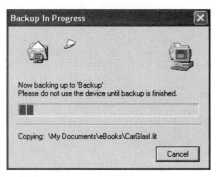

Figure 4.41 You can see how backup is proceeding.

5. Add a checkmark to "Automatically back up each time the device connects" if you want that option.

6. When you're ready, click Back Up Now. The Back Up in Progress window shows you how the backup is coming along (**Figure 4.41**).

✔ Tips

■ Restoring a backup can often be a nightmare—many settings have to all be correct before it will work. A great third-party backup program is Pocket Backup Plus from www.sprintesoftware.com. It runs directly on the device and, best of all, it has a scheduler, meaning you don't need to remember to run it. iPAQs come with Pocket Backup Plus already installed.

■ Be patient—if you have a lot of files, backing up takes a long time, up to many tens of minutes.

■ The first time you do an incremental backup, ActiveSync performs a full backup, because you're incrementing from nothing.

To restore from a backup:

1. Stop all programs on your device by tapping Start > Settings > System tab > Running Programs tab, and then tapping the Stop All button.

2. Connect your device to your computer.

3. In ActiveSync on your computer, click Tools > Backup/Restore > Restore tab to bring up the Backup/Restore dialog box (**Figure 4.42**).

4. Tap Restore Now.

   The Restore program begins.

5. When Restore is finished, tap OK.

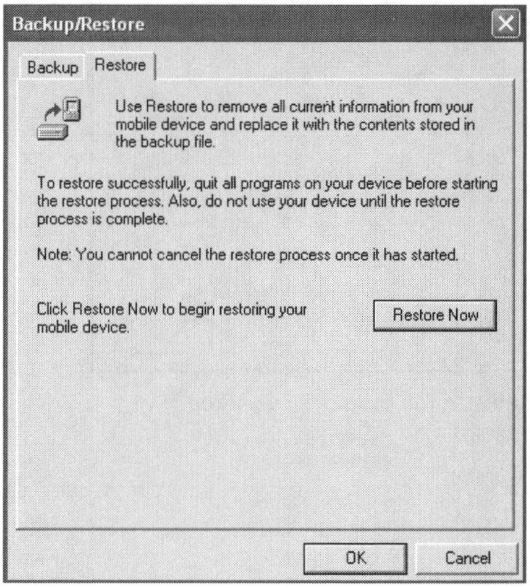

✔ Tip

■ Restore removes all current data from your device and replaces it with the data that was there the last time you backed up, so be careful that you really do want to restore. Once you begin the restore process, there's no turning back.

Figure 4.42 The Restore tab of the Backup/Restore dialog box is where you go to restore your device to its last backup state.

Backing up to storage cards and file stores

Your Pocket PC likely has a slot for an SD memory card and perhaps another one for a CompactFlash card. These kinds of flash memory storage cards are a good way to back up your device—and to store files, too, such as video and audio files. With a storage card, you back your device up using your Pocket PC's backup utility. Cards are available in memory sizes ranging from 32MB to 1GB. Insert the card, set it up (see Appendix C for more), and then back up to the card. Backup utilities for the Pocket PC vary from brand to brand. See your device's Help program or manual for how to back your device up to a card.

Some Pocket PCs allow you to back up and store files in internal Flash ROM—kind of a built-in virtual storage card. When something is in ROM, it is permanent, meaning it can't be lost if your device requires a hard reset (see Chapter 1). Look in your device's Help program or check File Explorer in the My Device folder for a special subfolder called File Store.

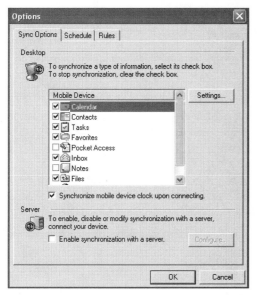

Figure 4.43 The Sync Options icon opens ActiveSync Options.

ActiveSync Options

ActiveSync offers flexibility in how synchronization works. You can control what types of files and data get synchronized and when, how to resolve conflicts, and how files are converted when they move between your computer and your device.

To choose what gets synchronized:

1. In the ActiveSync program on your computer, click the Options icon to display the Options dialog box (**Figure 4.43**). The Sync Options tab is selected by default.

2. In the Desktop area, click to check or uncheck boxes for the type of information you want ActiveSync to synchronize.

3. If your workplace has Microsoft Exchange Server with Exchange Server ActiveSync installed, and you're supposed to synchronize with it, click to put a check next to "Enable synchronization with a server" and click Configure to set it up.

Bear in mind that you can only synchronize items with one or the other—if you sync your Inbox with the server, for example, you cannot sync it with your computer.

To choose when your data will be synchronized:

1. Tap the Schedule tab in the Options dialog box for Schedule options (**Figure 4.44**).

2. Choose when you want ActiveSync to synchronize by clicking the drop-down box next to "When connected to my PC, sync."

   Your choices are Continuously, On Connection, and Manually.

3. If you synchronize with a server, choose how often by clicking the drop-down box in the Server schedule area.

4. In the Wireless schedule area, click the drop-down boxes to control how often ActiveSync will synchronize during peak times (when you receive the most email) and off-peak times. Click the Peak Times button to set up your peak times.

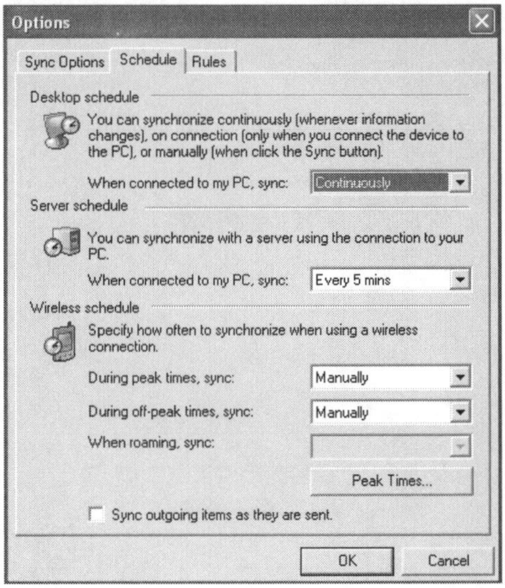

✔ Tip

- Put a check in the "Sync outgoing items as they are sent" check box at the bottom of the Schedule dialog box to automatically synchronize your Outlook Sent folder when you email from your device.

Figure 4.44 The Schedule tab lets you determine when ActiveSync occurs.

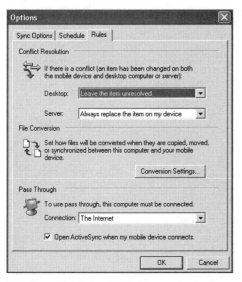

Figure 4.45 The Rules tab enables you to change certain ActiveSync behaviors.

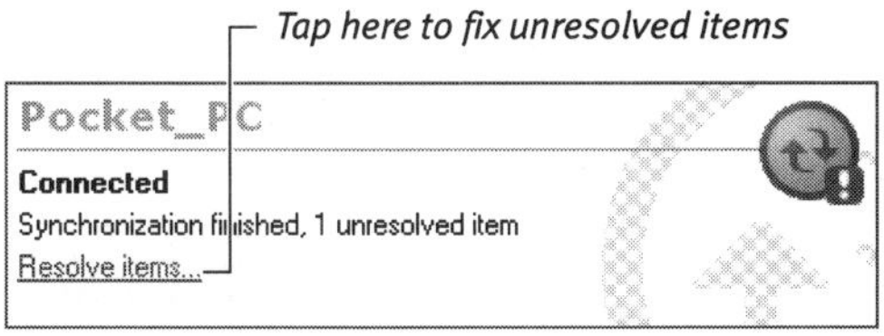

Tap here to fix unresolved items

Figure 4.46 ActiveSync has found a problem it needs human input to resolve.

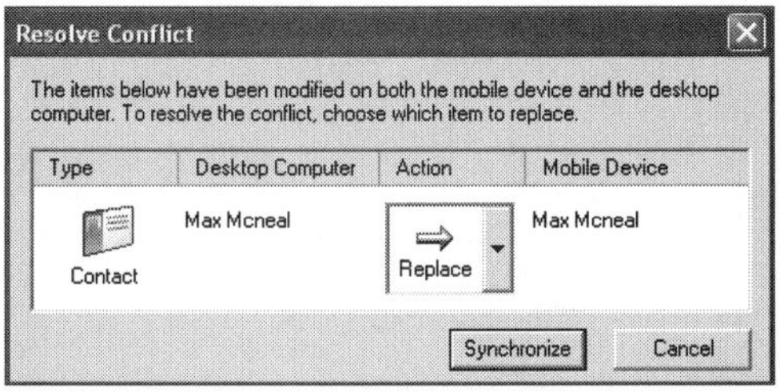

Figure 4.47 Conflict resolution in ActiveSync sometimes requires decisions from you.

To choose synchronization rules:

1. Tap the Rules tab in the Options dialog box to display Rules options (**Figure 4.45**).

2. In the Conflict Resolution area, click the drop-down boxes for Desktop and Server to set how to deal with unresolved items.

Unresolved items are items that have changed in both your device *and* your computer since your last synchronization. Choosing "Leave the item unresolved" lets you choose what to do on a case-by-case basis. Then, when you synchronize, ActiveSync alerts you that something is unresolved and offers a link to fix it (**Figure 4.46**). The link opens a window that lets you determine which version's change you want more—the one made on your device or the one on your computer (**Figure 4.47**).

continues on next page

ACTIVESYNC OPTIONS

95

3. In the File Conversion area, click Conversion Settings to open File Conversion Properties (**Figure 4.48**).

4. The default is to automatically convert files when they are synchronized, copied, or moved. Leave this option alone unless you don't want to convert files.

Files converted for Pocket PC use usually work better than unconverted files. You will rarely if ever have to change file conversion options, but in the Device to Desktop and Desktop to Device tabs, you can specify which file types get converted and how.

5. In the Pass Through area, leave the "Open ActiveSync when my mobile device connects" check box checked to enable your device to "pass through" your computer to a network to download email or browse the Web. Choose whether your device should connect to the Internet or a work network.

6. Click OK to save your changes.

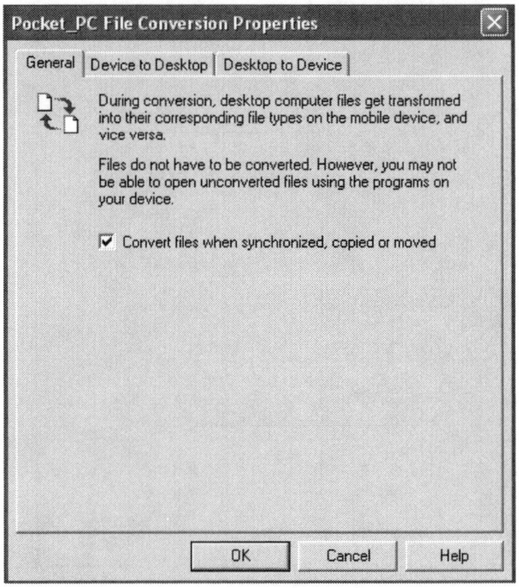

Figure 4.48 ActiveSync lets you control whether and how files are converted between your device and your computer.

MANAGING YOUR CONTACTS

Your Pocket PC comes equipped with an address book program called Contacts that beats the pants off a Rolodex for storing and organizing contact info for all the people you need to be in touch with. Contacts synchronizes with the Contacts module of the Outlook program on your computer—so, what you do to one happens to the other.

Contacts makes it easy to email anyone in your list. But it's not just for email addresses—even those Luddites in your life without email accounts can find a home in your contacts. You can organize contacts among family, friends, and business colleagues and navigate categories to quickly find the name you seek. Contacts can be sorted alphabetically, by the names you've looked up most recently, and by other categories you create, such as by business type or relationship.

Think of the Contacts application as a thorough address book that is more efficient to carry and use than a physical address book, and in many cases is easier to access than Outlook on your computer.

Entering Contacts

If you're creating more than one contact, it is probably faster and more efficient to create them on your computer in Microsoft Outlook and then synchronize with ActiveSync to get them onto your Pocket PC. If you want to create one contact or if you're away from your computer, you can create it easily directly on your device. You can also import contacts from other Personal Information Manager programs (PIMs) including ACT!, ECCO, Lotus Organizer, and Sidekick.

To create a new contact:

1. Press the Contacts hardware button on the face of your Pocket PC.

   or

   Tap Start > Contacts.

   The Contacts screen (**Figure 5.1**) appears.

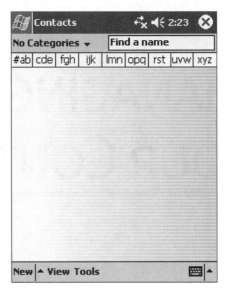

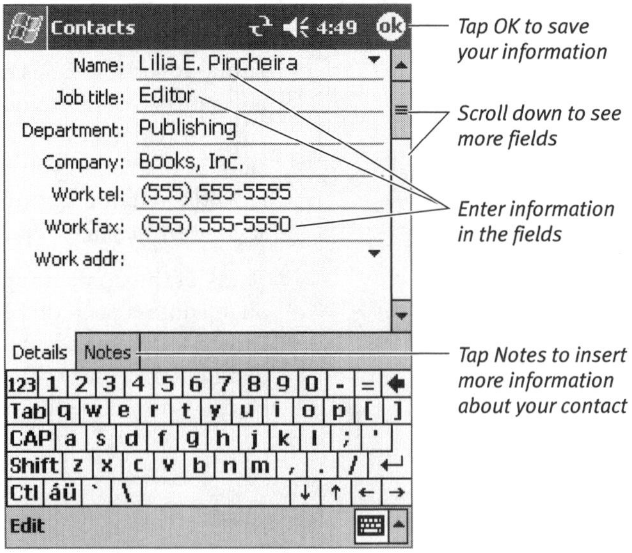

Figure 5.1 This is the tidiest your Contacts screen will ever look.

Tap OK to save your information

Scroll down to see more fields

Enter information in the fields

Tap Notes to insert more information about your contact

Figure 5.2 Fill in the relevant fields for your new contact.

All Contacts ▾	Find a name							
#ab	cde	fgh	ijk	lmn	opq	rst	uvw	xyz

Pincheira, Lilia   (555) 555-5555   ⋓

Figure 5.3 Your new contact appears.

2. Tap New at the bottom of the screen to access the New Contact form.

3. Use the soft (onscreen) keyboard (or your preferred text-entering method) to enter information into the applicable fields for the contact you are adding (**Figure 5.2**).

4. Tap OK.

    Your contact now appears on the Contacts screen (**Figure 5.3**).

To import contacts from other programs:

1. In Outlook (on your computer), click File > Import and Export... to bring up the Import and Export Wizard.

2. Click "Import from another program or file" and click Next.

3. Click the type of file you want to import and click Next.

4. Keep making the appropriate selections and clicking Next until you click Finish.

    Your contacts are imported into Outlook and are ready to use.

ENTERING CONTACTS

Navigating Contacts

Next to each column in the Contacts screen, what you see varies depending on which fields have been filled in for the contact. For example, if the contact has an email address entered, the address will show. If there is a work phone number and no email address entered, the phone number will appear. And if a contact has a mobile phone number and no email address or other number listed, you'll see it. Your contacts can be listed alphabetically by name or company.

To view contacts:

1. Tap Start > Contacts.

   The Contacts screen appears.

2. Tap the All Contacts drop-down arrow at the top left-hand side of the screen.

   The Show options menu appears (**Figure 5.4**).

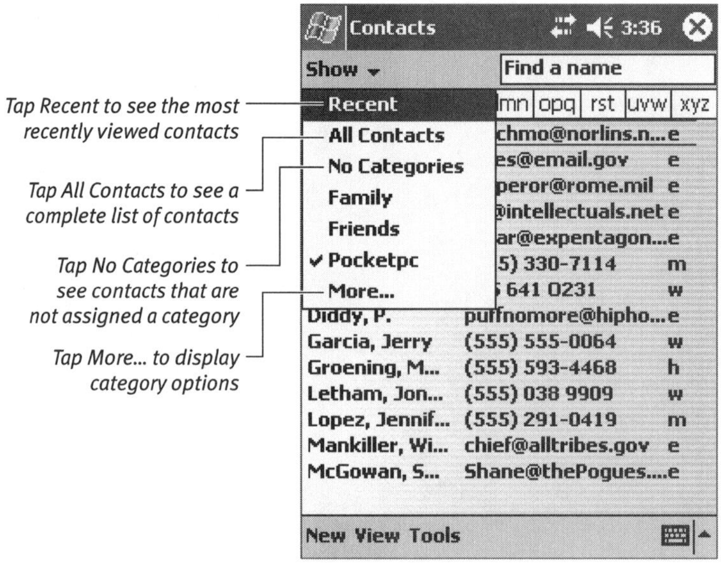

Tap Recent to see the most recently viewed contacts

Tap All Contacts to see a complete list of contacts

Tap No Categories to see contacts that are not assigned a category

Tap More... to display category options

Figure 5.4 The Show menu presents options for how your contacts are displayed.

Tap here in the blank space after the
letter to reveal the full contact info

🏁 Contacts	⁺✗ ◀€ 2:25	❌

Pocketpc ▾	Find a name

#ab	cde	fgh	ijk	lmn	opq	rst	uvw	xyz

Armstrong, Louis		e
Bastio	• satchmo@norlins.net E-mail	
Caesar, Julius	emperor@rome.mil	e
Chomsky, No...	NC@intellectuals.net	e
Clark, Wesley	4star@expentagon...e
Connor, Sarah	(555) 330-7114	m
Darywimple, ...	555 641 0231	w
Diddy, P.	puffnomore@hipho...e
Garcia, Jerry	(555) 555-0064	w
Groening, M...	(555) 593-4468	h
Letham, Jon...	(555) 038 9909	w
Lopez, Jennif...	(555) 291-0419	m
Mankiller, Wi...	chief@alltribes.gov	e
McGowan, S...	Shane@thePogues....e

New View Tools	🖊 ▲

Figure 5.5 Tap beside the letter to reveal the entire listing.

3. Tap a menu option to select how you want the contacts to be displayed.

   ▲ "Recent" displays a list of those contacts you accessed most recently.

   ▲ "All Contacts" displays all your contacts.

   ▲ "No Categories" displays those contacts not assigned to a category.

✔ Tips

■ In the Contacts screen, depending on what is shown, after each contact item you'll see an *e* (for email), a *w* (work), *h* (home), or an *m* (mobile) in the far right of the screen. Because of size limitations, often these are cut off from full view. To view the entire number or email address from the Contacts screen, tap in the blank space after the letter, and the numbers and email address associated for the contact will be displayed, as shown in **Figure 5.5**.

■ Once you add new categories, they will also appear in the Show options menu.

■ If you have added new categories, you will also see a More... option in the Show menu. Tapping this displays the category options screen.

■ When you make your selection in the Show menu, the menu name changes to that of the selection you made. If you aren't sure which categories are being displayed, you can always tell by looking at this menu name.

■ Tap an ABC tab at the top of the list of contacts to quickly move to the letter your contact begins with.

■ Use the navigation button (the big middle one) on the face of your device to quickly scroll up and down through your contacts. If you hold the edge of the button down (or up), it reaches a fast speed and displays each letter it passes in very large font right in the middle of the screen, so you can stop when you see the letter the contact begins with.

To find contacts:

◆ Scroll up and down your list of contacts until you see the one you want and tap it.

◆ Tap one of the ABC tabs at the top of the list of contacts to display those beginning with those letters.

◆ Tap the "Find a name" box to begin entering the name of a contact (**Figure 5.6**). For each letter you enter as you spell the name, Contacts narrows down the choices. Tap your choice when you see it.

To sort contacts:

◆ Tap View > By Name to sort contacts alphabetically by name.

◆ Tap View > By Company to sort contacts alphabetically by company.

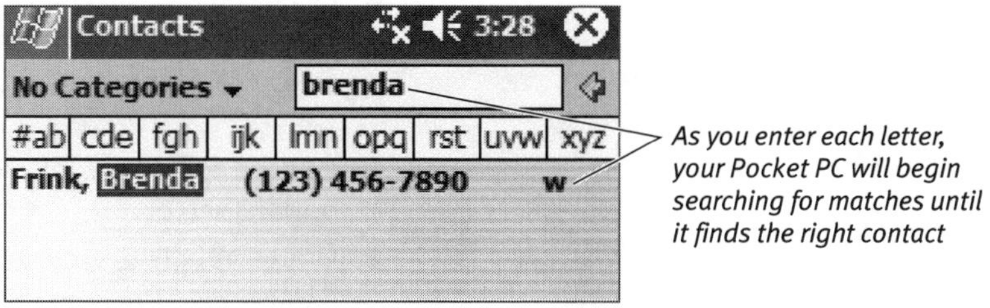

NAVIGATING CONTACTS

As you enter each letter, your Pocket PC will begin searching for matches until it finds the right contact

Figure 5.6 Type (or write) the name of the contact you want to locate, and your Pocket PC will find it for you.

Modifying Contacts

After creating or entering contacts, you can edit, copy, and/or delete them on your device. Copying contacts is a quick and easy way to enter contacts with the same address, phone number, or other details. When you copy a contact, you create a duplicate of an existing contact and then edit the fields that distinguish the new contact, such as the name.

Synchronize contacts with ActiveSync

When you install ActiveSync (see Chapter 4 if you haven't done so), it is automatically set up to synchronize your contacts with Outlook every time you synchronize. To check that this option is selected, in ActiveSync on your computer, click the Options button to access the Options screen, shown here.

Here, you can select which items you want ActiveSync to synchronize. Be sure the box next to Contacts is checked to enable synchronization. (Uncheck this box if for any reason you don't want your contacts synchronized.) Click OK to save your settings.

If you're not using Outlook as your email program on your computer, all is not lost. You don't have to use the same program for contacts and email. Many email programs, including Eudora and Pegasus Mail, will import your Outlook contacts. There are also third-party programs that enable synchronization with email applications other than Outlook (see Appendix A for more on these and Chapter 11 for more on email).

To edit contacts:

1. Tap the contact you want to edit.

   The summary screen for the contact appears.

2. Tap the Edit menu (**Figure 5.7**).

   The Contacts editing screen appears, and you are now able to edit the contact.

3. Tap the field you want to edit.

   A blinking cursor appears (**Figure 5.8**).

4. Make your changes or additions using the keyboard or your preferred text-entering method (**Figure 5.9**).

5. Tap OK to save your edits.

✔ Tip

- When you edit contacts on your Pocket PC, they will also be changed in Outlook on your computer the next time you synchronize with ActiveSync.

To copy contacts:

1. In the Contacts screen, tap the contact you want to copy.

   Tapping the contact will probably bring you to the contact's summary screen—just tap OK to return to the Contacts screen with the Contact selected.

2. With the contact selected, tap Tools > Copy Contacts.

   The copy of the contact appears immediately below the original.

3. Edit the new contact.

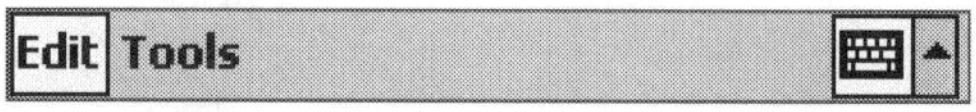

Figure 5.7 The Edit menu is how you access the different fields for editing.

Figure 5.8 Tap a field to edit, and the existing text becomes highlighted and a blinking cursor appears. You may now edit or replace the information in the field.

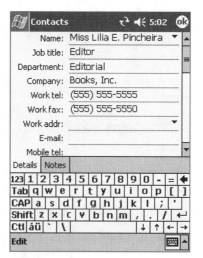

Figure 5.9 The field has now been changed. Tap OK to save edits.

MODIFYING CONTACTS

Name: Miss Lilia E. Pincheira
Job title: Editor
Title: Miss
First: Lilia
Middle: E.
Last: Pincheira
Suffix:
E-mail:
Tap this arrow...
To bring up this box and enter a title or suffix

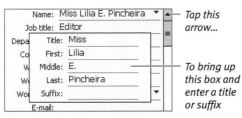

Figure 5.10 The Name subfield lets you get more specific regarding your contact's name.

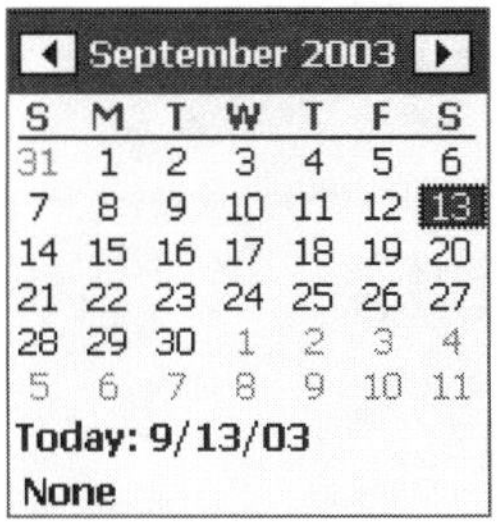

September 2003
S M T W T F S
31 1 2 3 4 5 6
7 8 9 10 11 12 13
14 15 16 17 18 19 20
21 22 23 24 25 26 27
28 29 30 1 2 3 4
5 6 7 8 9 10 11
Today: 9/13/03
None

Figure 5.11 The Calendar subfield lets you pick a date from a calendar.

To delete contacts:

◆ Tap and hold the stylus on the name in the list of contacts and tap Delete Contact in the pop-up menu that appears. Tap Yes to confirm your decision when prompted.

✔ Tips

■ The Name and Address fields have a downward-facing arrow next to them. Tap it to enter specific information in subfields, such as city and state in the Address field or title in the Name field (**Figure 5.10**).

■ Tap the fields relating to dates—Birthday and Anniversary—and then tap the downward-facing arrow that appears to access a calendar from which you can select dates (**Figure 5.11**).

■ Adding, editing, and deleting contacts on your device will also perform those actions in Outlook on your computer the next time you synchronize with ActiveSync.

Setting Contacts Options

You can change some aspects of how the Contacts application works on your device in the Contacts Options screen.

To set Contacts options:

1. In the Contacts screen, tap Tools > Options.

   The Contacts Options screen appears (**Figure 5.12**).

2. Tap the checkbox next to the options you want to set.

   An unchecked box means the option is disabled; a checked box means it's enabled.

   ▲ Tap the box next to "Show ABC tabs" to uncheck it. This will hide the ABC tabs on your Contacts screen.

   ▲ Tap the box next to "Show contact names only" if you want only the names to display in the Contacts screen (**Figure 5.13**).

   ▲ Tap the box next to "Use large font" to increase the font size on your Contacts screen (**Figure 5.14**).

✔ Tip

■ You can enter a default area code in the Country/Region drop-down list. If most of your contacts are in the same area code, doing this will save you time entering contacts. This is also where you set your default country or region.

Figure 5.12
Contacts Options let you control some aspects of what Contacts displays.

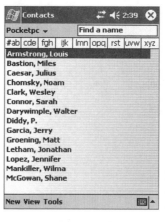

Figure 5.13
Showing only the names of your contacts is an option.

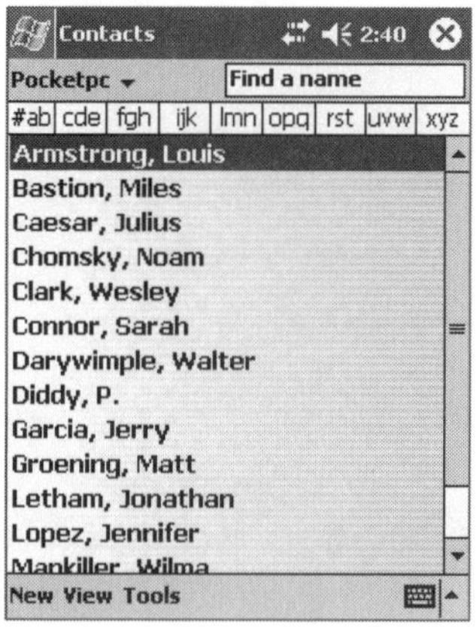

Figure 5.14
Selecting the larger font makes your contacts a little easier to read, but displays fewer of them at once.

No categories are assigned to this contact, but when you assign a category it will be listed here

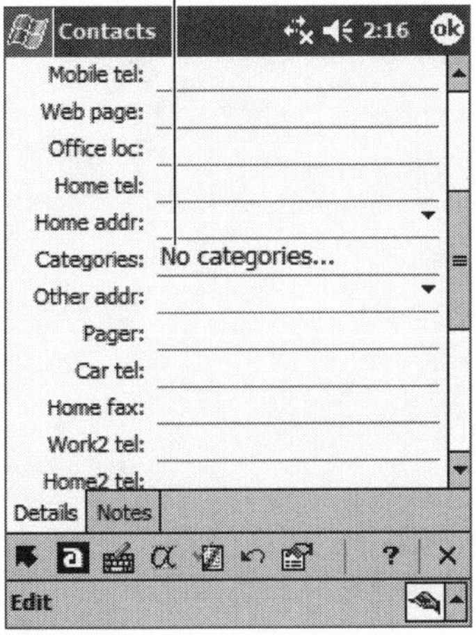

Figure 5.15 Keep scrolling until you come to the Categories field, where you can assign each contact to a category.

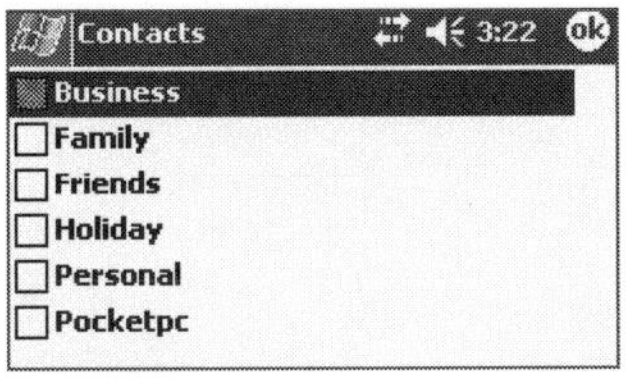

Figure 5.16 Here are the currently available categories.

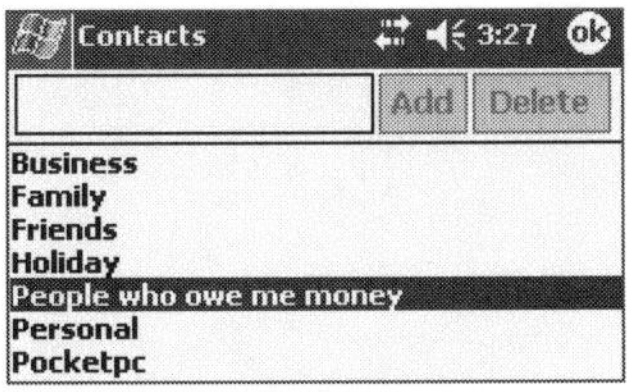

Figure 5.17 Our new category appears in alphabetical order with the rest of the categories.

Using Contacts Categories

Categories enable you to organize your contacts according to whatever criteria you like. When you assign a contact to a category, you make it possible to view all contacts in that category together.

To create a category:

1. In the Contacts screen, tap the contact you wish to assign to a category.

   The summary screen for the contact appears.

2. Tap the Edit menu to display the Contacts editing screen.

3. Use the scrollbar to move down the screen to the Categories field (**Figure 5.15**).

   By default, contacts are assigned to the No Categories category in the Categories field.

4. Tap the Categories field to display the current category options (**Figure 5.16**).

5. Tap the Add/Delete tab.

   A text box appears at the top of the screen.

6. Enter the name of the new category in the text box using the soft keyboard or whichever text-entering method you prefer.

7. Tap Add.

   Your new category appears, listed with the other contacts in alphabetical order (**Figure 5.17**).

USING CONTACTS CATEGORIES

To delete a category:

1. Follow steps 1–5 in the previous task.

2. Tap the category you want to delete.

3. Tap the Delete button.

The category disappears from the list.

✔ Tip

■ Deleting a category doesn't delete the contacts within that category—it just strips them of the category you deleted. If you want the contacts to be in a different category, you will have to reassign them to it, one contact at a time.

To assign contacts into categories:

1. Tap the contact you want to assign to a category.

The summary screen for the contact appears.

2. Tap the Edit menu to display the Contacts editing screen.

3. Use the scrollbar to move down the screen to the Categories field.

By default, contacts are assigned to the No Categories category in the Categories field.

4. Tap the Categories field to display the current category options.

5. Tap to put a check mark in the box next to the category you want to put the contact in and tap OK.

The contact is assigned the category.

✔ Tip

■ You can assign a contact to more than one category.

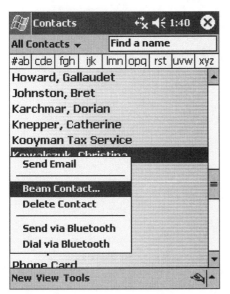

Figure 5.18 You can also enter contacts by accepting contacts that are beamed from another device to yours. You can also beam contacts from your device to another.

Beaming Contacts

You can send and receive contacts from other Pocket PCs via infrared beaming. This is very satisfying, because you don't have to do the work of creating them or synchronizing them with ActiveSync.

To beam contacts between Pocket PCs:

1. Press and hold the tip of the stylus on the contact you want to beam to another device.

A pop-up menu appears.

2. Tap Beam Contact... (**Figure 5.18**).

If the other device is in range (a few feet) and set up to accept beams, your contact will be sent and received via the infrared ports and automatically added to the other device's Contacts program.

✔ Tip

■ See Chapter 2 for more on how to send and receive beams.

BEAMING CONTACTS

Sending email from Contacts

One of the handiest features in Contacts is this: In the Contacts screen, press and hold the tip of the stylus on a contact to whom you'd like to send an email. Tap Send email in the pop-up menu that appears. Inbox opens and a new email is created with the contact's email address all filled in for you.

Printing contacts

You can print your contacts from Outlook on your computer, if you like. Double-click the Contacts module in the folder list and click File > Print. In the Print dialog box that appears, choose how you want the contacts to be printed in the Print Style area of the dialog box. Your choices are card style, different types of booklet styles, memo style, and phone directory style.

KEEPING YOUR SCHEDULE

We all have things to do, places to go, people to meet, and we need to keep track of it all. To help you do just that, the Pocket PC offers two scheduling programs: Tasks and Calendar. This chapter covers both of them.

Both Tasks and Calendar display and manage your to-do lists and appointment schedule in rather a lot of detail. Both programs synchronize with Outlook on your computer, so whatever you do in these programs on your Pocket PC also happens in the corresponding Outlook modules on your computer, and vice versa.

Both Tasks and Calendar let you organize your life into categories. You can use categories to organize tasks into different kinds of arrangements—shopping lists, for example. And both programs will alert you of your engagements and duties by issuing reminders in the form of bleeps and squawks, flashing lights, on-screen alerts, and/or the vibration of the little machine itself.

Together, the two programs offer extensive scheduling features that ought to be enough for even the busiest of folks. If you find them too limited, you might want to cut back on the coffee—or burrow deeper into geek-dom by purchasing a third-party planning and scheduling application.

Creating and Editing Tasks

Tasks lets you create lists of entries representing your errands, responsibilities, chores, and so forth—things that you must make happen in the future. You can create and edit new tasks, mark them completed, delete them, and assign reminders and categories to them.

Some tasks are simpler than others—by "simple task," we mean a straightforward phrase that, at a glance, reminds you of everything you need to know about the task. More complex tasks may involve entering additional information regarding priority, start times, due dates, sensitivity, and how often this task occurs.

To create a simple task:

1. Tap the Tasks item in the Today screen.
   or
   Tap Start > Programs > Tasks.
   The Tasks program launches and displays the main Tasks screen (**Figure 6.1**). If this is the first time you've run Tasks, there won't be any tasks showing.

2. Tap in the text box that reads, "Tap here to add new task."
   The text is replaced by a blinking cursor, and the soft (onscreen) keyboard appears.

3. Write or type your task using your favorite text-entering method (**Figure 6.2**).

4. Tap anywhere in the blank middle of the screen.
   or
   Tap the Enter key on the keyboard.
   The task is added to the list (**Figure 6.3**).

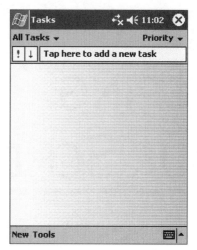

Figure 6.1 The main Tasks screen appears clean when you first launch it.

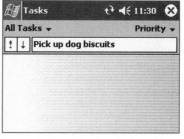

Figure 6.2 Enter the description of the task in the text box.

Figure 6.3 The task is entered into the task list, which means you really have to do it now.

CREATING AND EDITING TASKS

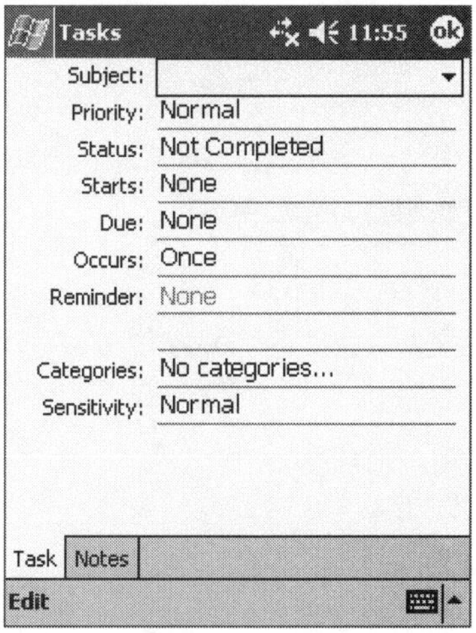

Figure 6.4 Edit the task details screen to reflect everything you think is important to record about the task.

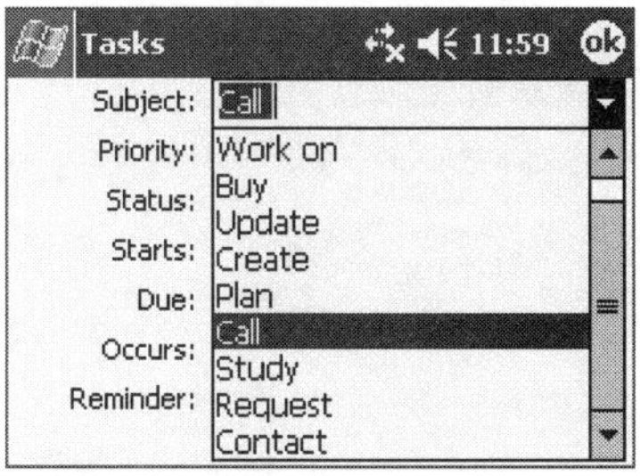

Figure 6.5 The Subject line offers some common starter verbs to help you name your task.

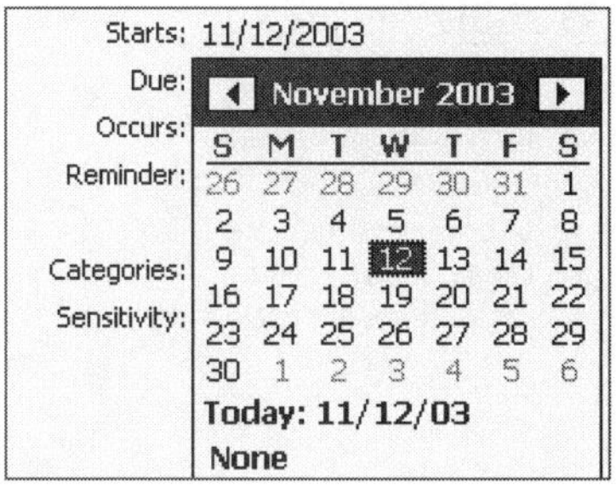

Figure 6.6 Some tasks may span several days or more, and the Start line lets you conveniently tap a date for when you want to start the task.

To create a detailed task:

◆ Tap the New menu in the Tasks screen.

 The task details screen appears, which you edit to customize all the particulars. (For how, see the next section.)

To edit a task:

1. Tap a task in the task list to select it, and then tap the Edit menu.

 The task details screen appears (**Figure 6.4**), offering nine different characteristics that you can assign to the task. Each of the nine items, when tapped, opens a drop-down menu where you can choose from among several options or lets you enter text directly.

2. Tap the middle of the Subject line to enter a new name for the task.

 or

 Tap the drop-down arrow on the right-hand side of the Subject line to choose from ten suggested verbs to get you started on naming the task (**Figure 6.5**).

3. Tap the Priority line to change the priority from the default Normal to High or Low.

4. Tap the Status line to change the status to Completed or Not Completed, if desired.

5. Tap the Starts line to choose a start date for the task, if any, from the calendar that pops up (**Figure 6.6**).

continues on next page

CREATING AND EDITING TASKS

6. Tap the Due line to select a due date, if any, from the calendar that pops up.

7. Tap the Occurs line to tell the Pocket PC that the task occurs once, weekly, monthly, annually, or in some other recurring pattern (**Figure 6.7**).

The default is that the task will occur once.

8. Tap the first Reminder line to choose whether you want the device to remind you of the task and, if so, tap the second line to choose when.

9. Tap the Categories line to assign the task to one or more categories.

10. Tap the Sensitivity line to choose between Normal and Private sensitivity.

11. Tap OK to finish editing the task.

To delete a task:

◆ Press and hold the tip of the stylus on a task and tap Delete in the pop-up menu that appears (**Figure 6.8**).

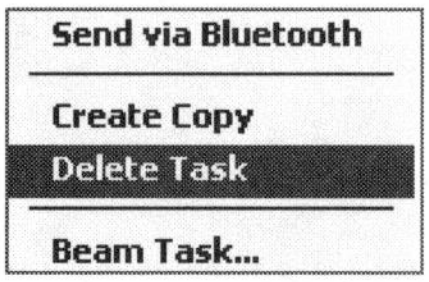

To mark a task as completed:

◆ Tap the check box next to the completed task to put a check mark in the box (**Figure 6.9**).

Checked tasks are considered completed.

✔ Tip

■ If the task is a recurring task, checking the box will automatically create the next task in the recurring series.

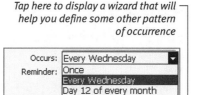
Tap here to display a wizard that will help you define some other pattern of occurrence

Figure 6.7 Some tasks occur regularly or in a pattern you can define in the task.

Send via Bluetooth

Create Copy

Delete Task

Beam Task...

Figure 6.8 Delete a task by tapping Delete in the pop-up menu.

Figure 6.9 Just like crossing items off your list, checking tasks means they are done. If you forget, the task turns red to show how angry it is at your negligence.

CREATING AND EDITING TASKS

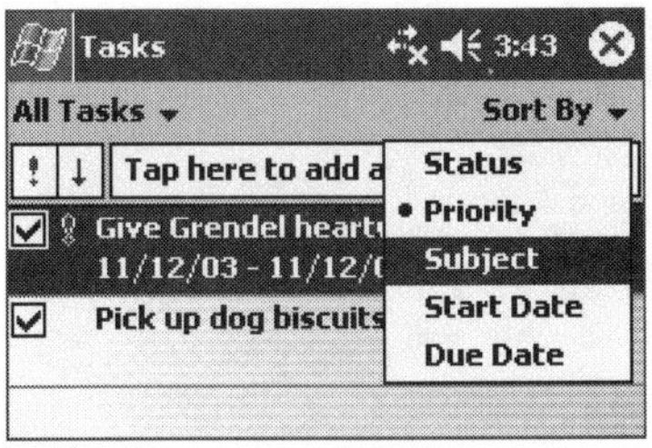

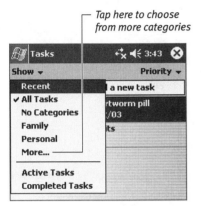

Figure 6.10 You can sort tasks by different gauges in the Sort By drop-down list.

Tap here to choose
from more categories

Figure 6.11 Show only certain kinds of tasks in the Show drop-down menu.

To sort tasks:

1. Tap the drop-down list in the upper right-hand part of the screen (**Figure 6.10**).

2. Tap Status, Priority, Subject, Start Date, or Due Date to sort tasks by that criterion.

   The tasks are arranged in the list according to the criterion you pick.

To display only certain tasks:

1. Tap the drop-down list in the upper left-hand part of the screen (**Figure 6.11**).

2. Tap Recent, All Tasks, No Categories, one of the current categories that are displayed, Active Tasks, or Completed Tasks to display on that kind of task.

   The tasks are displayed according to the preference you expressed.

✔ Tips

■ See later in this chapter for more on using categories in Tasks.

■ Tap Tools > Options to enable/disable reminders, choose whether to display start and due dates in the list screen, or use a larger font.

CREATING AND EDITING TASKS

Using Reminders in Tasks

Reminders are Tasks' way of alerting you to an upcoming task. Reminders can be in the form of messages that appear, audible alarms, flashing indicator lights, or physical vibration.

To set a reminder for a task:

1. Tap a task to select it and tap the Edit menu.

   The task details screen appears.

2. Tap the Due line to set a date (**Figure 6.12**).

3. Tap the first Reminders line and tap Remind Me in the drop-down list (**Figure 6.13**).

4. Tap the second Reminders line to choose the date you want to be reminded on.

5. Tap OK to have the reminder play at 8 a.m. on the due date.

✔ Tip

■ To get more precise, hour-specific reminders, use Calendar, not Tasks.

Figure 6.12 Choose a due date for your task to be completed.

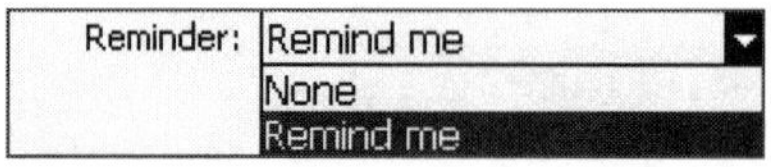

Figure 6.13 If you want your Pocket PC to remind you to do what you claim you're going to do, tap Remind Me.

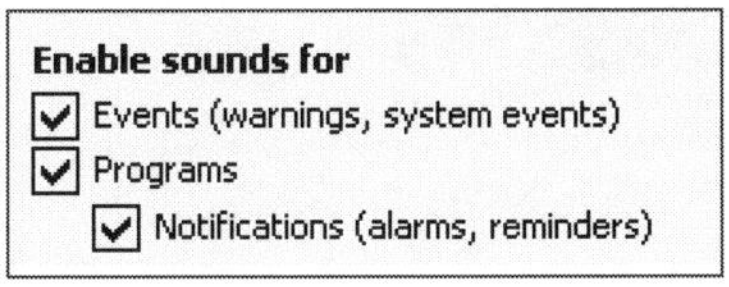

Enable sounds for
- ☑ Events (warnings, system events)
- ☑ Programs
  - ☑ Notifications (alarms, reminders)

Figure 6.14 You have to enable Notifications before Tasks can remind you to do something.

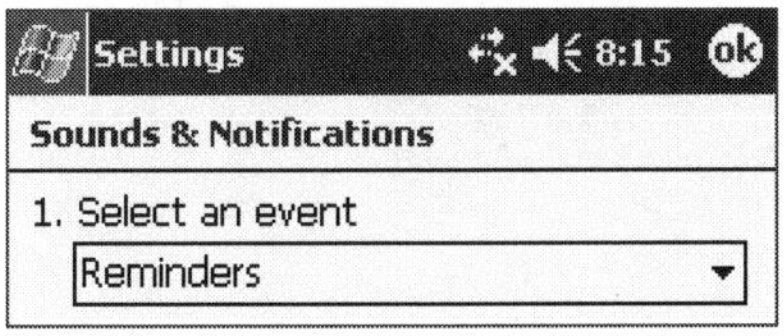

Settings	⁺✗ ◀€ 8:15	ok
Sounds & Notifications		
1. Select an event		
Reminders		▾

Figure 6.15 Choose Reminders in the drop-down list to enable settings for reminders.

To set different types of reminders:

1. Tap Start > Settings > Personal tab > Sounds & Notifications to open the Volume tab of the Sounds & Notifications settings screen.

2. Under "Enable sounds for," tap Programs, and then tap Notifications (**Figure 6.14**).

3. In the Notifications tab, under "Select an event," tap Reminders (**Figure 6.15**).

4. To have the reminder play a sound, check the Play Sound box, then tap the sound you want in the sound drop-down list. Try out sounds first with the play button.

5. To have the reminder display a message, check "Display message on screen."

6. For an indicator light reminder, check "Flash light for" and choose a length of time to flash the light.

7. For a buzzing reminder, check Vibrate. (Not all devices offer vibration.)

USING REMINDERS IN TASKS

Using Categories in Tasks

As do the other programs that synchronize with Outlook, Tasks offers categories as a way to help sort your information. You can create any kind of categories you like, based on whatever criteria are useful to you. Examples might include broad classifications such as "business" and "personal," or organizing by work project or freelance client, or more specialized ones for budgets, expenses, planning vacations, birthdays, pets, relatives, health care, taxes, education, hobbies—whatever. Once your tasks are in categories, they're much easier to find and keep an eye on, and it can be interesting to see how information tends to clump together. Also helpful is the fact that you can assign a task to multiple categories.

To assign a task to a category:

1. Tap the task to select it and tap the Edit menu.

   The task details screen appears.

2. Tap the Categories line to display the categories screen (**Figure 6.16**).

3. Tap to put check marks next to each category your task seems to belong to.

4. When you're done checking boxes, tap OK to finish.

   The task details screen reappears (**Figure 6.17**), and your task is assigned to the category or categories you chose (not all of them can be displayed at once).

✔ Tips

■ For shopping lists, enter each item as a task and group them all into a category such as Groceries. Then you can check off celery, for example, when it's purchased.

■ Tap the Add/Delete tab in the categories screen to add or delete categories (**Figure 6.18**). Tap a category and tap Delete to delete it, or start entering a new category in the text box.

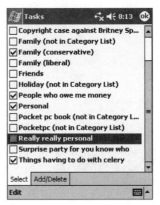

Figure 6.16 Choose a category or categories for your task.

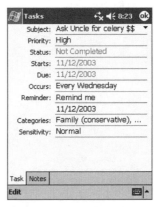

Figure 6.17 Your task now has categories assigned to it.

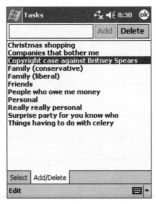

Figure 6.18 Create and delete categories in the Add/Delete tab.

Tap the Calendar item to launch Calendar

Figure 6.19 You can go to Calendar right from the Today screen.

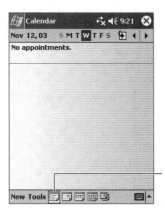

Note that the agenda view is selected

Figure 6.20 Someday you'll wish your Calendar were this clear.

About Calendar

Where Tasks is designed to track the various and sometimes random things you must do—such as adding a task to call for a haircut appointment when you look shaggy— Calendar is about the Big Picture, the grand sweep of what's coming up in the weeks and months and years ahead. This would encompass the hair appointment itself, as well as your other appointments, meetings, engagements, interviews, events, parties, trips—in other words, everything you would write down on your ... calendar. Except this one fits in your pocket, alerts you when something's coming up in time to do something about it, and is good to go for the next 996 years.

To view your Calendar:

◆ Press the device's Calendar program button.

or

Tap Start > Calendar.

or

Tap the Calendar item in the Today screen (**Figure 6.19**).

The Calendar screen appears (**Figure 6.20**), in one of five views (here, it's in agenda view).

✔ Tip

■ If it's your first time viewing the Calendar, it will display in agenda view—one of five views. Otherwise, it appears in the view you were looking at the last time you used it.

To change Calendar views:

◆ To see today's agenda in agenda view, tap the agenda view icon.

◆ To see today's hourly schedule in Day view, tap the Day view icon.

continues on next page

- To see the week's schedule in week view, tap 📅 the week view icon.

- To see the month's schedule in month view, tap 📅 the month view icon.

- To see the whole year in year view, tap 📅 the year view icon.

Anatomy of the Calendar screen

Here is the same appointment viewed by zooming out from the Calendar's day view, through week and month views, to year view. Let's make the appointment lunch on November 20, 2003.

Day of week

Go forward or back one day

Day of week and date

Go forward or back one week

Go to today (if viewing a different day)

Go to Today

Hour of day

Appointment (tap to see it in a banner at the top of the screen)

Day view is selected

Week view is selected

Go forward or back one month

Go forward or back one year

Today (tap to see it in day view)

Afternoon appointment

All day event

Today (tap to see it in day view)

Month view is selected

Year view is selected

Figure 6.21 Add an appointment with the pop-up menu.

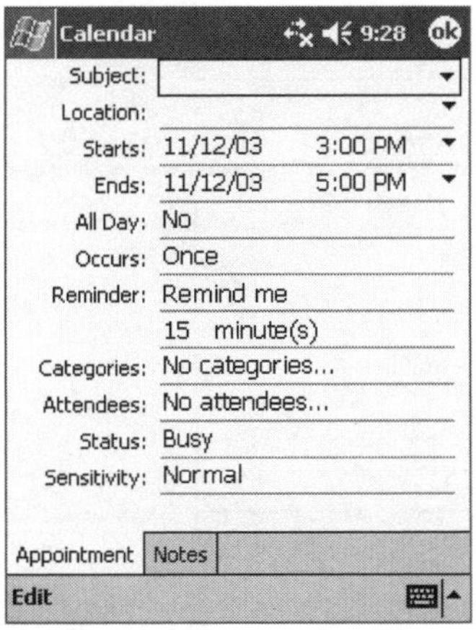

Figure 6.22 The appointment details screen is very similar to the task details screen—it's where you edit the information to reflect the appointment you want to add.

Figure 6.23 Now the appointment is entered and it appears in the list of appointments.

Creating and Editing Appointments in Calendar

Anything that's coming up is easy to add to or delete from the Calendar, and as with the Tasks program, you can specify an array of particulars and details for it. Appointments in Calendar can be either normal or what the program calls "all-day" events. All day events, such as a birthday, don't have a specific start or end time, and they don't show up as blocks of time in Calendar.

To create an appointment:

1. Tap the New menu.

   or

   In agenda, day, or week view, press and hold the stylus on the time slot (in agenda view, on any blank space) and tap New Appointment in the pop-up menu that appears (**Figure 6.21**).

   or

   In month or year views, tap the day of the appointment to bring up the day view, then press and hold the stylus on the time slot and tap New Appointment in the pop-up menu.

   The appointment details screen appears (**Figure 6.22**).

2. Name the appointment in the Subject line.

3. Enter any other pertinent details in the other lines. (See next section for more information on each line.)

4. Tap OK to finish.

   Your appointment is entered (**Figure 6.23**).

continues on next page

✔ Tip

■ A morning appointment appears in month view as a blue triangle pointing up and to the left; an afternoon or evening appointment shows up as a blue triangle pointing down and the right (**Figure 6.24**).

To delete an appointment:

◆ Press and hold the stylus on the appointment and tap Delete Appointment in the pop-up menu that appears.

To copy an appointment:

◆ Press and hold the stylus on the appointment and tap Copy in the pop-up menu that appears.

The appointment is copied to the clipboard and ready to paste into another time slot.

To paste an appointment:

◆ Press and hold the stylus on the desired time slot and tap Paste in the pop-up menu that appears.

The appointment is pasted into the Calendar and can be edited, if necessary, by tapping the Edit menu.

To edit an appointment:

1. Tap an appointment to display its summary and tap the Edit menu (**Figure 6.25**).

The appointment details screen appears, offering eleven different characteristics that you can assign to it (**Figure 6.26**).

Each of the eleven items, when tapped, opens a drop-down menu where you can choose from among several options or lets you enter information directly into it.

Morning appointment

Figure 6.24 You can tell by the triangles whether your appointment is in the a.m. or p.m.

Afternoon appointment

Tap here to open the appointment for editing

Figure 6.25 The summary screen gives you the appointment's basics.

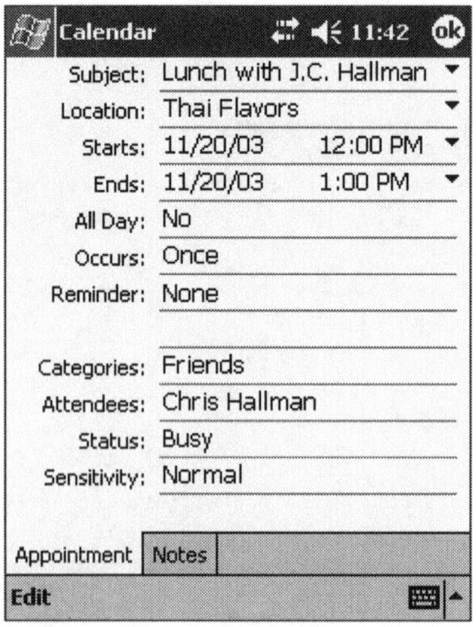

Figure 6.26 Here we've filled in particulars for an appointment in the appointment details screen.

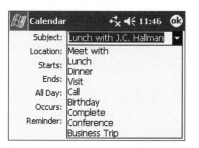

Figure 6.27 Calendar offers nine starter subjects to help you not have to type or write so much. Tap one and then add to it in the Subject text box.

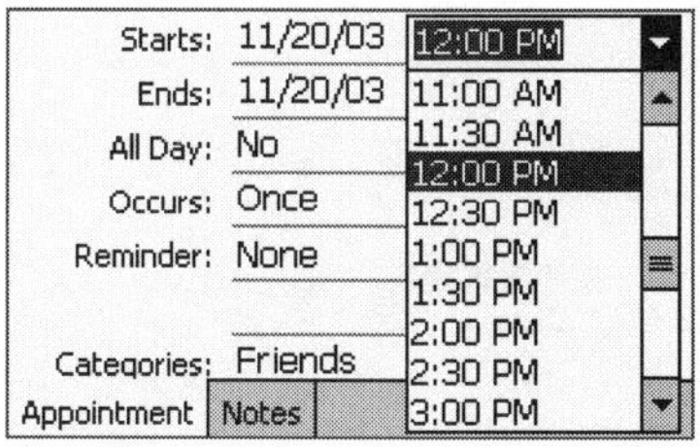

Starts:	11/20/03	12:00 PM
Ends:	11/20/03	11:00 AM
All Day:	No	11:30 AM
Occurs:	Once	12:00 PM
Reminder:	None	12:30 PM
		1:00 PM
		1:30 PM
		2:00 PM
Categories:	Friends	2:30 PM
Appointment	Notes	3:00 PM

Figure 6.28 Pick a start time from the drop-down menu.

Occurs:	Once
Reminder:	Once
	Every Thursday
	Day 20 of every month
Categories:	Every November 20
Appointment	< Edit pattern... >

Figure 6.29 How often will this appointment take place?

2. Tap the middle of the Subject line to enter a new name for the task.

   or

   Tap the Subject drop-down arrow to choose from nine types of events (**Figure 6.27**).

3. Tap the middle of the Location line to enter a new location.

   or

   Tap the Location drop-down arrow to select from some of your appointment locations.

4. Tap the date in the Starts line to choose a start date for the task from the little pop-up calendar that appears.

5. Tap the Starts line to enter a time or tap the drop-down arrow to pick one (**Figure 6.28**).

6. Tap the time in the Ends line to enter an end time or tap the drop-down arrow to pick one.

7. Tap the All Day line to choose whether the appointment will be an all-day event.

8. Tap the Occurs line to register that the task occurs once, weekly, monthly, annually, or in some other pattern (**Figure 6.29**).

   The default is that the task will occur once.

9. Tap the first Reminder line to choose whether to have the device remind you of the appointment and, if so, tap the second line to choose when. (See later in this chapter for more on reminders.)

continues on next page

CREATING AND EDITING APPOINTMENTS

10. Tap the Categories line to assign the task to one or more categories.

11. Tap the Attendees line to display a screen of your contacts, put a check mark in the box next to any attendee you want to attend the appointment (**Figure 6.30**), and tap OK to return to the Calendar details screen.

12. Tap the Status line to choose a status during the appointment (**Figure 6.31**). The default is Busy, meaning that to others you are "busy" during the appointment.

13. Tap the Sensitivity line to choose either Normal or Private.

14. Tap OK to finish editing the task.

You are returned to the Calendar view you were in before you began editing the task.

✔ Tip

■ When you make certain changes to an appointment that has attendees, Calendar asks whether you want to notify the attendees of the changes. (See later in this chapter for more on notifying attendees.)

To create an all-day event:

1. Create a new appointment.

or

Tap an appointment to display its summary and tap the Edit menu.

The appointment details screen appears.

2. Tap the All Day line and tap Yes in the drop-down menu that appears (**Figure 6.32**).

3. Tap the Reminder line, if desired, and choose a suitable amount of time to be reminded in advance of the event (**Figure 6.33**). (See next section for more on reminders.)

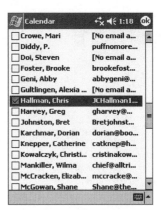

Figure 6.30 We want Chris, and only Chris, to buy us Thai food.

Figure 6.31 While at this appointment, we'll be busy— with chopsticks, even though you're supposed to eat Thai with a fork, we think.

Figure 6.32 Mom's birthday lasts all day, so we'll make it an all-day event.

Figure 6.33 If the Pocket PC reminds us of Mom's birthday ten days in advance, which should be enough time to buy a gift and mail it.

Figure 6.34 Calendar sensibly figures that some things are not so much appointments as they are events to be pondered and reflected upon all day long.

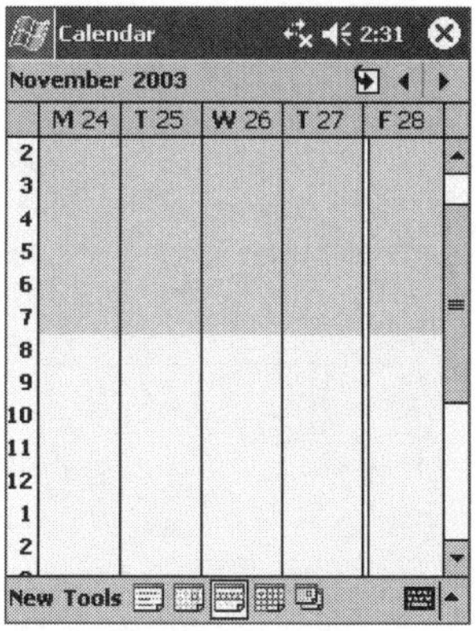

Figure 6.35 The all day event is indicated by a long thin bar on Friday.

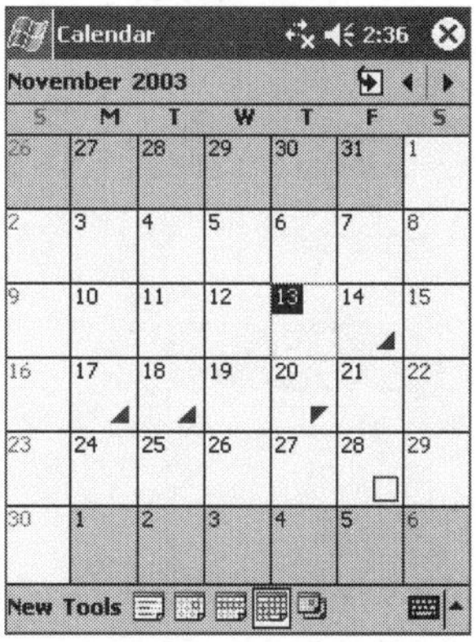

Figure 6.36 On November 28 in month view, Mom's birthday is represented by a blue square.

4. Tap the Status line and tap Free in the drop-down list that appears if the event is one that doesn't prevent you from other appointments. Otherwise, tap Tentative (if you're not sure yet), Busy (if the event stops you from attending to other appointments), or "Out of office" (in the case of a vacation, for example).

5. Tap OK to finish.

Your event appears in agenda and day views as a banner near the top of the screen (**Figure 6.34**).

In week view, the event is signaled by a long thin bar to the left of the day of the all day event (**Figure 6.35**).

In month view, the event is shown by a small blue square on that day—if you chose any status except Free (**Figure 6.36**). If you chose Free status, the event does not appear at all in month view.

✔ Tips

- Tap the banner in agenda or day view to display the summary page for the event, and from there tap the Edit menu to edit it.

- All day events are especially good for birthdays, vacations, holidays, seminars, and business trips.

Using Reminders in Calendar

Reminders in Calendar work, for the most part, just like they do in the Tasks program (discussed at the beginning of this chapter). Refer to the section "Using Reminders in Tasks" for more on reminders.

The only real difference is that Calendar reminders are more precise. In Tasks, a reminder will alert you at 8 a.m. on the morning the Task is due. But in Calendar, you can set the Pocket PC to remind you of an appointment or event *any* amount of time in advance.

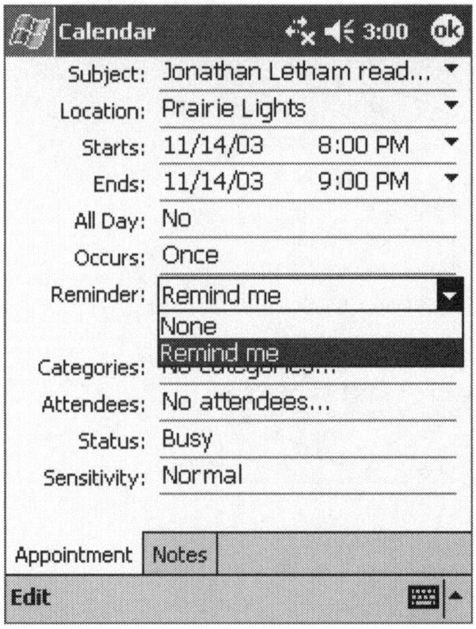

To set a reminder for an appointment:

1. Tap an appointment to display it in its summary screen and tap the Edit menu.

   The appointment details screen appears.

2. Tap the first Reminder line and tap Remind Me in the drop-down list (**Figure 6.37**).

3. Tap the number in the second Reminders line to choose the number of time units and tap the time unit to choose minutes, hours, days or weeks (**Figure 6.38**).

4. Tap OK to finish.

   You are returned to the view you were in before adding the reminder.

5. Tap the appointment to display it in the summary screen (**Figure 6.39**).

   The reminder is indicated by the little ringing bell icon.

✔ Tip

■ See the section "To set different types of reminders" earlier in this chapter to see how to set reminders that flash a message, blink lights, sound an alarm, and/or vibrate your Pocket PC. The vibrating reminder is almost frightening the first time you feel it—like unexpectedly turning on an electric shaver. Or something.

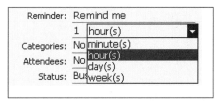

Figure 6.37 A Jonathan Lethem reading is definitely something you want to be reminded about.

Figure 6.38 An hour beforehand should do it. Note that in Tasks, you can only choose which day you want to be reminded, and then the reminder happens at 8 a.m. that day. Calendar is much more precise with reminders.

Figure 6.39 The little bell reminds us that we will be reminded when the time comes.

USING CALENDAR REMINDERS

Figure 6.40 Calendar lets you pick with category of appointments to display.

Using Categories in Calendar

Like the tasks in the Tasks program, and contacts in Contacts, appointments in Calendar can be assigned to categories that help you organize and track the different kinds of data you keep on your device. See "Using Categories in Tasks " earlier in this chapter for more on how categories can help sort your information.

To assign an appointment to a category:

1. Tap an appointment to display it in its summary screen and tap the Edit menu. The appointment details screen appears.

2. Tap the Categories line to display the categories screen and put a check mark next to each category you want to assign the appointment to.

3. Tap OK to finish.
   Your appointment is assigned to the category or categories you chose.

✔ Tips

■ To display only appointments in a certain category, tap Tools > Categories > Select tab and put a check mark in the check box beside the category of appointments you want to display (**Figure 6.40**). In Calendar, only appointments belonging to that category will be shown. To show all appointments again, remove check marks from all boxes.

■ Tap Tools > Categories > Add/Delete tab in the categories screen to add or delete categories. Tap a category and tap Delete to delete it, or start entering a new category in the text box.

USING CATEGORIES IN CALENDAR

Meeting Requests

If you use Outlook on your computer for email, you can create an appointment in Calendar and configure the Pocket PC to automatically invite attendees that you designate. After synchronizing, Calendar will ask Outlook to send an email message to your attendees inviting them to the meeting. If they accept, the meeting will be automatically added to their Calendar and they will be added as attendees to yours.

To send a meeting request:

1. Make sure the attendees have contacts entered for them in the Inbox program (see Chapter 5).

2. Connect your device to your computer if it isn't already.

3. In Calendar, tap New to create a new appointment.

   The appointment details screen appears.

4. Fill out any pertinent information (**Figure 6.41**).

5. Tap the Attendees line to show your contacts and put a check mark next to the attendee(s) you want to invite (**Figure 6.42**).

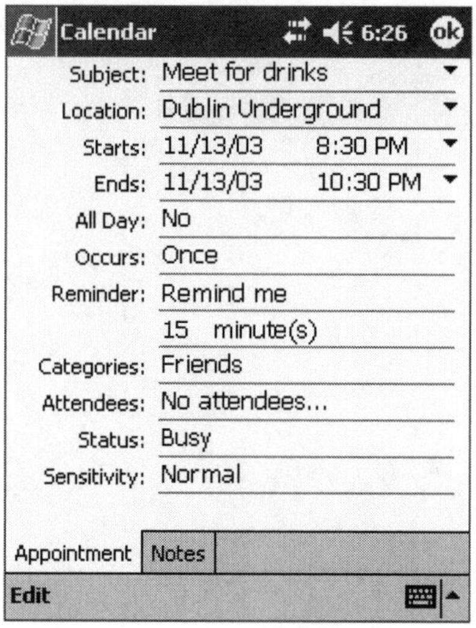

Figure 6.41 Start out creating a meeting request as you would any other appointment.

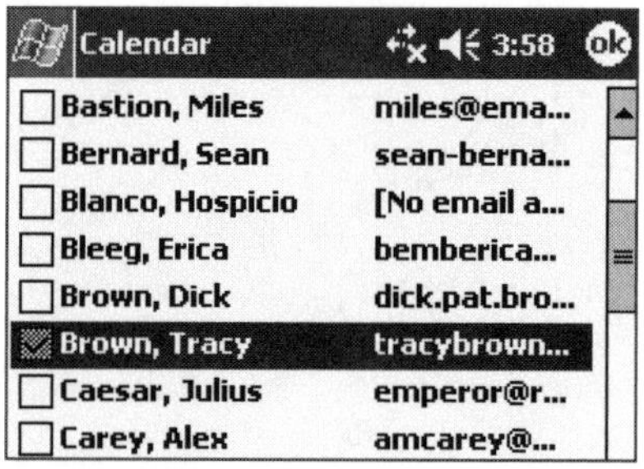

Figure 6.42 Choose an attendee from the list of contacts.

Figure 6.43 The appointment is entered and appears in the list.

6. Tap the Notes tab and enter a note (this will end up the body of your email).

7. Tap OK to finish and return to the Calendar screen (**Figure 6.43**).

8. Synchronize with ActiveSync if it does not occur automatically.

   Outlook creates an email inviting your attendee(s) to your meeting and places it in your Outbox in Outlook on your computer.

   If Outlook sends the email you're done.

9. In Outlook on your computer, double-click the email in your Outbox (**Figure 6.44**).

10. Click Send Update to send the email.

    If your attendee declines, you'll read about it in an email. If the invitation is accepted, you'll get an email, and both your Calendars will be updated to reflect the meeting!

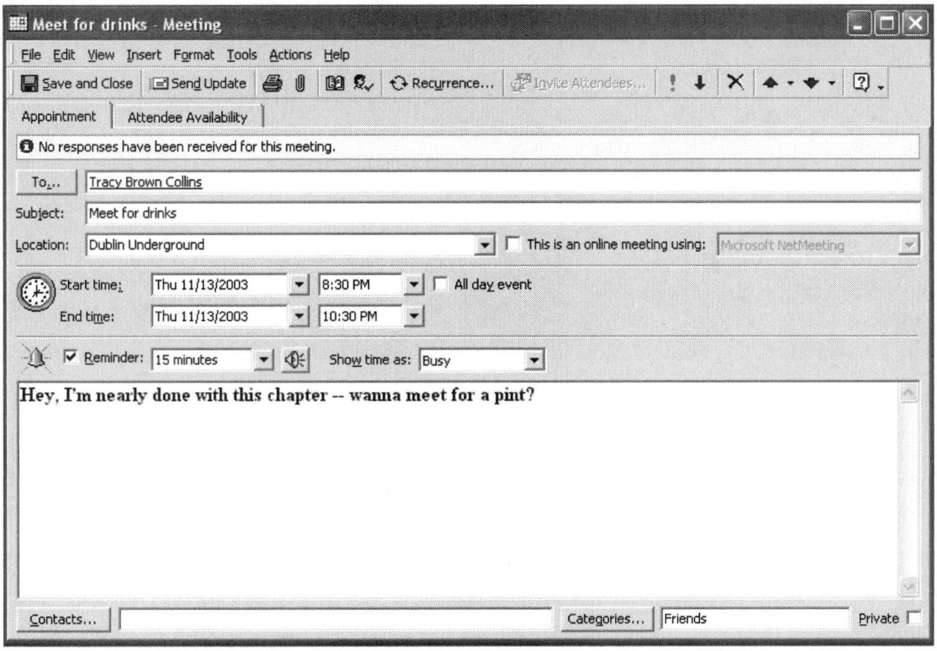

Figure 6.44 After synchronizing, the meeting invitation appears in your Outlook Outbox, ready to send.

Changing Calendar Options

In Calendar's Options screen, you can change several things about the way Calendar accepts and displays your schedule.

To change Calendar options:

1. In Calendar, tap Tools > Options.

   The Calendar Options screen appears (**Figure 6.45**).

2. Tap the "1st day of the week" drop-down box to choose Sunday or Monday as the first day of the week.

   Choosing Monday merely moves Sunday to the far right-hand side in week, month, and year views.

3. Tap the "Week view" drop-down box to choose among a 5-, 6-, or 7-day week.

   The default is a 5-day week. Choosing the other two smashes them into the week view.

4. Put a check mark next to "Show half hour slots" to display every half hour in day and week views (**Figure 6.46**).

5. Put a check mark next to "Show week numbers" to make the week of the year show up as a number in week and month views (**Figure 6.47**).

6. Put a check mark next to "Use large font" to display text on the screen in a larger font.

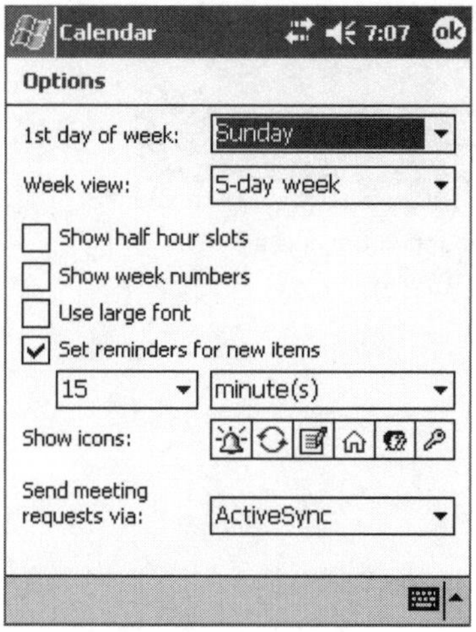

Figure 6.45 Change certain aspects of how Calendar looks and operates in Calendar Options.

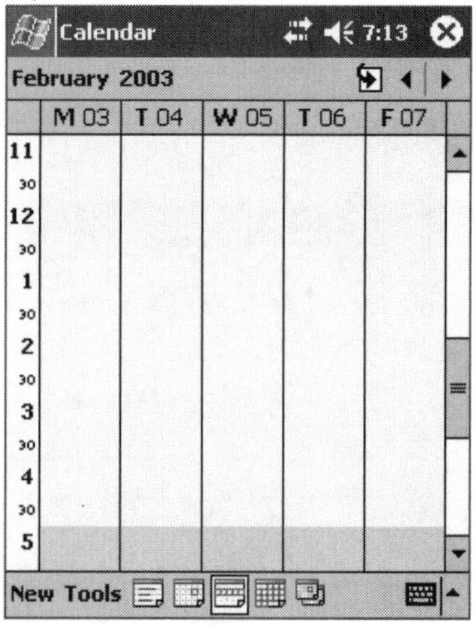

Figure 6.46 Here's how the week view looks when chopped up into half hours instead of just hours.

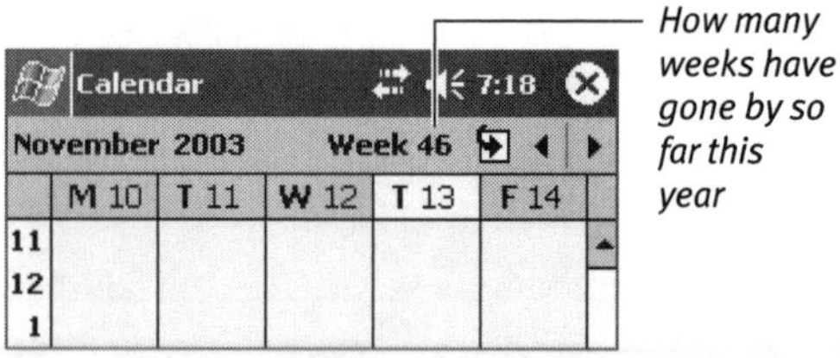

How many weeks have gone by so far this year

Figure 6.47 You can display the week number if you like.

CHANGING CALENDAR OPTIONS

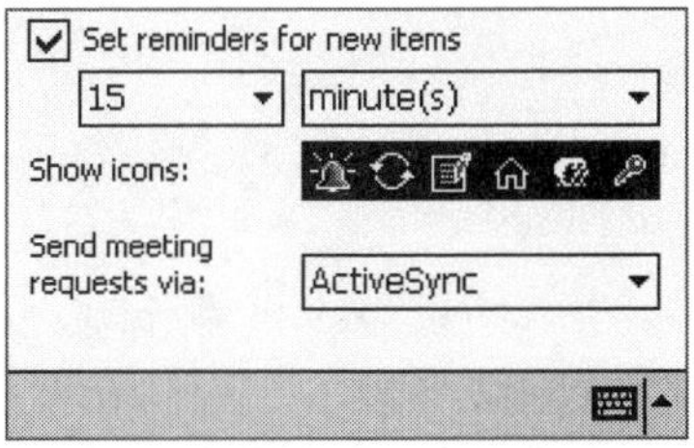

Figure 6.48 The icons darken when you tap them to show that they are selected.

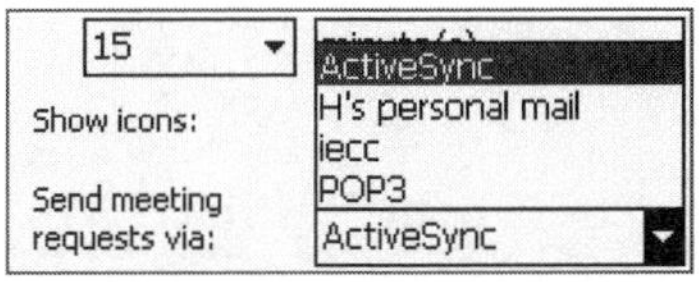

Figure 6.49 Choose how you want to send the meeting request.

7. Put a check mark next to "Set reminders for new items" to enable reminders in Calendar.

   The box is checked by default.

8. Next to "Show icons," tap to select (darken) and deselect (brighten) the icons you want to display in day view (**Figure 6.48**).

   Icons display in the summary screen by default. Icons include the following:

   ▲ Reminder icon means an appointment has a reminder set.

   ▲ Recurs icon means an appointment occurs more than once.

   ▲ Note icon means appointment has a note attached.

   ▲ Location icon means the appointment specifies a location.

   ▲ Attendees icon means the appointment includes attendees.

   ▲ Private icon means the appointment has been marked private.

9. Tap the "Send meeting requests via" drop-down list to choose how you want meeting requests to be sent (**Figure 6.49**).

   The default is ActiveSync, but you can choose among any of your Inbox accounts to send the meeting request directly from your Pocket PC.

CHANGING CALENDAR OPTIONS

Other organizer programs

The quest to create the perfect PIM—Personal Information Manager—continues. The Pocket PC's Calendar program is a very modest effort when compared to some.

SuperCalendar uses graphic indicators and icons to show how full current and upcoming days are. Coloring options let the user quickly check upcoming appointments. In day view, a pop-up balloon window shows attached notes and abbreviated appointments. Other features include word wrap and international calendars. It's a $10 download from www.scarybearsoftware.com.

DateLens is an interesting calendar program that focuses on drilling down and up through greater and lesser levels of detail, using animated transitions. It costs $15 and can be downloaded from www.windsorinterfaces.com.

VOCalendar lets you view your calendar graphically a month at a time, using any GIF, JPG, BMP, or PNG graphic you want, which are automatically reduced to fit into calendar days. This is probably the prettiest calendar around, for $19.95. Download from www.voscorp.com/asp/ppc/vocalendar/default.asp

To go even fancier and more powerful, you might try something like the $29.95 **Agenda Fusion 5**. It does calendar, contacts, and tasks—a time-management Swiss Army knife.

Agenda Fusion has supposedly won more awards than any other time management Pocket PC software. Get it from www.developerone.com.

TAKING NOTES

The Notes application is a handy electronic notepad you can use to jot your ideas and quickly document key points in meetings or interviews. Notes is for anything you want to get down on "paper" fast, without messing with the fancier formatting capabilities of Pocket Word. Notes does, however, come with a few installed templates that help jazz up and organize the content of your notes.

You can choose to enter text with the soft (onscreen) keyboard or write on your screen using the Pen tool. If you prefer to scribble down notes with the Pen, but later want to share your notes, you can convert your chicken scratches to type.

Notes can handle more than text, though. If you want to store your ideas as sketches or drawings, you can draw directly in Notes. You can also employ the Notes program's voice-recording feature and use your device as a Dictaphone.

And, as with all applications on your Pocket PC, it's easy to share notes via email and beaming, as well as to synchronize your Pocket PC's Notes files with Outlook on your computer.

Creating Notes

Whether you use the Notes program as a simple piece of electronic scrap paper or decide to take advantage of its many other capabilities, the first thing you'll want to do is create a note.

To create a note:

1. In the Today screen, tap New at the bottom left-hand corner of the screen and tap Note in the pop-up menu that appears.

   or

   Tap Start > Notes to start the program, then tap the New menu.

   A blank note appears (**Figure 7.1**).

2. Select an entry mode for your note.

   ▲ To enter text with the soft keyboard, Transcriber, or Block or Letter Recognizer, tap the ⌨▲ up arrow and choose your text input method.

   ▲ To handwrite with the stylus, tap the ✏ Pen icon. Lines appear as guides, just like ruled paper (**Figure 7.2**). The Pen works like Transcriber (see Chapter 3), except that your handwriting will not be *automatically* recognized.

Figure 7.1 A blank note is ready for you to start taking notes.

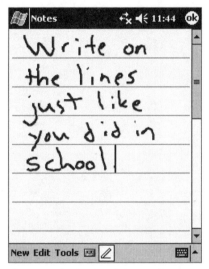

Figure 7.2 The Pen icon brings up lines to guide your handwriting.

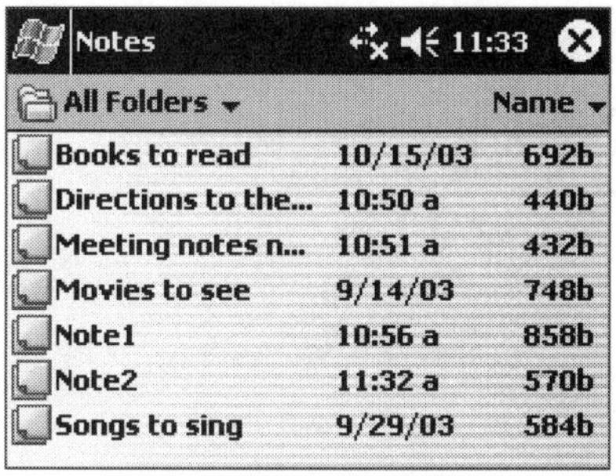

Figure 7.3 The Pocket PC automatically names your files.

3. Write your note using your chosen method.

4. Tap OK when you are done.

Your note is automatically saved. The filename is the first line of the note if you used the keyboard—otherwise, it's named Note1, Note2, and so on (**Figure 7.3**).

✔ Tips

- The default mode for Notes is Typing—using the soft keyboard rather than the Pen. See the section on customizing notes later in this chapter to change this default.

- Notes can be beamed like any other files. See Chapter 2 for more info.

To rename a note:

1. Press and hold the stylus on the filename in the Notes screen and tap Rename/Move from the pop-up menu that appears.

or

Tap the filename to select it and tap Tools > Rename/Move.

2. Enter the name you want for the file in the Name: field and tap OK.

The note is renamed.

CREATING NOTES

Converting Notes to Text

Using the Pen tool, you can write notes in your normal handwriting and keep them that way if you like. After all, so long as *you* can read them, and they're only for your eyes, then they're fine and useful as is. However, you can make the Pocket PC recognize your handwriting as text that you can email or place in a document.

To convert handwriting to text:

1. Enter a note using the 🖉 Pen tool or open an existing handwritten note.

2. Select the text you want to convert by tapping your stylus just before the first letter of the text, pausing for a second, and then dragging your stylus across the text you want to select.

   The text to be converted is highlighted (**Figure 7.4**).

3. Press and hold your stylus on the highlighted text and tap Recognize from the pop-up menu that appears (**Figure 7.5**).

   or

   Tap Tools > Recognize.

   Your handwritten text is converted to type (**Figure 7.6**).

✔ Tips

■ To convert an entire note rather than selected text, be sure that no text is highlighted and tap Tools > Recognize.

■ To help the device better interpret your handwriting, write your words big. There's no running out of paper or room, so don't be afraid to take up some space.

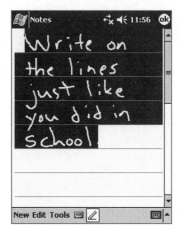

Figure 7.4 Once highlighted, selected handwritten text is ready to convert to text.

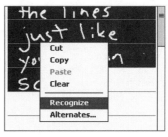

Figure 7.5 Recognize is what Notes calls the command that "reads" and interprets your handwriting.

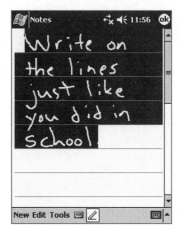

Figure 7.6 Your handwriting is recognized.

When Recognize gets it wrong

The Recognize tool doesn't always get it right.

If some words are not properly converted, select the word or words, and tap Tools > Alternates—or press and hold on the selected word or words and tap Alternates... from the pop-up menu that appears. A selection of alternate words is displayed, with your handwritten version at the top, as shown here.

Tap the correct word from the list. If the correct word does not appear on the list, as is the case here, you'll have to tap the ⌨️|▲ keyboard icon at the bottom right-hand corner of the screen and enter the word by hand using the soft keyboard.

CONVERTING NOTES TO TEXT

Drawing with Notes

If you're like us, your handwritten scribbles often include rough sketches, graphs and charts, or silly little drawings. For better or worse, the Notes program accommodates this tendency by allowing you to draw with the Pen tool.

To draw a sketch:

1. Open a new or an existing note.

2. Tap the ✎ Pen icon.
   Lines appear on your screen.

3. With the stylus, draw an object (**Figure 7.7**).
   When any section of your drawing crosses three of the lines on your screen, a box appears around your work to indicate that Notes recognizes it as a drawing.

4. Tap OK to save your note.
   A note that is a drawing only will be saved as Note1, Note2, and so on. A drawing that is added to a text note will still be named by the first line of text.

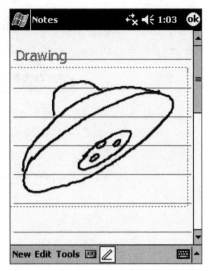

Figure 7.7 This flying saucer crosses at least three lines and is recognized as a drawing.

DRAWING WITH NOTES

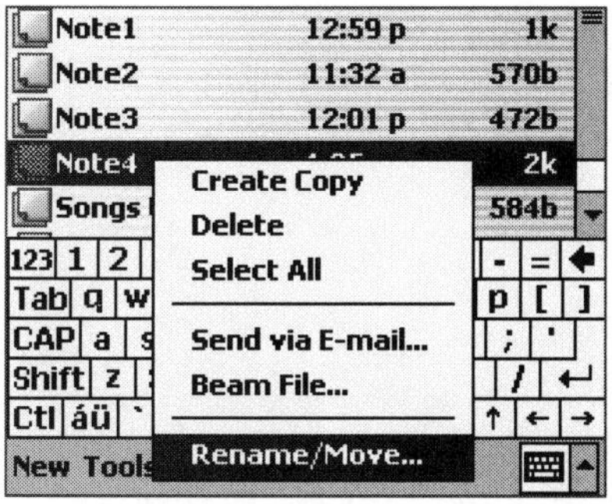

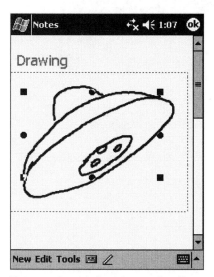

Figure 7.8 Rename a file in the pop-up menu.

Figure 7.9 Drag circle and square handles to reshape the drawing object. Tapping different parts of the drawing selects different elements of it for reshaping.

✔ Tips

- To rename a Note that is a drawing only, press and hold your stylus on the file in the Notes screen and tap Rename/Move from the pop-up menu that appears (**Figure 7.8**). Enter the name you want for the file in the Name: field and tap OK.

- To select a drawing, tap it. You'll see squares and circles ("handles") surrounding your drawing or the part of it you tapped, indicating that it is selected (**Figure 7.9**). Drag a circle handle to stretch or shrink the drawing up or down; drag a square to stretch it diagonally. Drag the center of the selection to move it. Tap Edit > Select All to select the entire note (to cut or copy).

- To undo a change, tap Edit > Undo. To repeat a change, tap Edit > Redo. The option will vary with what you are undoing or redoing (Undo/Redo Ink, for example.)

DRAWING WITH NOTES

Recording Notes

It's often easier and faster to record information with your voice than it is to write it down in the Notes program. For example, shopping lists, directions, dreams, ideas, and flashes of inspiration naturally lend themselves to being spoken into a microphone—just to get them out and safely recorded before they deteriorate in your brain. For these kinds of purposes, the audio recording capability of Notes comes in mighty handy.

To make an audio recording:

1. Open a new Note.

2. Tap the Recording icon.
   The Record/Playback toolbar appears at the bottom of the screen (**Figure 7.10**).

3. Tap the Record button.

   A beep lets you know your device is now recording.

4. Begin talking into the microphone on your device or bring the device within several feet of the source of the sound you wish to record.

   You should be able to record a human voice at ten feet or so without much problem. The less background noise, the better.

5. Tap the Stop button to stop recording.

   A recording icon appears in the note (**Figure 7.11**). Tapping this icon plays back your recording.

6. Tap OK to save your note.

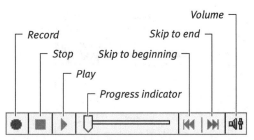
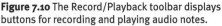

Figure 7.10 The Record/Playback toolbar displays buttons for recording and playing audio notes.

Figure 7.11 A recording icon indicates the presence of a recording within a note.

This recording is 10.6 seconds long ⌐

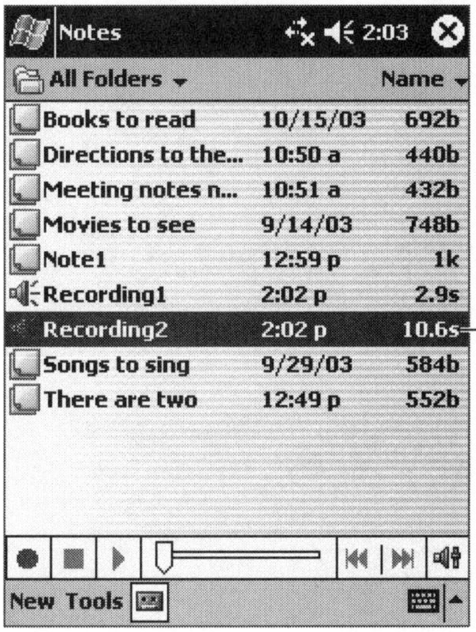

Notes	⚡✕ ◀€ 2:03	✕
All Folders ▾		Name ▾
Books to read	10/15/03	692b
Directions to the...	10:50 a	440b
Meeting notes n...	10:51 a	432b
Movies to see	9/14/03	748b
Note1	12:59 p	1k
Recording1	2:02 p	2.9s
Recording2	2:02 p	10.6s
Songs to sing	9/29/03	584b
There are two	12:49 p	552b

● ■ ▶ ──U────── ⏮ ⏭ 🔊

New Tools 📧 ⌨ ▲

Figure 7.12 With recordings, length rather than file size is displayed in the Notes lists screen.

A physical Record button?

Your device may have a physical Record button that can automatically start the Notes program and begin recording when you press it. This can be tremendously handy. Its location varies—for example, in an iPAQ 5000 series, you can record by pressing both sides of the physical volume control button. Check your device's manual for the location of a physical Record button. When you find it, hold it down until you hear a beep and keep holding to record. Releasing the button stops the recording.

✔ Tips

- Recording notes are saved as Recording1, Recording2, and so on. Rather than the file size in the far right of the Notes file list screen, the length of the recorded message is displayed (**Figure 7.12**).

- There's no limit to the length of a recording except your device's memory. If you plan to record something long, such as a lecture, you should make sure you have enough memory beforehand—otherwise, Notes will record right up until the recording eats up all the memory on the Pocket PC, without warning you first. Keep in mind, recorded notes take up roughly half a megabyte a minute. So, every ten minutes eats 5 MB of memory.

- To rename a recording file, press and hold your stylus on the file in the list screen and tap Rename/Move. Enter a more meaningful filename in the Name field.

- To add a recording to an existing note, simply tap the cursor where you want the recording icon to be placed and follow the steps in this section.

- You can also create a recording note without opening a new Note at all. This standalone method is the best way to do it if you plan to use the recording's .wav file on your computer, because an embedded recording in a note is hard to work with. Simply tap the 📧 Recording tool in the Notes list and begin recording. Your file will appear as a .wav file in the file list. From there, once connected with ActiveSync, you can drag it to your hard drive.

continues on next page

- To adjust the volume at which your recordings are played back, tap the volume control icon and, in the Volume box that appears, use your stylus to move the volume pointer up and down to adjust it (**Figure 7.13**).

- Change the recording format by tapping Tools > Options > Global Input Options > Options tab. Tap the down arrow under "Voice recording format" to select a format (**Figure 7.14**). You see a list of Mobile Voice and Pulse Code Modulation (PCM) formats. The Mobile Voice format is best for decent quality recordings that won't take up all of your storage space. For somewhat better sound quality, choose a PCM format—but be warned that these can consume up to 50 times more memory than the Mobile Voice format.

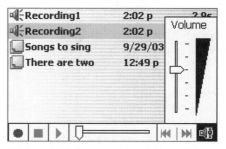

Figure 7.13 Adjust the volume of a recording with the Volume control.

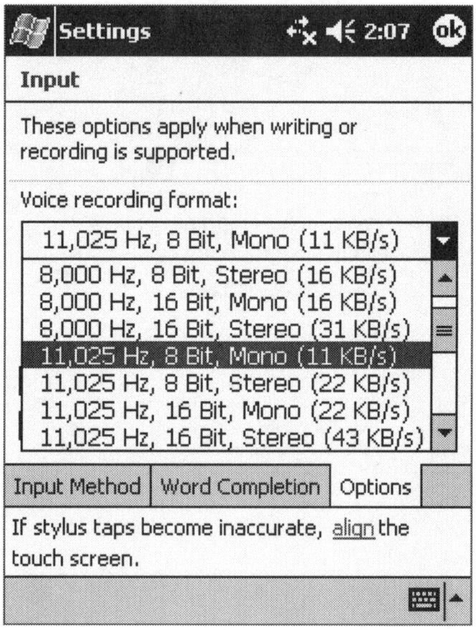

Figure 7.14 Choose a recording format in the Options tab. Try the default choice first before changing it.

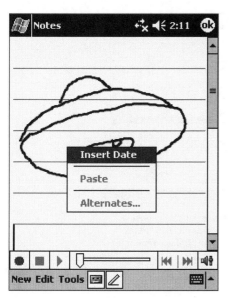

Figure 7.15 Inserting the date into a note is a good way to document when the note was created.

Modifying Notes

After you create a note, you may want to go back and modify it. And when notes start piling up on your device, there comes a time when you ought to organize them. You can also customize Notes to better suit the way you like to work.

To edit a note:

1. Open an existing note.

2. Add or change the text, drawing, or recording.

3. Tap OK to save your changes.

✔ Tips

- You can enter the date in any note by pressing and holding your stylus in a blank area of the screen and tapping Insert Date (**Figure 7.15**). This is handy if you want to keep track of information by date, such as when something was said in a meeting.

- There's no Save As option in Notes, so the changes you make when editing an existing note will overwrite the original note file.

To customize Notes:

◆ From the Notes list screen, tap Tools > Options.

The Options screen appears.

▲ Tap the down arrow under "Default mode" to tap Writing or Typing from the drop-down menu to set the default mode.

▲ Tap the down arrow under "Default template" and tap a new default template style from the drop-down menu that appears (**Figure 7.16**). See nearby sidebar for more.

▲ To set the default saving mode, tap the down arrow under "Save to" and tap "Main memory" (or "Storage card" or "File store," if those options are present) from the drop-down list that appears, depending on where you'd like your notes to be saved.

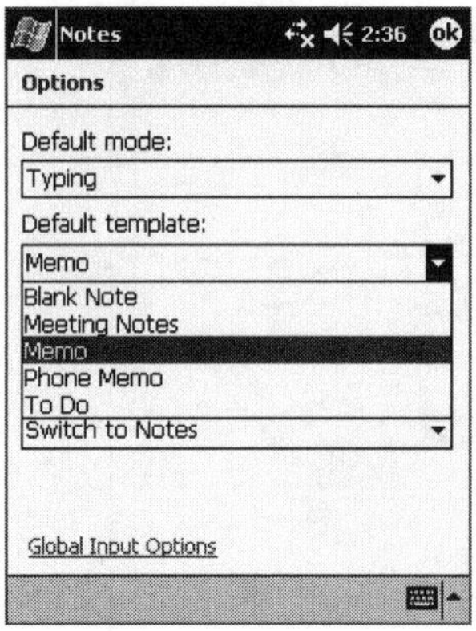

Figure 7.16 You can choose a different default than "Blank note" in the "Default template" drop-down box.

Using Notes templates

When you first create a new note, the default appearance is the Blank Note screen. You're not stuck with this appearance, however. The Notes application comes with four other template choices: Meeting Notes, Memo, Phone Memo, and To Do.

The **Meeting Notes** template is perfect for documenting meetings. The template includes fields for the subject, attendees, date, and action items.

The **Memo** template includes fields for the sender and recipients of the memo, and the date when the memo was sent.

Phone Memo includes fields for the date and time a call was received and for the message text.

The **To Do** list template is formatted in a handy bulleted list style that makes it easy to create a well-organized list.

To choose a template to be the default, tap Start > Notes. In the Notes file list screen, tap Tools > Options. The Options screen appears. In the "Default template" section, tap the down arrow to view the drop-down list. Tap a template in the list and tap OK. When you create a new note, it will appear in that template.

Figure 7.17 The Rename/Move screen is where you can save your note to different folders.

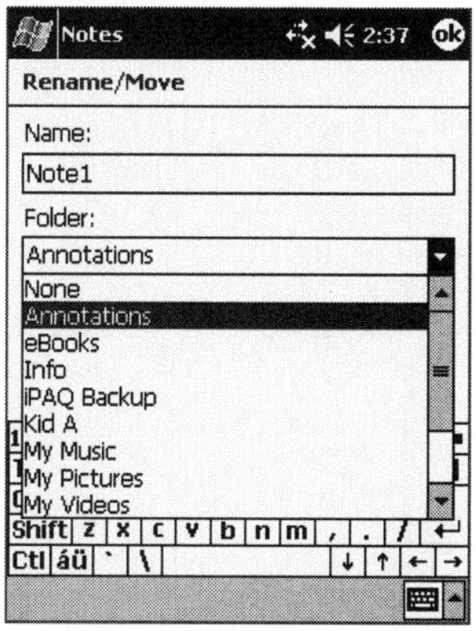

Figure 7.18 Pick a folder to hold your note.

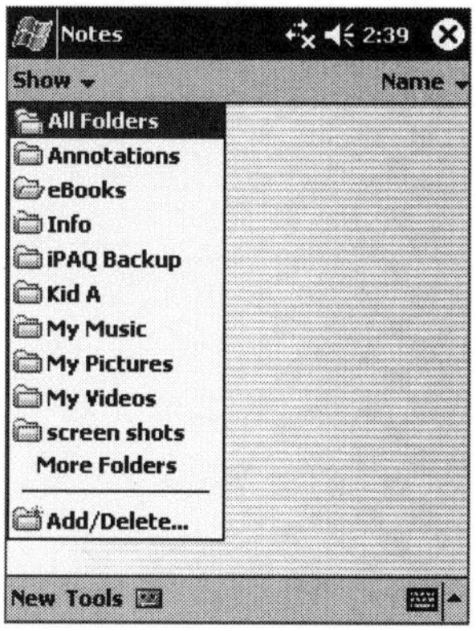

Figure 7.19 Tapping a folder in the drop-down list will reveal the notes it contains.

▲ When you press the Record button in another program, by default your Pocket PC immediately launches Notes. To remain in the application you are working in, tap "Stay in current program" from the "Record button action" drop-down list.

To organize notes in folders:

1. To save a note file in a folder other than the default (All Folders), press and hold a note file and tap Rename/Move from the pop-up menu that appears.

The Rename/Move screen appears (**Figure 7.17**).

2. Tap the down arrow under Folder.

A drop-down menu appears, listing all of your device's My Documents folders (**Figure 7.18**).

3. Tap the folder in which you want the note saved.

The note is saved in the folder of your choice.

✔ Tip

■ Organizing files by folder makes it easier to find a note you are seeking. To view the contents of a folder, simply tap it in the Notes list screen (**Figure 7.19**).

MODIFYING NOTES

To manage Notes folders:

1. From the Notes list screen, tap the down arrow next to All Folders (or whichever folder category is displayed).

   The folders drop-down menu appears.

2. Tap Add/Delete....

   The Add/Delete Folders screen appears (**Figure 7.20**).

3. Add, rename, or delete a folder:

   ▲ **To add a folder**: Tap New. A new folder appears named New Folder with a blinking cursor (**Figure 7.21**). Type the new folder name using the soft keyboard.

   ▲ **To rename a folder:** Tap a folder from the list and then tap Rename. Type the new folder name using the soft keyboard.

   ▲ **To delete a folder:** Tap a folder from the list and then tap Delete. A dialog box appears, asking you to confirm your decision to delete the folder permanently (**Figure 7.22**). Tap Yes or No.

4. Tap OK when you've finished adding, renaming, and deleting all the folders you want.

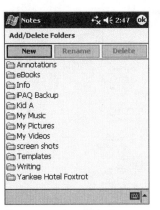

Figure 7.20 The Add/Delete Folders screen is where you manage your Notes folders.

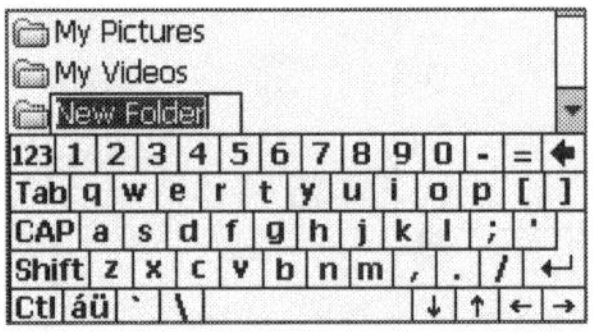

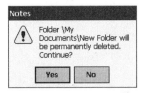

Figure 7.21 Type using the soft keyboard to rename the folder.

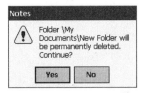

Figure 7.22 Deleting a folder will also delete the files it contains.

MODIFYING NOTES

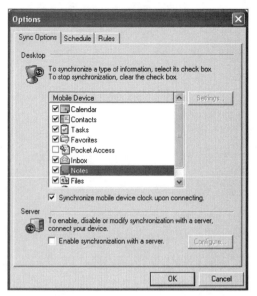

Figure 7.23 You choose whether to synchronize Notes in ActiveSync Options on your computer.

Synchronizing Notes

Like Contacts, Calendar, Inbox, and Tasks, the Notes program synchronizes with Outlook on your computer. All your notes, recordings, and drawings created in the Notes program will be copied to your computer and available to edit in Outlook's Notes module.

To synchronize Notes with Outlook:

1. Connect your Pocket PC to your computer.

2. In ActiveSync on your computer, make sure you have chosen to synchronize Notes by clicking Options > Sync Options tab, putting a check mark next to Notes, and clicking OK (**Figure 7.23**).

   The next time you synchronize your Pocket PC with ActiveSync, all your notes documents will be copied to your computer.

continues on next page

SYNCHRONIZING NOTES

✔ Tips

■ After you synchronize notes, they will appear in the Notes module in Outlook on your computer (**Figure 7.24**). Also, Notes that were in Outlook on your computer will appear on your Pocket PC.

■ There is a limitation to synchronizing: only notes residing in the main Notes folder can be recognized and synchronized. If you store your notes somewhere else or in a subfolder you create, they will not be synchronized or copied to your computer. A great product to help overcome this problem is HPC Notes from www.phatware.com.

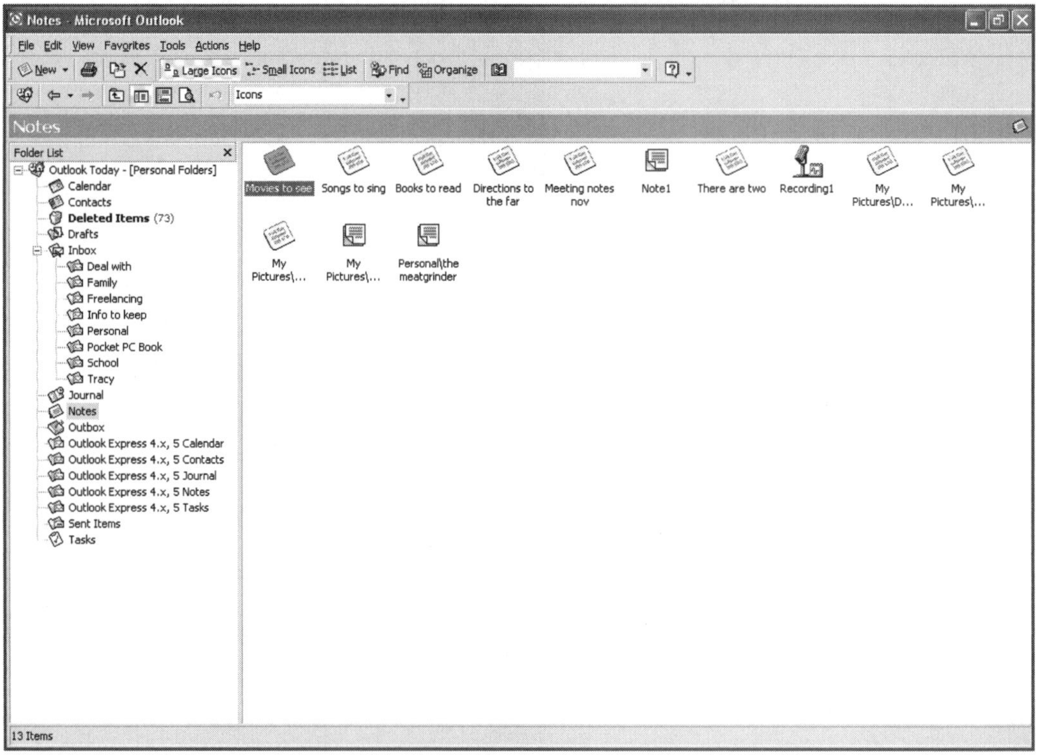

Figure 7.24 After synchronizing, your notes appear in the Notes module in Outlook on your computer.

POCKET WORD

Word processors have been around for decades, but they are still one of the computing world's "killer apps." Pocket Word, which comes pre-installed on your Pocket PC, is a small-scale version of the most popular word processor, Microsoft Word. With Pocket Word, you can quickly view and compose reports, letters, or memos, take notes in a meeting, or sketch out a quick flowchart using the program's built-in drawing tools. And if you need to make last-minute changes to a document, it doesn't matter whether you're on the train, bus, or at the opera: just tap to open the document on your Pocket PC and get to work.

In this chapter, you'll learn how to view, compose, edit, and format documents in Pocket Word. You'll also learn how to create sketches and drawings, install fonts, and share files between your Pocket PC and computer.

Pocket Word vs. Microsoft Word

If you use Microsoft Word on a PC or Mac, then Pocket Word will be familiar. This is both a blessing and a curse. Although it's comforting to see familiar Word commands and toolbars in Pocket Word's interface, don't get lulled into thinking that Pocket Word works exactly like its more powerful cousin.

Pocket Word was specifically designed for the small screen and limited memory of the Pocket PC. The program's designers had to make a lot of tough choices on which features to include and which to leave out. As a result, you might find yourself poking around for features that aren't there. (Where did that Print command go?)

The first notable difference is the file format of the applications' documents. Documents created in Word for your computer have a .doc extension, whereas documents created, opened, or edited in Pocket Word have a .psw extension. This is not something you have to worry too much about, though, because files are automatically translated from .doc to .psw and vice versa when you email, ActiveSync, or copy files between your computer and your Pocket PC.

However, a Word document created on your computer can lose key formatting features such as styles and tables if you make changes to it on your Pocket PC. Be on guard for this, but don't let it stop you from taking advantage of Pocket Word's editing and formatting capabilities. The last part of this chapter details features that are lost in translation and gives workarounds to the problem.

It's best to clear your head and approach Pocket Word as if it's a new program altogether. Our Dutch teacher used to tell us to "think in Dutch." Her point was that it's too hard to try to translate every word in a conversation. If you're an avid user of Word on the computer, it helps to forget most of what you know when using Pocket Word. There are so many differences between the programs that if you constantly try to compare the two, you'll go crazy. Better to learn to *think* in Pocket Word.

POCKET WORD VS. MICROSOFT WORD

Getting Started with Pocket Word

With Pocket Word, you can open Word-compatible documents on your Pocket PC. From there, you can make changes, save files in different formats, and even beam or email files using the program's menus.

To open Pocket Word:

1. Tap Start > Programs.

   Several program icons appear on the screen.

2. Tap Pocket Word.

   The first time you open Pocket Word, it opens a blank document (**Figure 8.1**). If you've used Pocket Word before and already have existing Pocket Word documents, you'll see files listed, as in **Figure 8.2**.

✔ Tip

■ If you leave a document open when you quit Pocket Word or turn off your device, the document will still be open the next time you open the program. (In fact, the program will still be running in the background.)

To create a new document:

◆ In Pocket Word, tap New on the menu bar at the bottom left-hand corner of the screen.

   or

   From your Pocket PC's Today screen, tap New at the bottom left-hand corner of the screen. Tap Word Document in the pop-up menu that appears.

   A blank document appears, as shown in Figure 8.1.

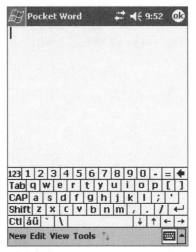

Figure 8.1 A blank page greets you if you have no existing documents on your device.

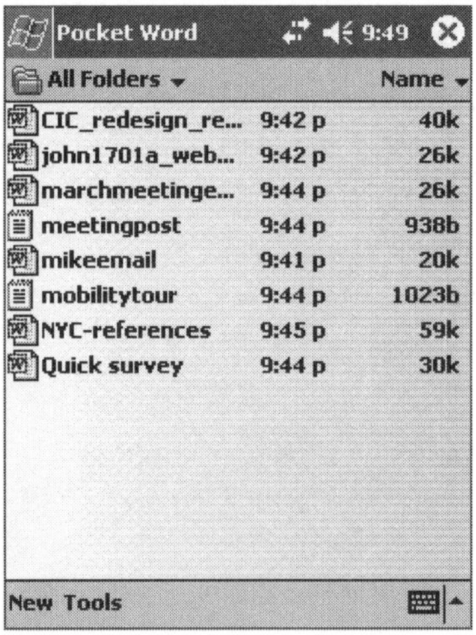

Figure 8.2 If you have documents in .doc, .pwd, or .txt formats, Pocket Word lists them for you.

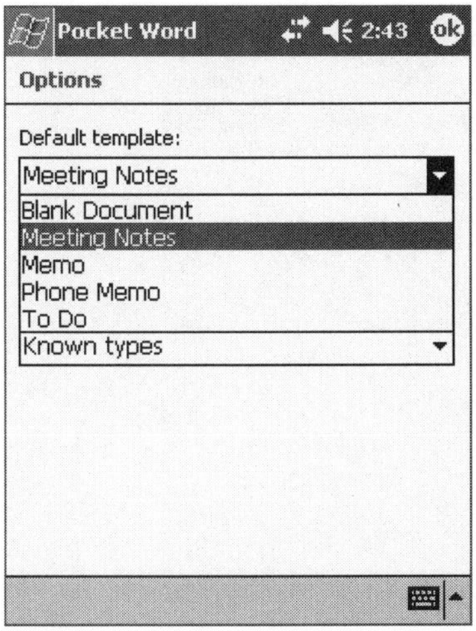

Figure 8.3 Pocket Word comes with five pre-formatted templates.

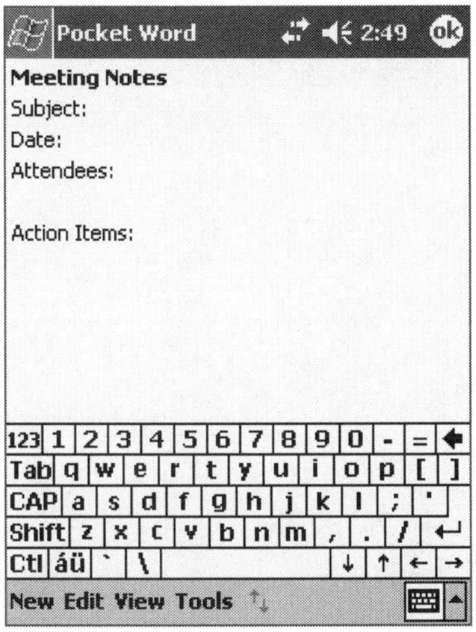

Figure 8.4 Once you choose a template, a new document is created, pre-populated with words and formatting.

To create a new document from a template:

1. In Pocket Word, tap Tools > Options. The Options screen appears.

2. In the Default Template pull-down menu, tap a template to select it from the list (**Figure 8.3**).

   Pocket Word comes equipped with five pre-set templates: Blank Document, Meeting Notes, Memo, Phone Memo, and To Do.

3. Tap OK.

4. Tap the New menu at the bottom left-hand corner of the screen.

   A new document appears (**Figure 8.4**), preformatted in the style of the template (in this case, Meeting Notes).

✔ Tips

■ Once you choose a new default template, every new document you create will use the default template you've chosen. You can always switch back to Blank Document as the default template.

■ You can easily turn any Pocket Word document into a template. Just copy or save it into the Templates folder by tapping Tools > Save Document As... and selecting Templates from the Folder: drop-down list.

To open a document:

1. Tap Start > Programs > Pocket Word to launch Pocket Word.

If the program opens into a blank document instead of listing files, tap OK to close it.

2. Tap a document in the list.

The document opens.

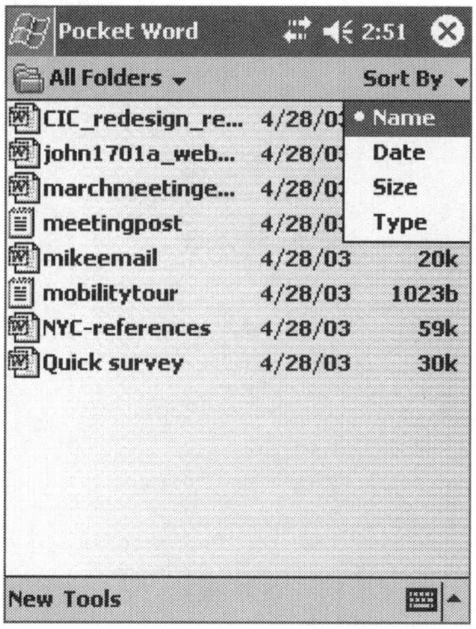

✔ Tips

■ You can change the way the list is sorted by tapping on the Name drop-down menu in the upper right-hand corner of the screen (**Figure 8.5**). Once you tap the menu, the menu title changes from Name to Sort By. You can now choose whether you want the files to be sorted by Name, Date, Size, or File Type.

■ Pocket Word's file list displays all readable documents in the My Documents folder and its subfolders. If you store files on an external memory card, make sure they are within a folder named My Documents (see Chapter 4 and Appendix C for more on memory cards).

■ By default, Pocket Word's file list looks for documents in All Folders within the My Documents folder. If you have a large number of documents, you can narrow the list by tapping the All Folders column head and choosing a specific folder from the drop-down list (**Figure 8.6**).

■ You can scroll quickly through your list of documents using the navigation button on the face of your device.

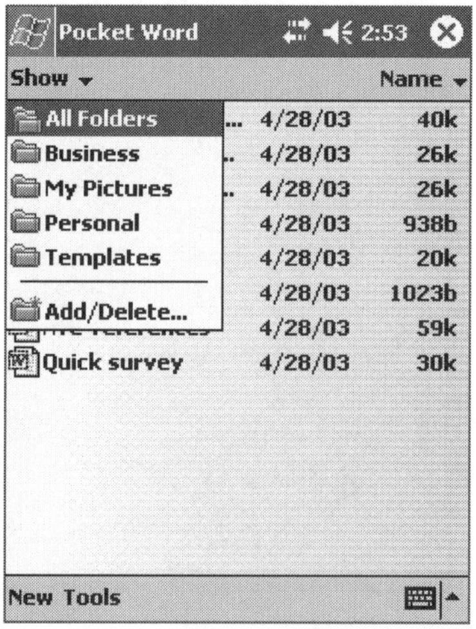

Figure 8.5 Sorting the document list by Name puts your documents in alphabetical order.

Figure 8.6 When you tap the All Folders icon, the Show menu appears, letting you narrow down the list of documents to a specific folder.

Saving Documents

On your computer, you probably already know that you should save your work early and often. On a Pocket PC, however, you don't have to be quite so vigilant. Before you even tap OK to close a document, your Pocket PC keeps the contents of that document saved in memory. Pocket Word names your file using the first few words in the document and stores it in the My Documents folder.

Although Pocket Word saves your work for you—even if you accidentally turn off your device—there are times when you will want to manually save your documents. If you are working in a Pocket Word document and tap New to open a new document, you are prompted to save the document you were working on. There are also times when you might want to give your document a more meaningful name or store it in a specific folder. Or you may need to change the file format before you email it to somebody.

To save a document:

1. Within a document, tap Tools > Save Document As... (**Figure 8.7**).
   The Save As screen appears (**Figure 8.8**).

2. Do one of the following:

   ▲ Change the document's name by typing a new name in the Name field.

   ▲ Move the document to a different folder by tapping an alternate folder from the Folder pull-down menu (**Figure 8.9**).

   If you tap None, the document is automatically saved to the My Documents folder.

   ▲ Change the document's file type by tapping a different one in the Type pull-down menu (**Figure 8.10**).

   ▲ Tap the Location pull-down menu to choose whether to store your file in your Pocket PC's main memory or on an external storage card (if you have one).

3. Tap OK to save your document (or tap Cancel if you don't want to save it).

✔ Tips

■ If you don't plan on emailing your document from your Pocket PC, keeping your document in the default Pocket Word format is usually the best option, because ActiveSync will convert it to a .doc file when you synchronize with your computer. But if you're going to email it, you should tap Rich Text Document (.rtf), Plain Text Document (.txt), or one of the provided Word Document (.doc) formats. That way, you can rest assured that your friends can open and read the file without a hitch. Microsoft Word cannot directly open a Pocket Word document.

Figure 8.7 The Save Document As command lets you choose your file's name, format, and location.

Figure 8.8 Give your document a more meaningful name in the Name field.

Figure 8.9 Choose None to save your document in the My Documents folder, where all documents are stored by default.

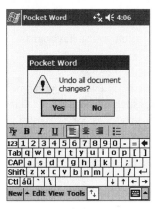

Figure 8.10 You can convert file types with the Type pull-down menu.

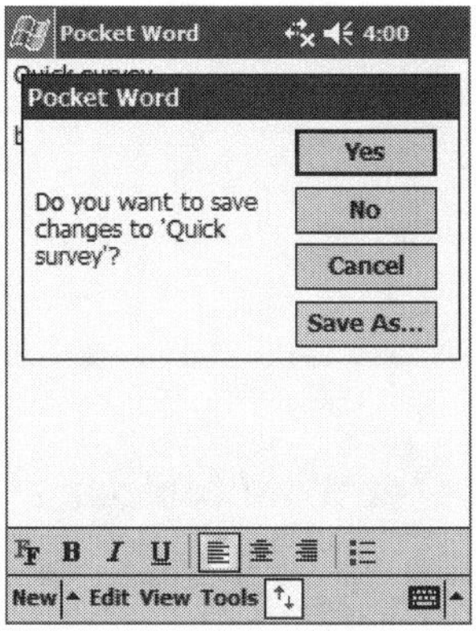

Figure 8.11 This dialog box asks you to save changes before creating another document.

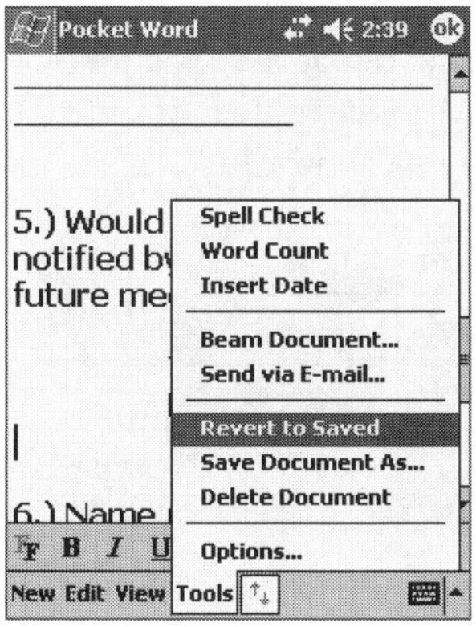

Figure 8.12 Revert to Saved can rescue your document by returning it to its last saved state.

Figure 8.13 You get one more chance to abort reverting to a previous saved state.

- If you are working in a Pocket Word document and tap New to open a new one, a dialog box appears, prompting you to save changes to the original document (**Figure 8.11**). Tap Yes to save changes to an existing file or to save a new file; tap No if you do not want to save. Tap Cancel if you want to change your mind about opening a new document. Tap Save As... and you are brought to the Save As screen.

To revert to a previously saved document:

1. Before closing a document, tap Tools > Revert to Saved from the pop-up menu (**Figure 8.12**).

   A dialog box appears asking whether you want to undo all document changes (**Figure 8.13**).

2. Tap Yes.

   Your document remains on the screen, but all the changes you made since opening the document are removed.

✔ Tip

- You cannot undo the Revert to Saved command, so think carefully beforehand.

Entering and Formatting Text

Pocket Word offers four different modes for entering data in the program: Typing, Writing, Drawing, and Recording. All these modes are available through the View menu (**Figure 8.14**).

Typing mode lets you enter text using the Pocket PC's soft (onscreen) keyboard. In Writing mode, you can use the stylus to write in freehand on the screen. You can either save your words in freehand format, or you can use Pocket Word's Recognize command to convert your freehand writing into text. You'll also find a number of tools for formatting your text and some handy features for spell-checking and counting words in your document.

To enter text with the keyboard:

1. Open a document.

2. If the soft keyboard is not showing, tap the  keyboard icon at the bottom right-hand corner of the screen.

   The icon *should* look like a small keyboard. If it doesn't, tap the small up arrow next to the icon and tap Keyboard in the pop-up screen.

3. Use the stylus to type on the keyboard.

✔ Tips

- In addition to the soft keyboard, you can enter text using Block Recognizer, Letter Recognizer, or Transcriber. (See Chapter 3 for more on these input methods.)

- As with Word on a computer, you can save time by using keyboard shortcuts, such as Ctl+B for bold, Ctl+I for italics, Ctl+X to cut, and so on. These keyboard shortcuts work with the soft keyboard as well as external keyboards.

Figure 8.14 The View menu lets you quickly switch among Pocket Word's four modes: Writing, Drawing, Typing, and Recording.

Using the Pocket Word toolbar

You can make instant formatting changes with the program's handy formatting toolbar. This toolbar, which should look familiar to you from Microsoft Word, appears near the bottom of the screen, above the menu bar. You can show or hide the toolbar by tapping the up-and-down arrow icon on the menu bar, shown here.

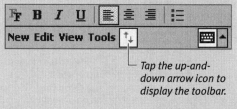

Tap the up-and-down arrow icon to display the toolbar.

The toolbar offers one-click access to commands and formatting options, and is usually the quickest way to make changes to your text.

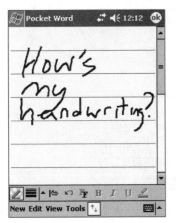

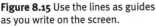

Figure 8.15 Use the lines as guides as you write on the screen.

Figure 8.16 Tap Recognize to see if Pocket Word can understand your chicken scratches.

- If you plan on working with longer documents in Pocket Word, spend a little extra money on an external keyboard. (See Appendix C for more).

To write in Writing mode:

1. In a document, tap View > Writing.

2. Write in cursive or script as clearly as you can, using the ruled lines on the screen as a guide (**Figure 8.15**).

   As your writing nears the bottom of the screen, the page scrolls down automatically.

✔ Tip

- The auto-scrolling feature is particularly useful. It's like having a small notepad that never runs out of paper. Writing mode is perfect for taking notes in meetings or interviews.

To convert handwritten words to text:

- ◆ After jotting down some words in Writing mode, tap Tools > Recognize (**Figure 8.16**).

   Your writing now appears as text. Chances are you see a few recognition mistakes. If your writing is as bad as ours, the recognized words may not quite match the words you typed, in which case you will want to correct the recognition errors.

✔ Tip

- See Chapter 3 for tips on entering handwritten text in your Pocket PC.

ENTERING AND FORMATTING TEXT

To correct recognition errors:

1. After converting handwritten words to text, tap the [icon] keyboard icon in the bottom right-hand corner of the screen to display the soft keyboard.

2. Make corrections with the soft keyboard.

or

Place your cursor within text and tap Tools > Alternates.

You'll see your original script and then a pop-up list of alternate words (**Figure 8.17**).

3. Tap the correct word in the list.

The correct word replaces the incorrect word.

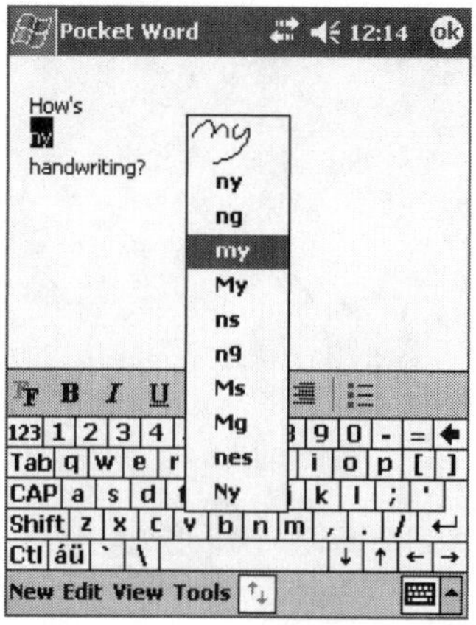

✔ Tips

■ Sometimes the correct word doesn't appear in the list of alternates. Use the soft keyboard method to enter the correct word in these cases. Or make the Pocket PC suggest up to three more words by tapping Start > Settings > Input > Word Completion tab and tapping 4 in the "Suggest __ words" drop-down box.

■ If Pocket Word has trouble recognizing your printed script, try writing in cursive—and vice versa.

Figure 8.17 The first item on the pop-up list is your original scrawl.

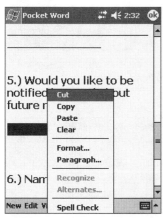

Figure 8.18 Press and hold on selected text to cut or copy it. A pop-up menu appears.

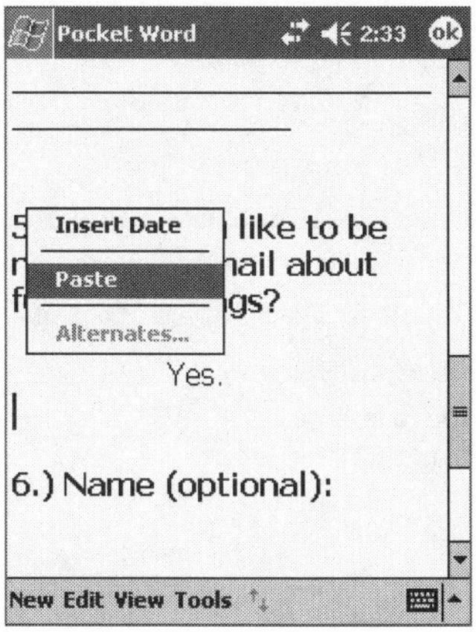

Figure 8.19 Paste text by pressing and holding the stylus where you want it to go.

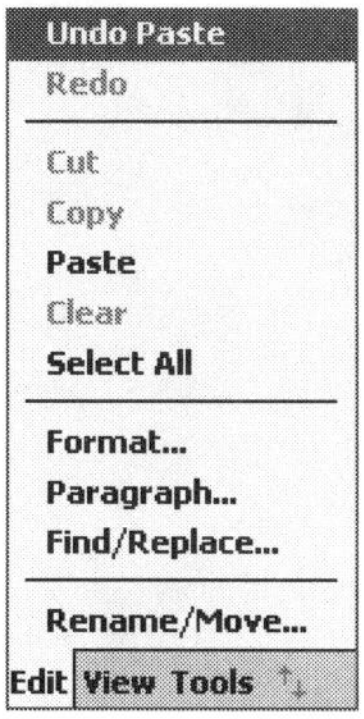

Figure 8.20 The Undo command is smart—it tells you exactly what action you're about to undo.

To cut, copy, and paste text:

1. Select text by pressing the tip of the stylus just before the beginning of a text block and dragging to the end of the text you want to cut, copy, or paste.

You can drag up and down as well as right and left.

2. With the text selected, press and hold the tip of the stylus on the selected text block and tap either Cut or Copy from the pop-up menu (**Figure 8.18**).

or

Tap Edit and then tap Cut or Copy.

As with Word on your computer, Cut removes the text from the document and places it in the clipboard. Copy leaves the text in the document and places it in the clipboard.

3. At the point in your document where you want to paste the text, press and hold and tap Paste from the pop-up menu that appears (**Figure 8.19**).

or

Tap Edit > Paste.

Your text (and all its formatting) is copied or moved to the new location.

To undo/redo an action:

◆ Undo your last action by tapping Edit > Undo (**Figure 8.20**).

or

◆ Tap the 🔄 Undo button in the toolbar (if it is showing).

✔ Tips

■ Pocket Word often lets you undo actions multiple times.

■ You can also redo actions by tapping Edit > Redo.

■ If you delete a file, you cannot undo the deletion.

ENTERING AND FORMATTING TEXT

To format text:

1. In a document, drag the stylus over the text you want to format with a different style, text size, or font.

   The text is highlighted.

2. Tap the up-and-down arrow icon on the menu bar.

   The formatting toolbar appears (**Figure 8.21**).

3. On the toolbar, tap the B (bold), I (italics), or U (underline) icon on the toolbar. For more formatting options, tap the FF (formatting) icon on the left side of the toolbar.

   The text is formatted.

✔ Tips

■ You can also tap Edit > Format (**Figure 8.22**) to display the Format screen (**Figure 8.23**). Check or uncheck the boxes for Bold, Italic, Underline, Highlight, or Strikethrough. Tap the drop-down menus to change the font, font color, or font size. Tap OK to close the Format screen.

■ See the sidebar "Using the Pocket Word toolbar" for an alternate way to format text.

To change paragraph alignment:

1. Tap anywhere within a paragraph, or tap and drag to select multiple paragraphs.

2. If the toolbar is not already visible, tap the ↑↓ up-and-down arrow icon on the menu bar to display it.

3. On the toolbar, tap either the left, center, or right alignment icons (**Figure 8.24**).

Figure 8.21 The toolbar appears when you tap the up-and-down arrow icon.

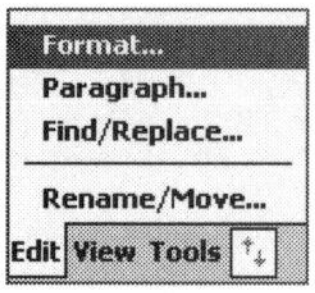

Figure 8.22 Pocket Word gives you a couple ways to format text. You can use the toolbar or choose Edit > Format—both provide the same results.

Figure 8.23 In addition to styling your text, you can change its font or size in the Format screen.

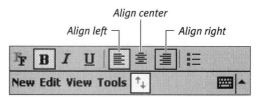

Figure 8.24 The toolbar is the quickest way to align your text.

✔ Tips

- To start a new paragraph with the same alignment, just tap the return key on the soft keyboard.

- You can also use the Edit menu to change a paragraph's alignment. To do so, select the text you wish to format and tap Edit > Paragraph to display the Paragraph screen. In the Alignment pull-down menu, tap Left, Center, or Right. Then tap OK. The paragraph will be correctly aligned.

Adding fonts to your Pocket PC

Pocket PCs come with only four fonts installed: Courier New, Tahoma, Bookdings, and Frutiger Linotype. The Pocket PC 2003 operating system maps the fonts used in a computer's document to the closest font on the Pocket PC—which is usually Tahoma. Don't worry, when a file is copied back to the computer, it reverts back to the original TrueType font.

This arrangement works so well that many people never notice that their fonts are making this behind-the-scenes switch. But if you're particular about how your fonts look onscreen, you can copy TrueType fonts from your computer to your Pocket PC and use them in Pocket Word and other applications. One warning though: TrueType font files can eat up a lot of memory on your device. The font family for Times New Roman, for example, consumes about a megabyte of memory. But if you want, here's how to install TrueType fonts on your Pocket PC:

1. Connect your Pocket PC to your computer using ActiveSync.

2. In ActiveSync on your computer, click the Explore button and navigate to the My Pocket PC\Windows\Fonts directory on your device.

3. In separate window on your computer, navigate to the Fonts directory at C:\Windows\Fonts.

4. Drag a font file (with a .ttf suffix) from the computer's Fonts directory to the Pocket PC's Fonts directory.

5. After the font file finishes copying, do a soft reset on your Pocket PC (see Chapter 1 for how to do a soft reset).

The font is installed on your Pocket PC, ready for you to use in Pocket Word and other programs.

ENTERING AND FORMATTING TEXT

To adjust paragraph indentation:

1. Tap anywhere within a paragraph.

2. Tap Edit > Paragraph.

3. In the Indentation Left: and/or Right: boxes, tap the up or down arrows to change the indentation in increments of $\frac{1}{10}$th of an inch (**Figure 8.25**).

4. To tweak the indentation of only the first line or to create a hanging indent after the first line, tap First Line or Hanging in the Special drop-down menu. Adjust the spacing in increments of $\frac{1}{10}$th of an inch by tapping the up or down arrows in the By: box.

5. Tap OK.

   Your paragraph adopts the indentation you set (**Figure 8.26**).

To create a bulleted list:

1. Tap anywhere within a paragraph, or tap and drag to select multiple paragraphs.

2. If the toolbar is not already visible, tap the up-and-down arrow icon on the menu bar to make it appear.

3. Tap the Bullets icon, located on the right-hand side of the toolbar.

   The paragraph (or paragraphs) are bulleted and slightly indented (**Figure 8.27**).

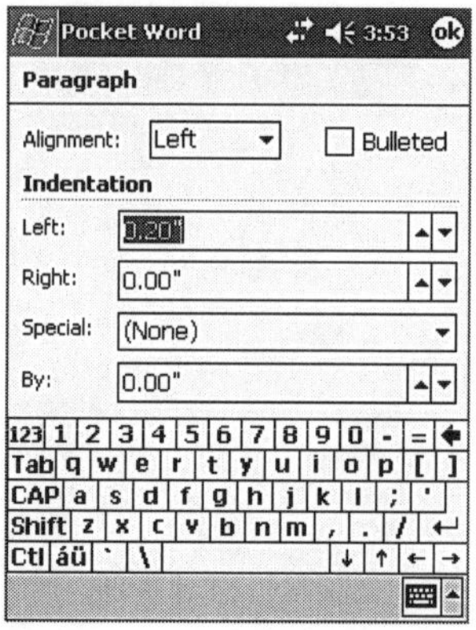

Figure 8.25 The Paragraph screen lets you fine-tune indentation.

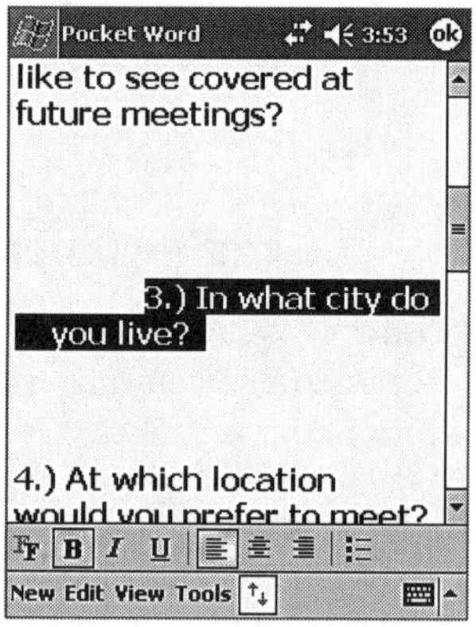

Figure 8.26 Both lines are indented, but we set the first line to indent more than the second.

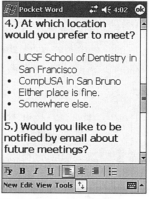

Figure 8.27 Tap the bullet icon to apply bullets to your paragraph(s).

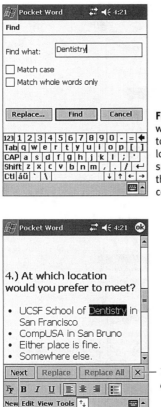

Figure 8.28 Don't waste time trying to scroll around, looking for a specific word. Use the Find/Replace command instead.

Tap here to cancel search

Tap here to find the next occurrence of the word

Figure 8.29 Tap the Next button to find the next occurrence of the word. Tap the X box if you're done looking.

Figure 8.30 Type the replacement word or phrase.

To find text:

1. In a document, tap Edit > Find/Replace.

2. In the "Find what:" box, type the word or words you want to find (**Figure 8.28**).

   If desired, check the check boxes for Match Case or Match Whole Words Only to narrow your search.

   For simple searches, these options are often unnecessary and may even cause you to miss the word you're seeking.

3. Tap Find.

   If present, the word (or words) will appear in your document.

4. To find the next occurrence of the word, tap Next. To stop searching, tap the X (**Figure 8.29**).

   If the text you're searching for was not found, you'll see the error message "No matching item found."

To replace text:

1. In a document, tap Edit > Find/Replace to display the Find screen.

2. Tap Replace.

3. In the "Find what:" box, enter the word or words you want to replace.

4. In the "Replace with:" box, enter the replacement text (**Figure 8.30**).

5. To refine your search, check the check boxes for Match Case or Match Whole Words Only, if you want.

   For simple searches, these options are unnecessary and may even cause you to miss the word you're looking for.

continues on next page

ENTERING AND FORMATTING TEXT

6. Tap Find to find the text.

The first occurrence of the text you're searching for will be highlighted (**Figure 8.31**).

You'll get an error message if the text wasn't found.

7. If you want to replace this occurrence of the text, tap Replace.

▲ If you want to skip this occurrence without replacing it, tap Next.

▲ If you're sure that you want to replace all occurrences, tap Replace All.

▲ Tap the X to abandon the search.

A dialog box alerts you when there are no more occurrences of the text (**Figure 8.32**).

8. Tap OK to close the dialog box.

The original text is changed to the replacement text, with formatting intact (bold words will be replaced by bold words, for example).

To check spelling:

1. From anywhere within a document, tap Tools > Spell Check.

If your spelling is perfect, a pop-up menu appears, informing you that the spell check is complete.

Otherwise, the spell checker highlights the first word it doesn't recognize and offers alternative spellings (**Figure 8.33**).

2. Tap an alternative word to accept its spelling.

▲ Tap Ignore to bypass the word.

▲ Tap Ignore All to bypass all occurrences of the word in the document.

▲ Tap Add to add the word to the spell checker's dictionary.

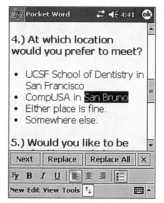

Figure 8.31 Pocket Word has found what we're looking for.

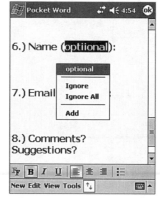

Figure 8.32 A dialog box announces when your search is done.

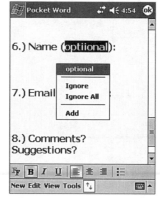

Figure 8.33 The suggested alternative (or alternatives) appears in the pop-up menu.

Figure 8.34 Pocket Word lets you know when it's finished spell checking your document.

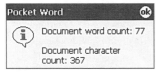

Figure 8.35 Sure, you can count the words yourself, but the Word Count command can do it faster.

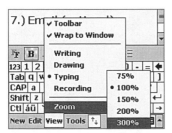

Figure 8.36 Text on a Pocket PC screen can often appear quite tiny. Zoom in to save yourself the eye strain.

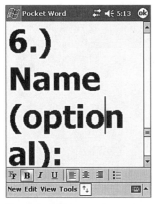

Figure 8.37 The actual text size hasn't changed, but our view has.

The spell check will continue in this manner until you reach the end of your document. A dialog box will tell you when the spell check is complete (**Figure 8.34**).

3. Tap OK to close the dialog box.

✔ Tips

■ You can check the spelling of only part of a document by using the stylus to tap and drag over a portion of the text to select it before you run a spell check.

■ No matter where you are in a document, Pocket Word goes back and checks words at the start of your document.

■ You can interrupt a spell check by tapping outside the pop-up suggestion menu. A dialog box warns you that the spell check is not complete. Tap OK to close it.

To count the number of words:

1. In a document, tap Tools > Word Count. A dialog box appears, telling you how many words and characters are in your document (**Figure 8.35**).

2. Tap OK to close the dialog box.

To change the zoom level:

1. In a document, tap View > Zoom.

2. Tap a zoom level from the pop-up list (**Figure 8.36**) to select it.

Your text appears larger or smaller, depending on the zoom level you selected (**Figure 8.37**).

✔ Tip

■ Zooming doesn't affect the actual font size of your text. It only changes the appearance of the current view.

ENTERING AND FORMATTING TEXT

Recording and Playing Audio in Pocket Word

Pocket Word's Recording mode lets you record and play audio files in your documents. We use this feature to make "notes to self" while writing, in the same way we use Word's Comments feature on the computer. You may also find it faster to dictate a to-do list to your Pocket PC, say, than to type it. It's pretty fun to play around with, however you use it.

To record a voice annotation:

1. Tap View > Recording (**Figure 8.38**).

    In the toolbar that appears, tap the red circular 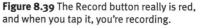 Record button, located in the lower left-hand corner of the toolbar (**Figure 8.39**).

    A tiny beep emits from your Pocket PC.

2. Speak into the microphone to create your recording.

3. To stop recording, tap the black square ■ Stop button on the toolbar.

✔ Tips

- Some Pocket PCs have a hardware record button along one side. You can record by pressing and holding this button and releasing when you're through recording. Two quick beeps will indicate that recording has stopped, and a 🔊 speaker icon will appear in your document. With other models, pressing both sides of the hardware volume control works the same as pressing a hardware record button.

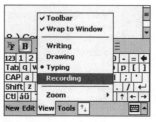

Figure 8.38 Tapping View > Recording gets you into Recording mode.

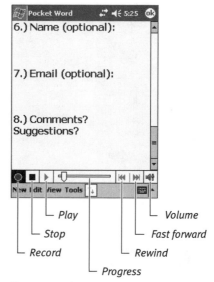

Figure 8.39 The Record button really is red, and when you tap it, you're recording.

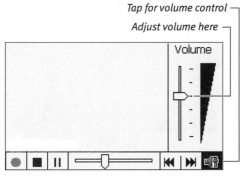

Tap for volume control ⌐
Adjust volume here ⌐

Figure 8.40 The Volume icon on the right end of the toolbar lets you adjust the volume.

- You can add multiple voice annotations to a document.

- Voice annotations will stay embedded in your document when you copy it to your computer.

- You don't have to be in Pocket Word or Notes to record. You can record audio files anytime, even if the device is off, by pressing and holding the hardware record button (if you have one) or the hardware volume button (if you have that).

To play a voice annotation:

◆ Tap a 📢 speaker icon in a Pocket Word document to play a voice annotation.

You can use the toolbar buttons to pause, rewind, and forward the audio. Tapping the toolbar button on the far right triggers a pop-up control that you can slide up and down to adjust the volume (**Figure 8.40**).

✔ Tip

- You can play audio in three of Pocket Word's modes: Writing, Typing, and Recording. The odd mode out is Drawing mode, where audio icons are dimmed to indicate that you can't play them.

RECORDING AND PLAYING AUDIO IN WORD

Creating Drawings

In Pocket Word's Drawing mode, you can create simple sketches with circles, triangles, rectangles, and straight and freeform lines. You can also move objects and color them. This is a handy way to draw a map for friends when giving directions to your house, or to accompany a document with a simple diagram.

Of course, the drawing feature has a few limitations. For starters, drawings made in Pocket Word are embedded in documents, and you can't convert them into .bmp or .jpg images until you copy the documents to a computer.

To draw:

1. In a document, tap View > Drawing. Gridlines fill the screen and the zoom level changes to 200 percent (**Figure 8.41**).

2. If it's not already visible, tap the up-and-down arrow icon on the menu bar to make the drawing toolbar appear (**Figure 8.42**).

3. Draw on the screen using the stylus (**Figure 8.43**).

✔ Tip

■ Tap the Undo icon or Edit > Undo Ink to erase the last object you drew. Undo as many times as you want to delete several objects.

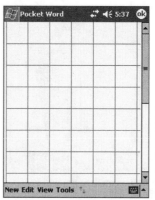

Figure 8.41 The gridlines you see when you enter Drawing mode aren't actually part of the drawing; they're there to help guide you.

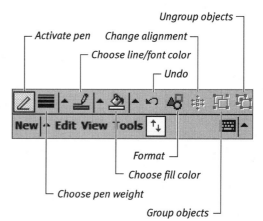

Figure 8.42 In Drawing mode, the toolbar is your best friend. This is where you'll find pen tools, fill colors, line width settings, and other basic drawing tools.

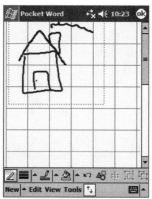

Figure 8.43 The screen is not touch-sensitive, so it doesn't matter how hard or soft you press.

CREATING DRAWINGS

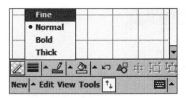

Figure 8.44 To make your lines thinner or thicker, tap the Pen weight icon.

Figure 8.45 The bounding boxes and circles let you know the object is selected.

To change line thickness:

1. Tap the Pen Weight icon (second from the left) on the toolbar.

A pop-up menu appears (**Figure 8.44**).

2. Tap on the thickness you want.

✔ Tip

■ You can change the line thickness of previously drawn objects by selecting them before following the steps listed above. See the next task.

To select an object:

◆ Press and hold the stylus on an object, count to three, and then let go.

Small squares and circles border the object, indicating that it is selected (**Figure 8.45**).

✔ Tip

■ Notice that only the section of the drawing that you tapped is selected—in this case, the house, but not the chimney or the roof. Each time you lift the stylus and draw again, your Pocket PC will consider what you draw to be a separate object from what you drew previously. See the next task for how to select multiple objects.

Advanced drawing with Pocket Artist

If you just want to doodle or make a sketch or a street map or a room layout, then Pocket Word certainly beats drawing on a cocktail napkin. But if you plan to do a lot of drawings with your Pocket PC, you should check out Conduits Technologies Pocket Artist at www.conduits.com. This program comes packed with hundreds of tools, and lets you open and save drawings in a variety of formats.

CREATING DRAWINGS

To select multiple objects:

1. Tap the ⧄ Pen icon on the far left of the toolbar.

   The small square that bounded the icon will disappear, indicating selection mode.

2. Use the stylus to drag diagonally across the objects you want to select, then let go.

   Squares and circles border the objects, indicating they are selected (**Figure 8.46**).

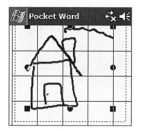

Figure 8.46 Multiple objects are selected.

✔ Tip

■ Working in selection mode can be tricky. After working with a selected object (moving it, coloring it, and so on), you must tap the Pen icon again to go back to drawing mode. In drawing mode the Pen icon has a box around it; in selection mode it doesn't.

To move objects:

1. Select an object or objects.

2. Drag the selected items to a new location (**Figure 8.47**).

3. Lift the stylus when the object is where you want it.

Figure 8.47 The rectangular outline shows the move in progress.

To cut and copy objects:

1. Select an object or objects.

2. From the Edit menu, tap either Cut or Copy.

To paste objects:

1. Cut or copy an object.

2. Tap Edit > Paste.

   You can paste the object into the same drawing or into a new drawing.

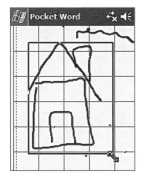

Figure 8.48 Dragging a bounding square out makes the object bigger.

Figure 8.49 Dragging a bounding circle distorts the shape.

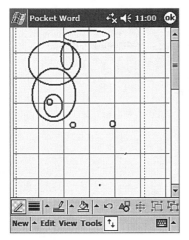

Figure 8.50 Drawing mode lets you transform any object into four basic shapes.

To resize or distort objects:

◆ Select an object or objects and then do one of the following:

◆ To make it smaller or larger, drag a bounding square in or out (**Figure 8.48**).

◆ To distort its shape, drag an inner bounding circle in or out (**Figure 8.49**).

To turn an object into a rectangle, circle, triangle, or line:

1. Select an object or objects.

2. Press and hold on the selected objects and tap Shape in the pop-up menu that appears.

   Another pop-up menu lists the shapes Rectangle, Circle, Triangle, and Line.

3. Tap the shape you want.

   The object is transformed into a new shape (**Figure 8.50**). In this case, every object has been converted to a circle.

✔ Tip

■ This tool is fun to play with, and it's also quite useful for turning shaky doodles into sharp-looking diagrams.

To color objects:

◆ Select an object or objects and then do one of the following:

◆ To change the object's color, tap the Line/Font icon on the toolbar and tap a color in the pop-up menu (**Figure 8.51**).

◆ To fill an object's insides with color, tap the Fill Color icon on the toolbar and tap a color in the pop-up menu (**Figure 8.52**).

To group and ungroup objects:

1. Select two or more objects.

2. Tap the 🔲 Group Objects icon on the toolbar.

   When objects are grouped, they can be selected and manipulated as if they were a single object.

✔ Tip

■ To ungroup objects, tap the Ungroup Objects icon at the right end of the toolbar.

To align objects:

◆ Select two or more objects.

◆ Tap the 🔲 Alignment icon in the toolbar and tap an alignment option from the pop-up menu that appears (**Figure 8.53**). The objects snap into alignment.

✔ Tip

■ This is another tool that can help the artistically challenged. For example, if you center two objects vertically and then center them again horizontally, the smaller object will become centered inside a larger object, like circles on a dartboard.

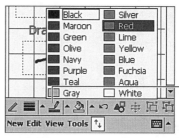

Tap the Line/ Font icon to display the pop-up menu

Figure 8.51 Choose a line or font color by tapping the Line/Font icon.

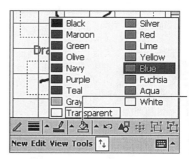

Tap the Fill Color icon to display the pop-up menu

Figure 8.52 Choose a fill color by tapping the Fill Color icon.

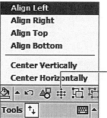

Tap the Alignment icon to display the pop-up menu

Figure 8.53 Align objects with the Align icon.

Table 7.1

What's Lost in the Translation	
POCKET WORD WON'T DISPLAY:	WILL FORMATTING BE CONVERTED BACK?
Annotations	No
Borders	Yes
Columns	No
Comments	No
Footnotes	No
Footers	No
Frames	No
Gutter size	No
Headers	No
Index formatting	Some
OLE objects	No
Page margins	Yes
Page setup settings	No
Paper size	Yes
Pictures	No
Shading	No
Style sheets	No
Table formatting	No
Table of contents formatting	Some

The TextMaker word-processing alternative

SoftMaker's TextMaker is a Pocket PC word processor that lets you edit and save a Word document without losing formatting.

With TextMaker, which starts at $49.99, you can create and format tables, work with style sheets, and do just about anything can in Word on your computer.

You can download a trial version of the program at `www.softmaker.de`.

Sharing Documents with your Computer

Can Pocket Word read and write documents that are compatible with Word on desktop computers? The answer is yes—sort of. Your Pocket PC preserves formatting for bold, hidden text, paragraph spacing, superscript, bullets, italics, simple numbered lists, subscript, headings, paragraph alignment, strikethrough, tabs, and indentation.

However, a lot of formatting is lost when ActiveSync converts a Word document to a Pocket Word document. This formatting loss also happens when you open a .doc file and change it on the Pocket PC.

For example, let's say you have a .doc file with a formatted table. Pocket Word can't display tables, so it lists the table as tabbed text. If you close the file without making any changes, the table (and all other formatting) will be preserved when you copy it back to a PC. However, if you make even the *slightest* change to the table, such as adding one space, you'll get an option asking you to save it in Desktop Word or Pocket Word format. Even if you pick Desktop, when you open the document on your computer, it will have lost the formatting—the table will be permanently converted into tabbed text.

Therefore, be very careful when working with heavily formatted documents. It's best to only work on copies of .doc files on your Pocket PC. To do this, ActiveSync a copy of the .doc files to your Pocket PC, but keep the original document in a separate folder on your computer. It's also a good idea to familiarize yourself with the way Pocket Word handles formatting (**Table 7.1**).

If you're planning to work with documents often, take a look at TextMaker, a full-featured word processor that preserves all of Word's .doc formatting (see sidebar).

POCKET EXCEL

Pocket Excel is a scaled-down version of Microsoft Excel, the electronic spreadsheet program that comes with Microsoft Office.

Pocket Excel, like its big brother version that is likely on your computer, is best at manipulating text and numeric values such as prices, statistics, dates, and percentages, using formulas that perform certain calculations in various cells.

With Microsoft Excel, you can also include graphics—such as pie charts—and apply shading and colors to cells to better organize and format the information in your workbook. The Pocket version doesn't support graphs, though it does contain the formulas needed to perform the most common and practical functions.

The idea behind Pocket Excel is that you can copy Excel workbooks from your computer to your Pocket PC and update and edit them while you are away from your desk. As with Pocket Word, when you synchronize your device with your computer, the file—a Pocket Excel workbook (with a .pxl extension)—is automatically converted into a Microsoft Excel workbook (with an .xls extension), and vice versa.

In this chapter, we'll look at how to create workbooks, enter data, formulas, and functions, and how to share your workbooks.

Getting Started with Pocket Excel

Excel is a clever program, and Pocket Excel is no slouch. It uses familiar commands to do the things you would expect—plus it offers the fabulous Fill command, a sort of artificial intelligence that can do for you automatically what you otherwise would have to slog through yourself. And isn't that what computing is for?

To launch Pocket Excel:

◆ Tap Start > Programs > Pocket Excel.

A blank Excel document, called a *workbook*, appears (**Figure 9.1**).

If you see a list of files instead, you need to create a new workbook.

To create a workbook:

◆ In Pocket Excel, tap the New menu.

or

In the Today screen, tap New and tap Excel Workbook in the pop-up menu (**Figure 9.2**).

A blank workbook appears, as in Figure 9.1.

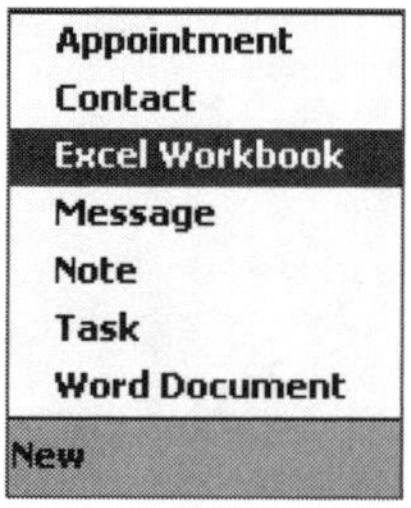

✔ Tips

■ By default, a new workbook has three *worksheets*, pages made up of grids of small squares called *cells*. Each cell is named according to the row of letters running horizontally across the top of the screen and the column of numbers running down the side, so you have cells B1, C6, and ZZ100.

■ Pocket Excel worksheets have 256 columns and 16,384 rows, which should be enough.

continues on page 180

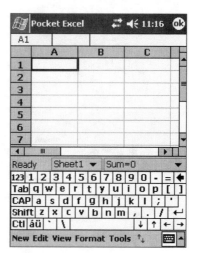

Figure 9.1 When you first launch Pocket Excel, a blank document is automatically created.

Figure 9.2 You can also create an Excel workbook straight from the Today screen.

A tour of Pocket Excel's screen

Here's a quick look at a typical Pocket Excel screen, with the different parts of it labeled for easy reference.

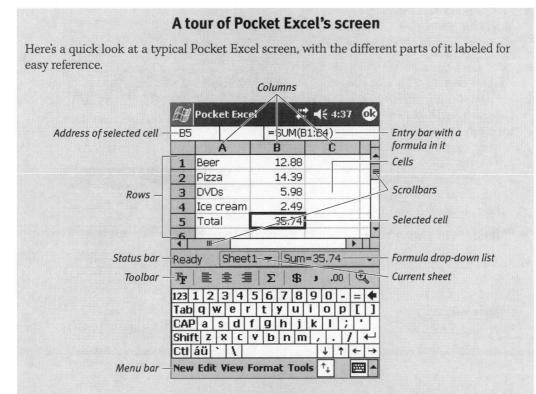

The Pocket Excel toolbar contains many useful commands, but it is hidden by default. You can view it by tapping the Show/Hide Toolbar icon at the bottom of the screen. The toolbar will appear just above the menu bar. The toolbar includes formatting options and commands that we will be discussing throughout the chapter for cell formatting, text alignment, a short-cut to the common SUM formula, number formatting, and zoom.

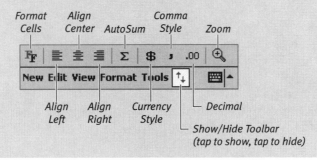

- Move among worksheets by tapping the Sheet1 drop-down list and tapping the sheet you want to view (**Figure 9.3**).

- Add, remove, reorder, or rename worksheets within a workbook by tapping Format > Modify Sheets. In the Modify Sheets screen (**Figure 9.4**), tap the sheet to modify in the left column, then tap Rename to rename it; tap Insert to add a new worksheet (the new one appears above the sheet you tapped); tap Delete to delete a worksheet; and tap Move Up or Move Down to reorder worksheets.

To enter data in a workbook:

1. Tap the cell you want to enter text or numbers into.

   A border appears around the cell (**Figure 9.5**).

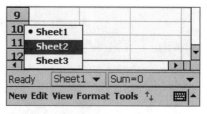

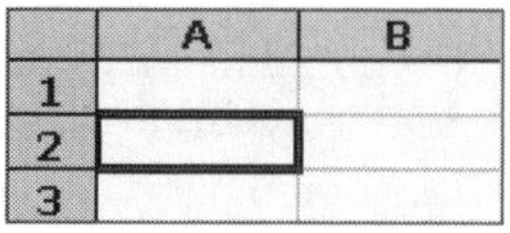

Figure 9.3 Tap the Sheet 1 drop-down list and tap the sheet you want to view.

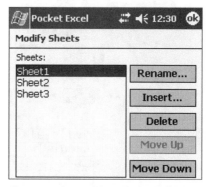

Figure 9.4 The Modify Sheets screen lets you manage your worksheets.

Figure 9.5 Here, the cell A2 is selected and ready for data.

What's missing in Pocket Excel?

Microsoft Excel, Pocket Excel's computer counterpart, is an extremely powerful spreadsheet program. It's heavily loaded with advanced features and capabilities that most users not only will never use, but won't even realize are there. But even some of the more basic of Excel's features are lacking in Pocket Excel. Among the features you may miss are Excel's charting abilities, macros, in-cell editing, cell protection, passwords, and pivot tables. However, you can find third-party programs and add-ons that provide some of these capabilities. See the sidebar "Alternatives to Pocket Excel" later in the chapter.

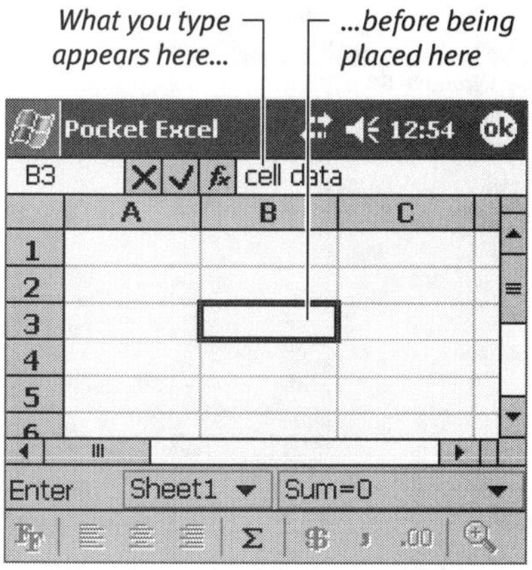

What you type appears here... ...before being placed here

Figure 9.6 Type data to be entered into the cell in the entry bar.

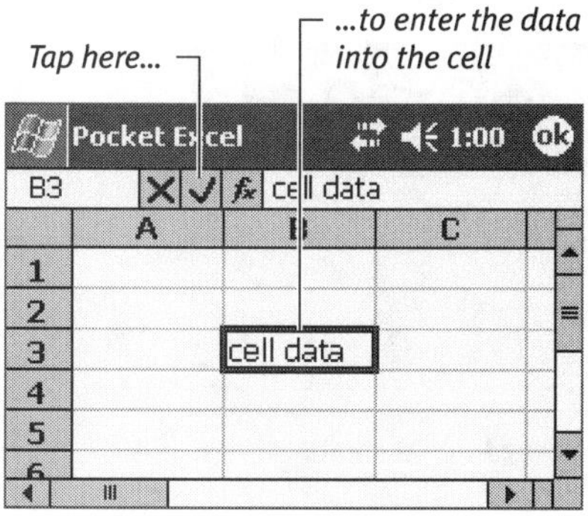

Tap here... ...to enter the data into the cell

Figure 9.7 When you tap the check mark, Pocket Excel puts the data into the selected cell.

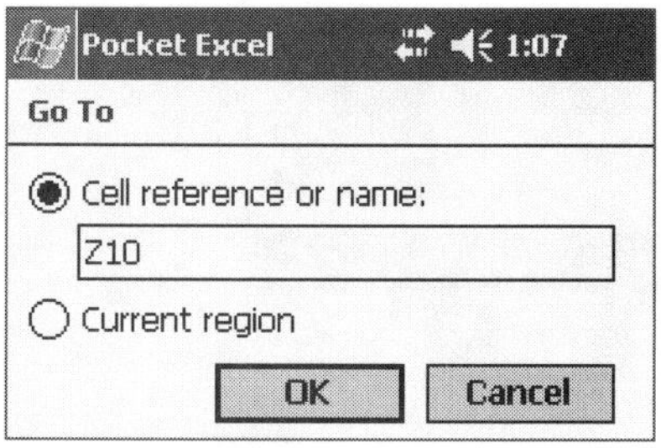

Figure 9.8 The Go To command lets you zip instantly to any cell.

2. Begin entering text or numbers using the soft (onscreen) keyboard.

As you type, a blinking cursor appears in the entry bar at the top of the screen (**Figure 9.6**). This is where the information you enter appears before it is placed in the cell.

3. Tap the check mark to the left of the entry bar or tap Enter on the soft keyboard to enter the data into the cell.

Your text appears in the cell (**Figure 9.7**).

✔ Tips

- Tap the X rather than the check mark to cancel text you enter in the entry bar.

- Tap the ⌨▲ keyboard icon up arrow to change text-entering methods.

- If the cell you want to enter text or a formula into is not visible on the screen, use the scrollbars to scroll down or over to find the cell you want.

- You can also use the Go To option to tell Excel which cell you want by name (for example, Z10). Tap Tools > Go To and enter the cell you want (**Figure 9.8**). Tap OK, and you are brought to that cell.

- You can edit cells in a worksheet by tapping the cell you want to edit, tapping your stylus at the end of the text in the entry bar, and then modifying the text using the soft keyboard or another text-entry method.

- To enter symbols, such as a currency symbol or a character from another alphabet, tap a cell in which you want the symbol to appear, then tap Tools > Insert Symbol, select your font from the Font drop-down list and the symbol from the Subset list, and then tap Insert.

GETTING STARTED WITH POCKET EXCEL

181

To copy and paste data from cells:

1. Tap the cell that contains the data (text or formula) you want to copy.

2. Tap Edit > Copy (**Figure 9.9**).

   or

   Press and hold the stylus on the cell and tap Copy from the pop-up menu that appears.

3. Tap the cell where you want to paste the data.

4. Tap Edit > Paste.

   or

   Press and hold the cell and tap Paste from the pop-up menu that appears.

✔ Tips

■ Copied formulas automatically adjust themselves to their new columns or rows. For example, if a formula in cell A3 adds cells A1 and A2, and you copy the formula to B3, it will automatically add cells B1 and B2. (See the section "Working with Formulas" for more on formulas.)

■ To copy and paste among multiple cells at once, just tap the first cell and drag to the last cell you want to copy or paste (**Figure 9.10**). You must paste text into an equal number and the same shape of cells that you copied it from or you will receive an error message (**Figure 9.11**).

■ To select an entire workbook for copying, tap Edit > Select All, then Edit > Copy.

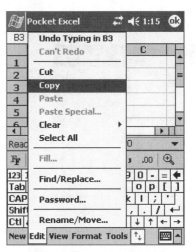

Figure 9.9 Use the Edit > Copy command to copy the contents of a cell.

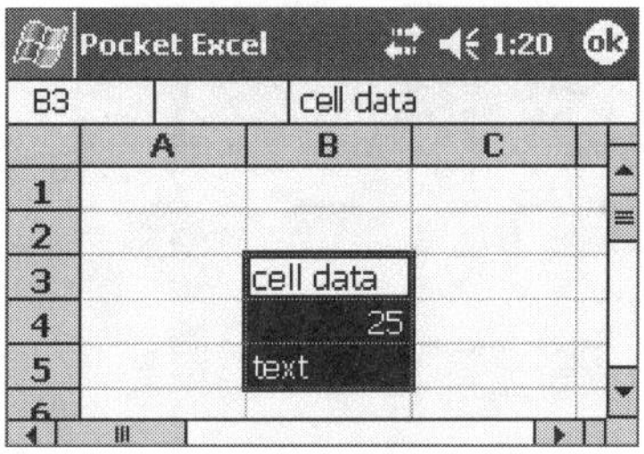

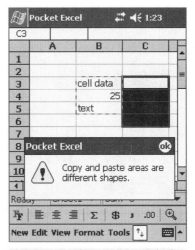

Figure 9.10 Drag through multiple cells to select them.

Figure 9.11 You have to paste multiple cells into a group of cells of the same number and shape.

Using the Fill command

If you are entering a sequential range of numbers or, in some cases, words (days of the week, for example) in a row or column, the Fill command can save you a lot of mind-numbing typing. Simply enter the first number or word in the range, then drag your stylus to select the range of cell where you want Pocket Excel to fill in the rest of your series, as shown here.

Then tap Edit > Fill... to access the Fill screen.

Under Direction, select whether you are "filling" a range of cells Up or Down or Right or Left (this will depend on whether you selected in a row or a column).

♦ Tap the Copy radio button to copy the existing cell content.

♦ Tap the Series radio button to automatically continue the series of numbers or dates.

Under "Series type," tap AutoFill to have Pocket Excel analyze the data and determine what sort of series you are entering.

♦ Tap Date if you want to enter a range of dates—you can select Day, Month, or Year from the drop-down menu.

♦ Tap Number for a range of numbers, and tap a "Step value" (e.g., 1 if you want sequential numbers, 2 if you want a series such as 1, 3, 5, etc.).

♦ Tap OK, and the cells you selected are "filled," as shown here.

To save a workbook:

1. With a workbook open, tap Tools > Save Workbook As... (**Figure 9.12**).
   The Save As screen appears (**Figure 9.13**).

2. Choose from the following options:

   ▲ Name the worksheet in the Name field.

   ▲ To save the worksheet to a particular folder, choose one from the Folder drop-down list. The default (if you choose None) is to save it in the device's My Documents directory.

   ▲ Change the file type by tapping one in the Type menu (you have three older Excel file types to choose from, or you can save it as an Excel template).

   ▲ In the Location drop-down list, choose "Storage card" (if you have one installed) to save the workbook on an external storage card or "Main memory" to store it in your Pocket PC's main memory.

3. Tap OK to save the workbook.

✔ Tips

■ When you close a workbook without choosing Save As, the document is automatically saved as Book1, Book2, and so on.

■ If you are working in a workbook and tap New to open a new one without saving your changes to the first one, you will be prompted to do so (**Figure 9.14**).

Sharing your workbooks:

◆ With the workbook you want to share open in Pocket Excel, tap Tools > Send via E-mail... A new email message with the file attached opens.

◆ Tap Beam Workbook... to beam your file to another device.

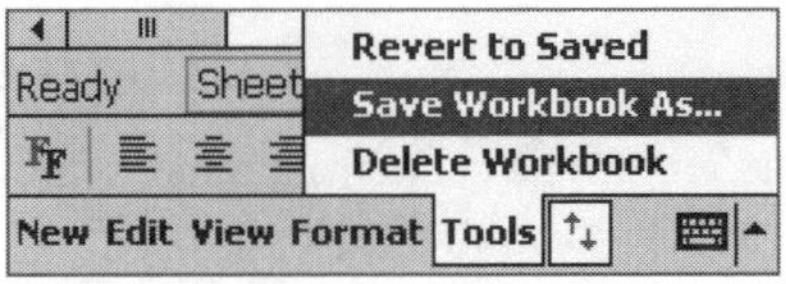

Figure 9.12 The Save As... command, instead of being in the File menu as it is in Windows programs, is in the Tools menu.

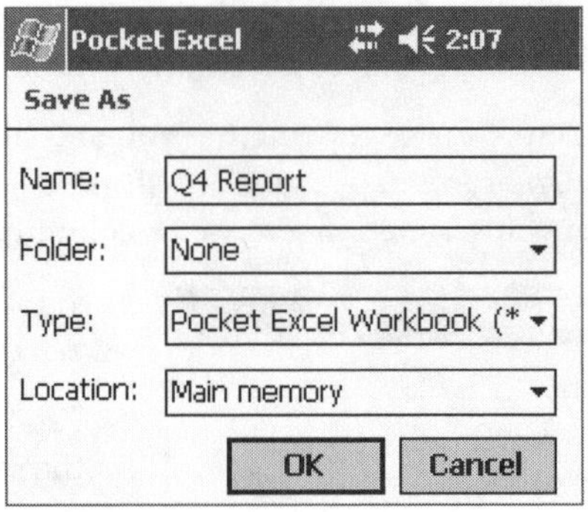

Figure 9.13 The Save As screen lets you pick where, how, and under what name to save your workbook.

Figure 9.14 If you forget to save your workbook, Pocket Excel thoughtfully reminds you to do so.

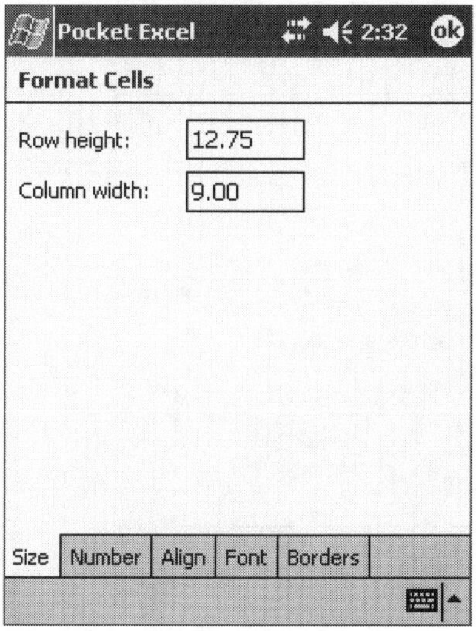

Figure 9.15 The Size tab lets you adjust the height and width of your rows and columns, respectively.

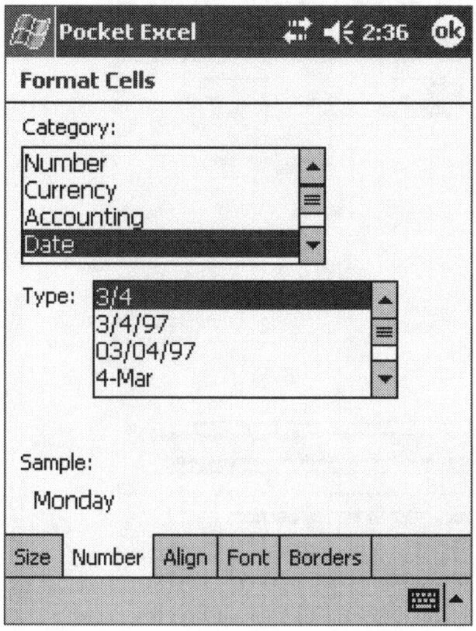

Figure 9.16 You can format your dates in Excel to look just the way you want.

Working with Cells, Rows, and Columns

To paraphrase Vidal Sassoon, when your workbooks don't look good, *you* don't look good. That's why Excel offers quite a bit of formatting and editing power—to make your cells, rows, and columns not just accurate in their data, but attractive and professional-looking.

To format cells:

1. Tap the cell you want to format.

   or

   Select a group of cells by dragging your stylus across the cells you want to format.

2. Tap Format > Cells.

   or

   Press and hold the stylus on the selected cell or group of cells and tap Format Cells in the pop-up menu that appears.

   The Format Cells screen appears, with the first tab, Size, selected (**Figure 9.15**).

3. From the tabs at the bottom of the screen, tap the specific cell characteristic you want to format.

   Size: You can alter the size of any cell. Cell height can range from 0 to 409. Cell width ranges from 0 to 255. Decimals are acceptable for both height and width.

   Number: Choose how you want numbers to appear in a specific cell. Numbers can represent percentages, time, fractions, and so on. For monetary units, choose Currency from the Category list. Most categories have other specific options as well. Date, for example, offers several different appearances for dates, such as "3/4/03" and "4-Mar" (**Figure 9.16**).

continues on next page

WORKING WITH CELLS, ROWS, AND COLUMNS

Align: The Align tab sets the arrangement of text in a cell (**Figure 9.17**). Choose Left, Center, Right, or across a selection. Arrange text vertically to the Top, Center, or Bottom of a cell. Checking "Wrap text" wraps lines of text to fit in a cell (you may only see the amount of text that will fit in the cell, but the rest of the text is still there).

Font: Tap Font to format the font of text in a cell (**Figure 9.18**).

Borders: Borders help the appearance and usability of workbooks. Select the border color from the Borders drop-down list and select which sides of the cell you want to have a border. You can also add shading to a cell on this page with the Fill drop-down list (**Figure 9.19**).

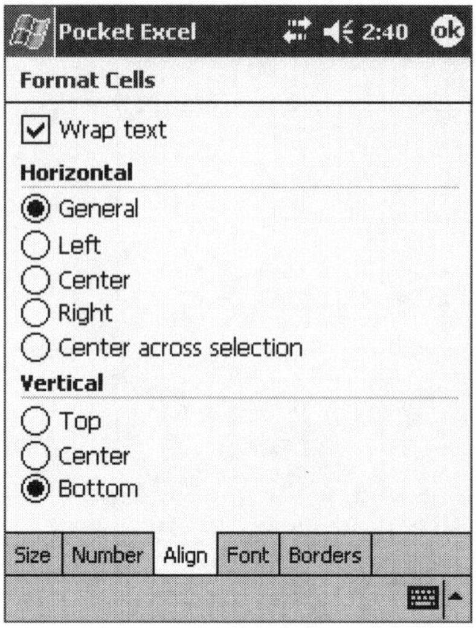

Figure 9.17 Use the Align tab to align text vertically or horizontally within a cell.

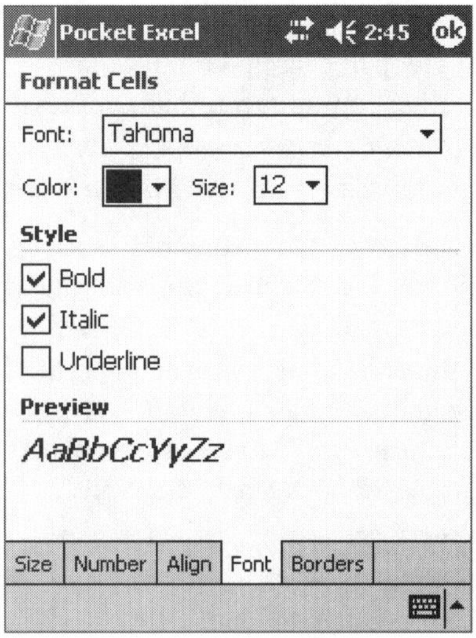

Figure 9.18 In the Font tab, choose the font, color, size, and style of your text. The Preview feature lets you see your changes before making them final.

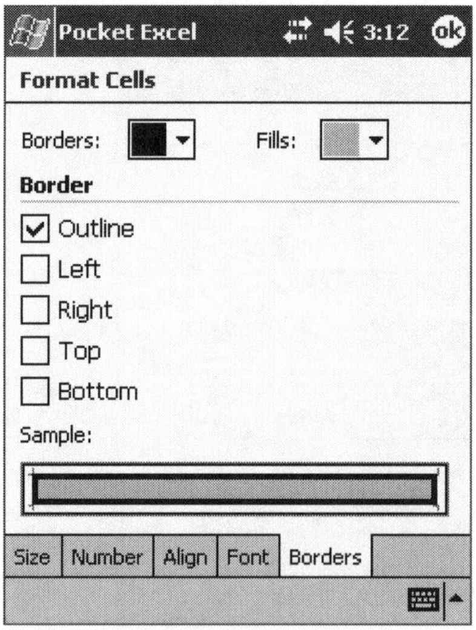

Figure 9.19 Borders and fills can add a bit of color and pizzazz and also help make your spreadsheet easier to read.

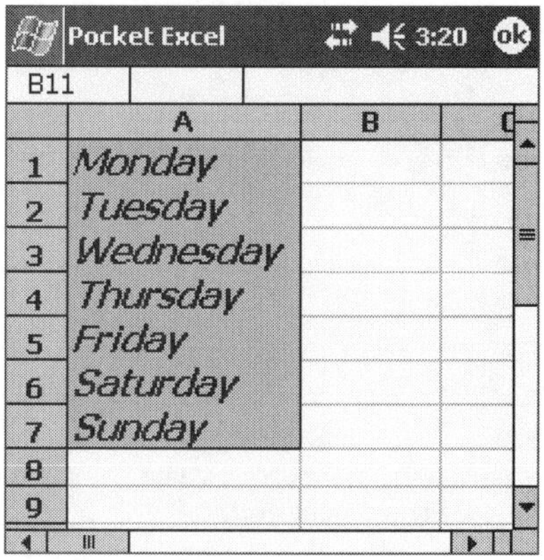

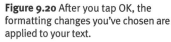

Figure 9.20 After you tap OK, the formatting changes you've chosen are applied to your text.

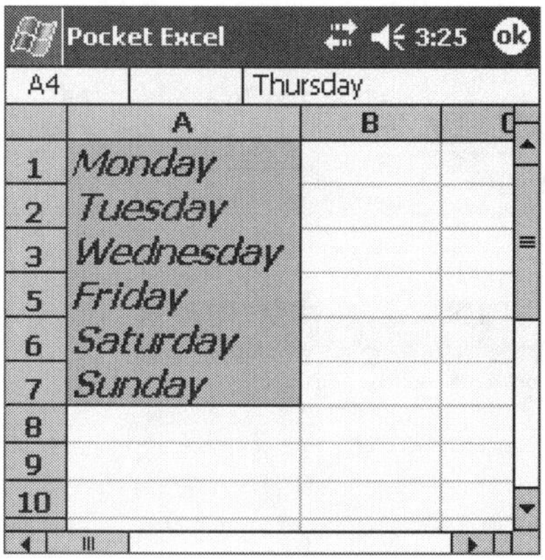

Figure 9.21 Hidden cells, rows, or columns are still there—you just can't see them until you unhide them.

4. When you have set your formatting options, tap OK.

Your cell or group of cells is now formatted (**Figure 9.20**).

✔ Tip

■ When formatting, you are formatting the cell itself rather than the text that appears there (except for Font formatting). If you format blank cells, text you add will automatically be formatted according to how the cell has been formatted.

To format rows and columns:

◆ To hide a row, tap any cell in the row and tap Format > Row > Hide.

The row is hidden (**Figure 9.21**).

◆ To hide a column, tap any cell in the column and tap Format > Column > Hide.

The column is hidden.

◆ To unhide a row or column, tap any cell in the row or column and tap Format > Row > Unhide or Format > Column > Unhide.

The row or column reappears.

◆ Tap a cell and tap Format > Row > AutoFit, and the row will automatically adjust its height to fit the tallest text entry in the row.

✔ Tip

■ Hiding rows or columns can be very useful if you only want to view specific sections of the workbook without seeing them all. See the section "Adjusting the View" later in the chapter for more on changing how you view workbooks.

WORKING WITH CELLS, ROWS, AND COLUMNS

To delete cells, rows, or columns:

1. Tap a cell that you want to delete or that is in a row or column that you want to delete.

2. Tap Format > Delete Cells.

or

Press and hold the stylus on a cell and tap Delete from the pop-up menu that appears.

The Delete Cells page appears (**Figure 9.22**).

3. Tap one of the following:

▲ "Shift cells left" to delete the cell and shift the rest of the cells left.

▲ "Shift cells up" to delete the cell and shift the rest of the cells up.

▲ "Entire row" to delete the entire row.

▲ "Entire column" to delete the entire column.

✔ Tips

■ Deleting cells, rows, and columns will actually delete the cells themselves, not just the text within a cell. To merely clear the content of a cell but leave the cell, press and hold a cell or cells and tap Clear in the pop-up menu that appears (**Figure 9.23**).

■ To clear some but not all data from a cell or group of cells, tap the cell or cells, tap Edit > Clear, and tap All if you want to clear the cell completely, Formats to clear formatting only, and Contents to clear text but not formatting (**Figure 9.24**).

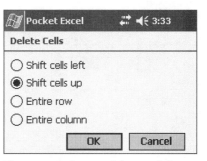

Figure 9.22 Before you delete a cell, you have to choose how you want Excel to deal with the hole it will leave in the grid.

Figure 9.23 To get rid of cell contents and return the cells to the blank state they were in before, use Clear.

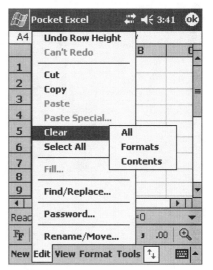

Figure 9.24 You can get even pickier about what exactly to clear from a cell with the Edit > Clear command.

WORKING WITH CELLS, ROWS, AND COLUMNS

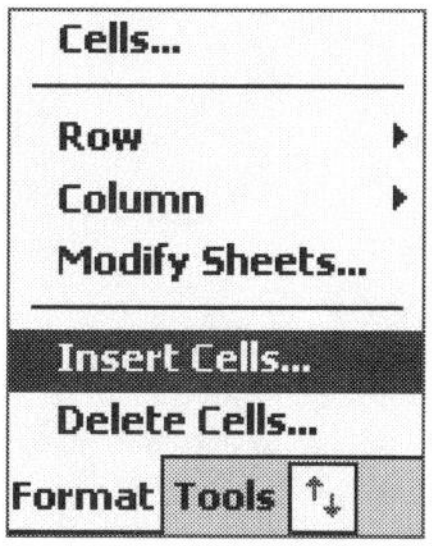

Figure 9.25 You can insert more cells, rows, and columns into a workbook where you like.

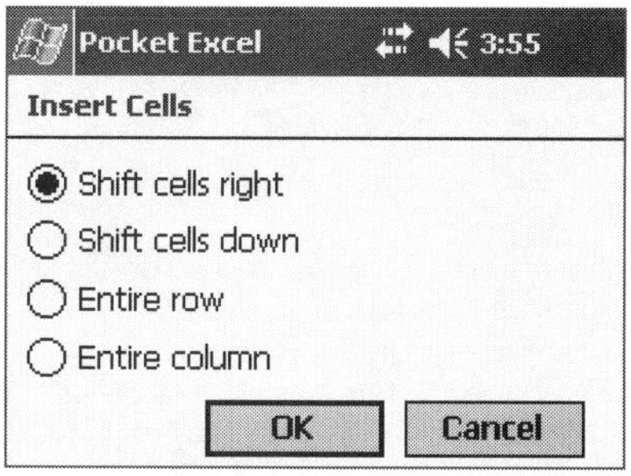

Figure 9.26 The Insert Cells screen lets you get more specific about what you want to insert.

To insert cells, rows, or columns:

1. Tap a cell on the workbook that you want to insert a cell, row, or column next to.

2. Tap Format > Insert Cells... (**Figure 9.25**).
   or
   Tap and hold a cell and tap Insert from the pop-up menu that appears.
   The Insert Cells page appears (**Figure 9.26**).

3. Tap one of the following:
   - ▲ "Shift cells right" to insert the cell and shift left.
   - ▲ "Shift cells down" to delete the cell and shift down.
   - ▲ "Insert row" to insert an entire row.
   - ▲ "Insert column" to insert an entire column.

✔ Tips

- A new column will appear to the left of the column in which you selected a cell. A new row will appear above the cell you selected.

- You will have to adjust any formulas that are impacted by the addition or deletion of a cell. Formulas do not "travel" with cells as you move them up and down by inserting and deleting rows—they are always assigned to the letter and number cell coordinates, such as B5.

WORKING WITH CELLS, ROWS, AND COLUMNS

To sort data:

1. Drag to select the cells you want to sort.

2. Tap Tools > Sort (**Figure 9.27**).

   You can sort by up to three columns.

3. Select the column or columns by which you want to sort in the three drop-down lists that appear (**Figure 9.28**).

   If you only want to sort by one column, tap None in the "Then by" lists.

✔ Tips

■ Uncheck the Ascending check box if you want your data sorted in descending order.

■ Tap "Exclude header row from sort" to sort data by row content rather than header.

Figure 9.27 If you prefer, you can sort your data by choosing a specific column (or columns).

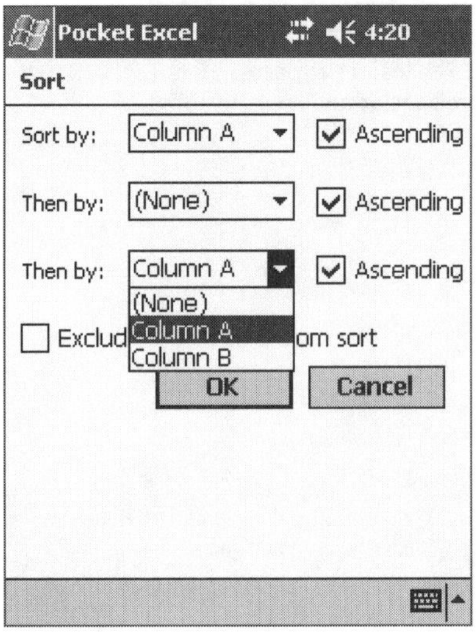

Figure 9.28 All three Sort By drop-down lists let you choose how to sort.

Filtering data with AutoFilter

The AutoFilter tool in Pocket Excel enables you to customize data in a worksheet into subsets so you can easily view the information you need without having to wade through data you don't.

For example, if you have a large database of addresses and phone numbers and you are only interested in viewing a list of people in the 415 area code, you can use this tool to "filter" your data to view contacts with that area code. Here's how to do it, using area codes as an example:

1. Tap the cell at the top of the column that holds the data you want to filter.

   Upside-down arrows appear across the tops of the columns in your worksheet.

2. Tap the upside-down arrow at the top of the column you want to filter your worksheet by.

   A drop-down list appears, offering you the choice to view all of the data, the top ten items, or to set a custom filter. Tap "Custom..."

   The Custom AutoFilter screen appears.

3. You can select from several ranges in the first drop-down list ("is greater than or equal to," "is not equal to," and so on).

   In the second drop-down list, select from a list of the various options that appear in the column. Tap the one you want.

   Tap the And radio button to select another range from the first list or another one (area code) from the second list. This will search for an occurrence of both area codes together. Tap Or if you want to search for instances for one or the other area code.

4. Tap OK.

   Your worksheet is now filtered to your specifications.

WORKING WITH CELLS, ROWS, AND COLUMNS

Working with Formulas

Formulas give Excel its power. A formula is an equation, starting with an equals (=) sign, that performs operations on your data. The operations can be mathematical, as in addition, subtraction, multiplication, and division, and can use numbers, text, or cell addresses.

You can enter formulas by hand, but a good way to introduce yourself to them is the Insert Function screen (Tools > Insert Function), which is a collection of formulas. Browse the various formulas to see what they do, then insert them into your workbook right from the list.

Categories of formulas are listed in the Category drop-down list, and predefined formulas, called functions, are also listed alphabetically in the Function drop-down list. When you tap a function in the list, a brief explanation of what it does appears at the bottom of the screen.

Alternatives to Pocket Excel

SpreadCE is a power user program for Excel users. It's very powerful and, unlike Pocket Excel, supports drawing objects and charts. Download a shareware version for free from www.byedesign.freeserve.co.uk and if you like it, you can register it for $20.

For users who want graphing and charting features within Pocket Excel, DeveloperOne makes **AutoGraph**, a clever little program that allows you to take your Pocket Excel data and generate seven types of graphs from it. Get it for $9.95 from www.developerone.com/autograph/

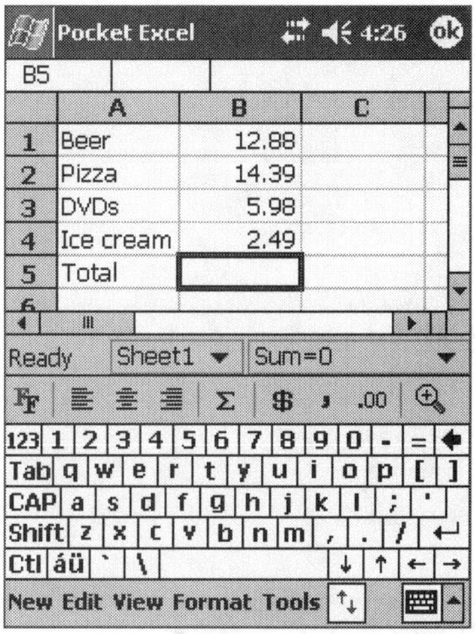

Figure 9.29 Select the cell where you want the formula to make the calculation.

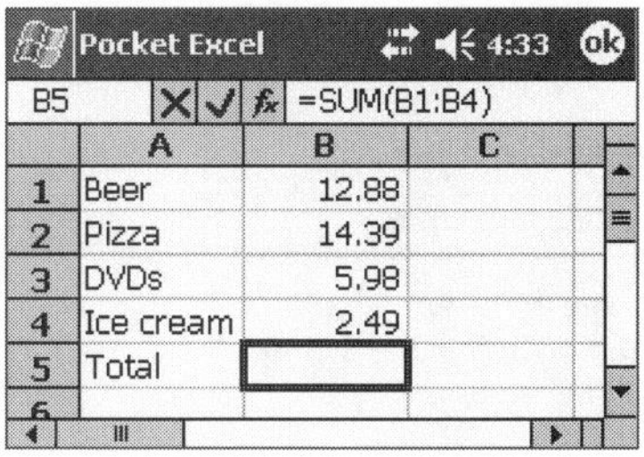

Figure 9.30 Enter the formula in the entry bar, beginning it with the equals (=) sign.

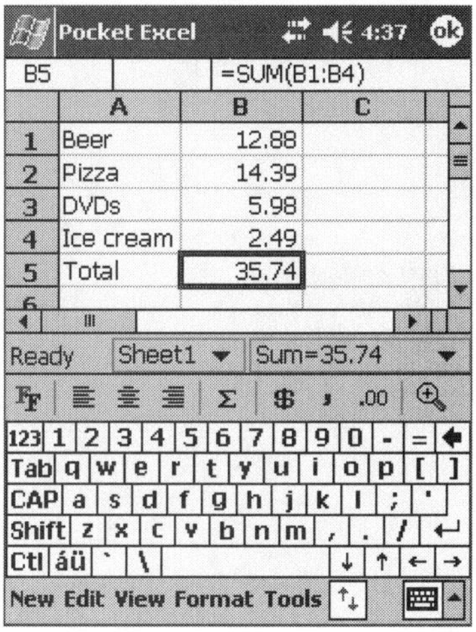

Figure 9.31 The formula tells us that a night in is not as cheap as it used to be.

To insert formulas manually:

1. Tap the cell where you want the result of the formula you apply to appear.

   For example, in **Figure 9.29**, we want the total of all of the expense amounts to appear in the cell next to the word Total.

2. Enter the formula in the entry bar (**Figure 9.30**).

   Remember, a formula begins with the equal sign (=). If you don't know which formula you want, see the next section.

3. Tap the check mark next to the entry bar, and the calculated result of your formula appears in the selected cell (**Figure 9.31**).

✔ Tips

- Tap the Σ AutoSum button in the toolbar to quickly add up a total for values in a group of cells.

- Much of Pocket Excel's functionality relies on learning and effectively applying formulas. But don't worry about learning all the formulas right away. It's a good idea to get a sense of what various formulas can do, but only commit them to memory on a need-to-know basis. You'll soon know the formulas you use most like you know your own phone number. Excel Help on your computer gives a good primer on formulas.

- Formulas are automatically recalculated whenever any changes are made to the cells where the formula is applied. This is an easy way to see how budgets, schedules, and so on will be impacted by a change in any of the amounts entered into cells.

- You can also insert formulas using the Insert Function tool (see the next section for how).

WORKING WITH FORMULAS

To use Insert Function:

1. Tap the cell in which you want the result of the formula to appear.

 A border appears around the cell to show that it is selected.

2. To access the Insert Function screen, either:

 ▲ Tap Tools > Insert Function.

 or

 ▲ Tap the *fx* button next to the entry bar. (If you don't see it, tap in the entry bar, and the flashing cursor and *fx* button appear).

 The Insert Function screen appears.

3. Tap the formula you want to apply to the cell. We'll pick AVERAGE (**Figure 9.32**).

 The formula it displays is a model, and the information in parentheses is to be replaced by your data. Here, in the parentheses, the AVERAGE function wants numbers (or cell coordinates) separated by commas. Do that in the entry bar, using your data.

4. Tap OK.

 You return to your worksheet, and the formula appears in the entry bar.

5. Following the example pattern, plug in your cell data in the parenthesis (**Figure 9.33**).

6. Tap the check mark or tap Enter.

 The results appear in the cell in which you entered the formula (**Figure 9.34**).

✔ Tip

■ If you're applying a function to a range of cells, for example a column of four cells, instead of listing each one with a comma between, a shortcut is to enter the first, then a colon, then the last cell in the range, like so: A1:A5.

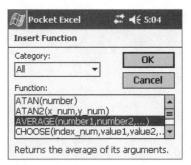

Figure 9.32 Tap a function, and its description appears below the function list.

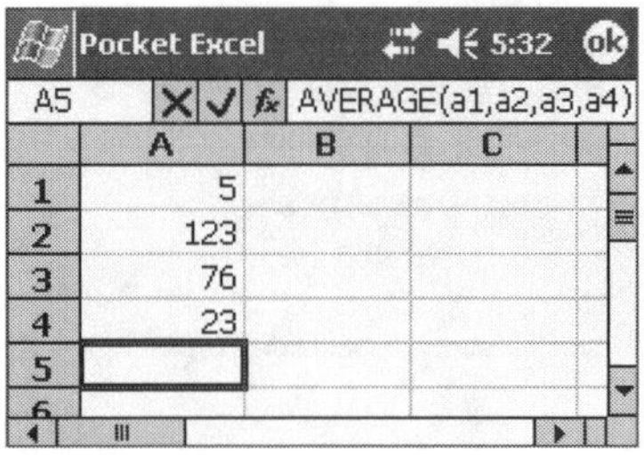

Figure 9.33 We see in the entry bar how to enter the function to find the average of numbers or cells.

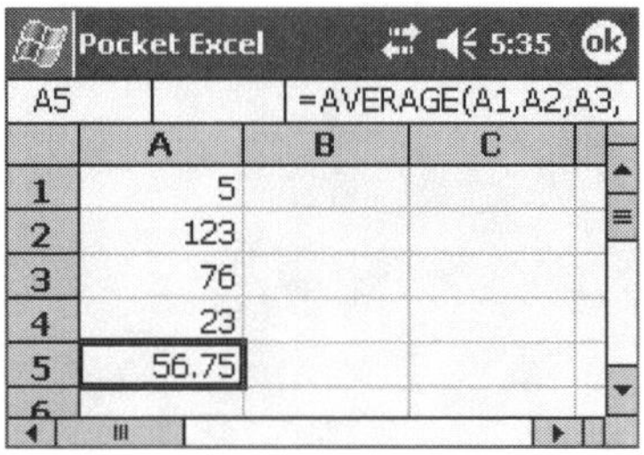

Figure 9.34 The function calculates the average according to the formula we entered in the entry bar.

WORKING WITH FORMULAS

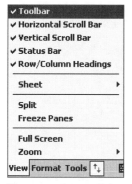

Figure 9.35 Access all the view possibilities through the View menu.

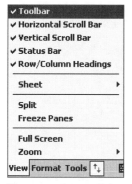

Figure 9.36 Use Full Screen to maximize your view in Pocket Excel.

Adjusting the View

You are not stuck with the cluttered scroll-athon that many Excel worksheets seem so desperately bent on becoming. The View menu gives you some options and tricks that let you display your worksheets more usefully.

To adjust workbook views:

1. To select items to view and hide, tap View (**Figure 9.35**).

2. Tap the items you want to view and clear the check box for those you want to hide:

   Toolbar: Tap to view or hide the toolbar.

   Horizontal/Vertical Scroll Bar: Tap to view or hide the horizontal or vertical scrollbar on the screen.

   Status Bar: Tap to view or hide the status bar.

   Row/Column Headings: Tap to view or hide the letter and number headings that run down rows and across columns.

   ▲ To view a different worksheet, tap View > Sheet and then tap the sheet you want.

   ▲ Tap View > Full Screen, and your worksheet fills the screen (**Figure 9.36**). Tap Restore to return to normal view, or just tap View > Full Screen again.

   ▲ To zoom, tap View > Zoom and then tap a percentage from the menu that appears. Tap Customize to insert your own percentage.

continues on next page

ADJUSTING THE VIEW

✔ Tips

■ To simultaneously view two parts of a worksheet that are separated, you can insert a *split*, which breaks the screen into separate panes, by tapping View > Split. Each pane has scrollbars so you can view column or row headings in one and data in the other (**Figure 9.37**). You can move the split bars left and right and up and down. Tap View > Remove Split to get rid of the split. Drag the split bars to move them as you like.

■ *Freezing* is similar to splitting. Tap View > Freeze to freeze the upper and left-hand sections of your screen so you can scroll through the document while keeping headers visible. Tap View > Unfreeze to undo this.

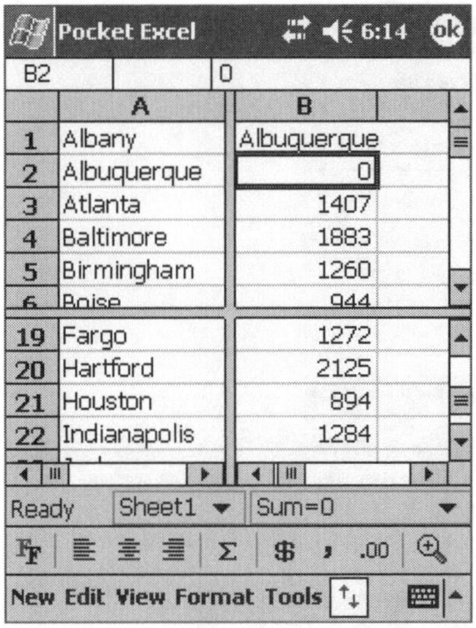

Figure 9.37 Maintain your headings while spanning distant cells with a split.

GETTING ONLINE

There are four popular ways of connecting your Pocket PC to the Internet: through your computer's ActiveSync connection, through a Bluetooth-enabled mobile phone connection, via a Bluetooth connection to a computer, or over a Wi-Fi networking connection. This chapter walks you through all four of these methods.

Every Pocket PC can connect to the Internet through the computer's ActiveSync connection, assuming the computer is online. The question is: why do that when the computer is right there? To use Bluetooth, your device must have Bluetooth built in or added via a Bluetooth card. To connect with Wi-Fi, your Pocket PC needs either built-in Wi-Fi or a Wi-Fi networking card.

(If you have a Smartphone or Pocket PC Phone Edition, see your documentation for specific information on setting up your model for data connections. There will probably be a separate connection package agreement with your carrier involved.)

Connecting to the Internet with ActiveSync

If your computer is connected to the Internet, and your Pocket PC is connected to your computer with ActiveSync, then your Pocket PC is connected to the Internet—as long as the ActiveSync Pass Through option is enabled.

To enable Pass Through in ActiveSync:

1. In ActiveSync on your computer, click the 🗐 Options icon.

   The Options screen appears (**Figure 10.1**).

2. Click the Rules tab.

3. In the Pass Through section at the bottom of the screen, make sure the Connection drop-down list is set to The Internet.

4. Click OK.

   Internet access is now enabled.

To connect to the Internet with ActiveSync:

1. Connect your computer to the Internet.

2. Connect your Pocket PC to your computer.

3. Check your Pocket PC connection by tapping (on your device) Start > ActiveSync (or Start > Programs > ActiveSync) and make sure it says "Connected" (**Figure 10.2**).

   or

   On your computer, in the ActiveSync Details screen, make sure it says "Connected" (**Figure 10.3**).

   Your Pocket PC is now on the Internet.

✔ Tip

■ Note that the 📶 connectivity indicator at the top of the Pocket PC screen shows a connection present with two arrows in opposite directions. With no connection, it displays 📶.

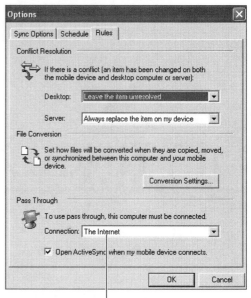

Connection must be set to The Internet

Figure 10.1 Enable Pass Through to the Internet in ActiveSync Options.

Device is connected to computer

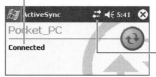

Connectivity indicator shows a PC connection

Figure 10.2 This Pocket PC is certifiably connected to a computer via ActiveSync.

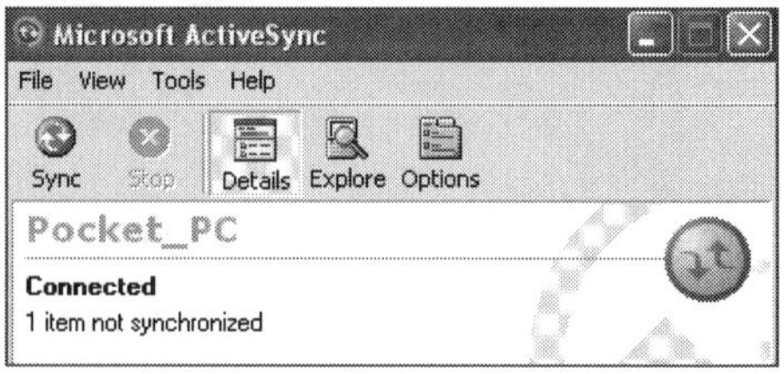

Figure 10.3 This computer is certifiably connected to a Pocket PC via ActiveSync.

Figure 10.4 The mobile phone's Bluetooth options are turned on.

Figure 10.5 The Bluetooth Connection Wizard is the gateway to creating a Bluetooth Internet connection.

What's GPRS?

Just as the modem came along and had to deal with using the ill-equipped telephone voice network to transfer computer data, so it goes with the cellular world. The General Packet Radio Service (GPRS) is a step toward a much-needed upgrading of the speed of data transfer over mobile phones. Right now, the standard rate of mobile phone data transmission is a sluggish 9.6 Kbps—about a third as fast as today's slowest computer modem. With the GPRS service, that rate goes up to 40 Kbps. Much better, but still slow. A 384 Kbps mobile data service known as Global System for Mobile Communication (GSM) is envisioned for the near future.

Connecting to the Internet with a Bluetooth-enabled Mobile Phone

The following two Bluetooth sections were prepared from material written by Mauricio Freitas, published at www.geekzone.co.nz *and are used by kind permission of the author.*

If your mobile phone and Pocket PC are both Bluetooth-enabled, you can use the mobile phone to dial up an Internet connection for your device. Here, we show how to configure and use a Bluetooth-enabled mobile phone to connect an iPAQ Pocket PC to the Internet. The phone we're using for this example is a Nokia 3650, but the steps on the Pocket PC will be the same or similar for other mobile phones.

You need to set up a dial-up account with a General Packet Radio Service (GPRS) service or an Internet Service Provider (ISP) before you can connect to the Internet with a mobile phone.

To set up Internet access with a Bluetooth-enabled mobile phone:

1. Make sure the phone is in discoverable mode (**Figure 10.4**).

2. Tap Start > Bluetooth Manager. The Bluetooth Manager program starts.

3. Tap New > Connect! The Bluetooth Connection Wizard launches (**Figure 10.5**).

4. Tap "Connect to the Internet" and tap Next.

5. In the screen that appears, tap the radio button next to "Connect via a dialup device" and tap Next.

continues on next page

6. In the Device screen that appears, tap in the Device box to make Bluetooth start trying to detect the mobile phone (**Figure 10.6**).

The Pocket PC begins searching for the mobile phone, using Bluetooth. This may take several seconds. If successful, the phone's icon will appear in the Device box in the Device screen.

7. Tap the phone's icon when it appears.

The next screen in the Bluetooth Connection Wizard appears (**Figure 10.7**).

8. Tap to put a check mark next to "Create a shortcut for this connection."

Creating a shortcut will place an icon for the connection on the first screen in the Bluetooth Manager, where it will be easy to access from now on.

9. Tap Finish.

10. In the Dial-Up Connection screen that appears, tap New Connection....

11. In the New Dial-Up Connection screen that appears, fill in the various fields (**Figure 10.8**).

▲ Give the new connection a name in the Connection Name text box.

▲ If the phone call to your GPRS service or ISP is a local call, leave the "Country code" and "Area code" boxes blank. (If you need it, the country code for the United States is 01.)

▲ Enter the phone access number of your provider.

Tap in the box to begin searching

Figure 10.6 The Device screen is where your device begins searching for any nearby Bluetooth brethren.

Figure 10.7 Go ahead and create a shortcut in Bluetooth Manager for your mobile phone's icon.

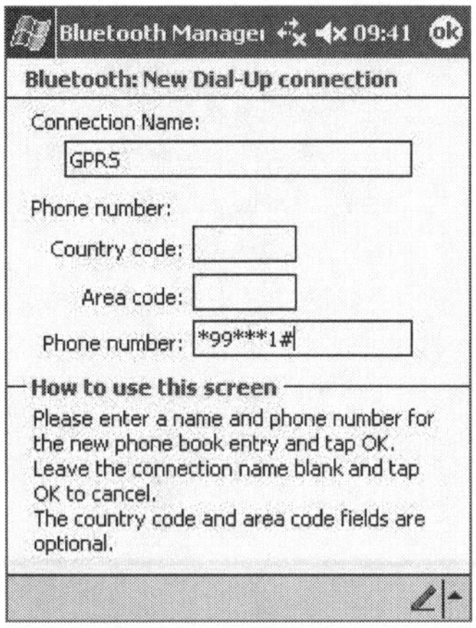

Figure 10.8 Enter your dialup information.

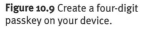

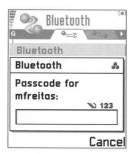

Figure 10.9 Create a four-digit passkey on your device.

Figure 10.10 Your mobile phone must use the same passkey as your Pocket PC.

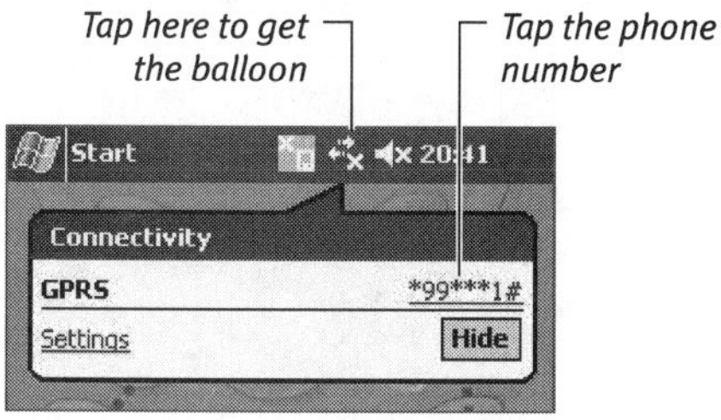

Tap here to get the balloon ⌐   ⌐ Tap the phone number

![Connectivity balloon screenshot]

Figure 10.11 Tap the phone number in the Connectivity balloon to begin dialing.

![Bluetooth accept connection request screenshot]

Figure 10.12 You must accept the request on your mobile phone in order to connect.

12. Tap OK.

13. In the Authentication screen that appears, enter a passkey (**Figure 10.9**). A four-digit numeric passkey is recommended.

14. Tap OK.

15. On your mobile phone, enter the same passkey (**Figure 10.10**).

Your Pocket PC and mobile phone are now set up to connect to the Internet.

To connect to the Internet with a Bluetooth-enabled mobile phone:

1. Tap the ▦ Connectivity icon at the top of the screen.

2. In the Connectivity drop-down balloon that appears, tap the phone number (**Figure 10.11**).

The balloon will indicate that it is dialing the connection, and the mobile phone will display a connection request.

3. On the mobile phone, choose Yes to accept the dialing request (**Figure 10.12**).

The connection will be made, and the Pocket PC will be connected to the Internet. From there, Web surfing, email, and Instant Messaging are available.

✔ Tip

■ To disconnect, tap the ▦ Connectivity icon again and tap Disconnect.

CONNECTING WITH BLUETOOTH-ENABLED PHONE

Connecting to the Internet with a Bluetooth-enabled Computer

If you have Bluetooth on your Pocket PC, but don't have built-in Wi-Fi on your device, probably the cheapest way to get your Pocket PC connected—other than ActiveSync, which largely defeats the advantage of having a handheld device by only providing Internet access while your device is connected to your computer—is to share your computer's connection with a Bluetooth USB adapter.

For $25 to $30, you can buy one of these adapters (sometimes called a "dongle") that plugs into a USB port on your computer. With some setup, you can share your Internet connection with your Pocket PC. Then you can have Internet access on your device as long as it's within 30 feet or so of the computer (the range of Bluetooth).

The following section explains how to do this, using an iPAQ Pocket PC and a TDK USB Bluetooth adapter on a Windows XP computer. If you have a different Bluetooth adapter, the steps may differ. See Appendix C for more on Bluetooth adapters.

Just what is Bluetooth?

Bluetooth is a short-range wireless data communications system. With Bluetooth, two devices can "talk" to each other over special radio waves. The idea behind Bluetooth is to have a cheap technology with low power consumption that is easy to implement in different devices.

The technology uses the unlicensed 2.4 GHz radio spectrum. Although it uses the same frequency as Wi-Fi (802.11b), Bluetooth doesn't conflict with Wi-Fi because Bluetooth uses frequency hop, changing frequency 1,600 times a second.

Bluetooth-enabled devices can share files and services. Examples of some of the devices available are mobile phones, printers, USB dongles, headsets, car kits, digital cameras, Palm devices, Pocket PCs, and network access points.

Figure 10.13 My Network Places is in the Start menu.

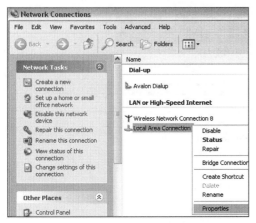

Figure 10.14 Open the Local Area Connection Properties.

Figure 10.15 You have to enable Internet Connection Sharing in order for your device to share your computer's connection.

To set up your computer to share its Internet connection over Bluetooth:

1. Purchase and install a Bluetooth USB adapter and the software that came with it.

   Make sure the adapter supports the LAN Access profile. Some models, such as 3COM's, don't support the LAN profile. Others, including Ambicom's and Widcomm's, do.

2. On your computer, right-click the My Network Places icon and click Properties in the pop-up menu (**Figure 10.13**).

3. In the Network Connections screen, right-click the Local Area Connection (or the connection that connects to the Internet) icon and click Properties in the pop-up menu (**Figure 10.14**).

4. In the Advanced tab, check the option to enable Internet connection sharing and click OK (**Figure 10.15**).

5. In your Bluetooth software on your computer, enable the option to allow other devices to access the Internet using the computer's connection.

   This option's location will vary among different types of Bluetooth software. See your documentation if you can't find it.

   Your computer is now ready to share its connection with your Pocket PC.

To set up your Pocket PC to access the Internet with Bluetooth:

1. If your Pocket PC doesn't have Bluetooth built in, install your Bluetooth card and set up its software.

2. Make sure Bluetooth is turned on. On the iPAQ, tap the Bluetooth icon at the bottom right-hand corner of the Today screen and, in the pop-up box that appears, tap Turn Bluetooth ON if that is showing (**Figure 10.16**).

   If it says Turn Bluetooth OFF, leave it alone. That means Bluetooth is on.

3. Tap Bluetooth Manager to start the Bluetooth Manager.

4. Tap New > Connect! to start the Bluetooth Connection Wizard (**Figure 10.17**).

5. Tap Connect to the Internet to select it, and then tap Next.

6. Tap the radio button next to "Connect via a LAN or a computer permanently connected to a Local Area Network" and click Next.

7. Tap anywhere in the Device box.

   The Pocket PC starts searching for the computer. When it finds it, the computer's icon will appear in a "Please select a device" screen.

8. Tap the computer's icon.

9. In the shortcut-creation screen that appears, tap to put a check mark next to "Create a shortcut for this connection."

   The shortcut will in the future appear in the first Bluetooth Manager screen.

10. Tap Finish.

    Bluetooth attempts to connect.

    When it succeeds, a balloon appears on your computer, indicating that a PIN code needs to be entered.

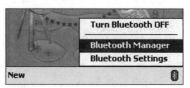

Figure 10.16 Access the Bluetooth Manager by tapping the tiny Bluetooth icon.

Figure 10.17 Start the Bluetooth Connection Wizard.

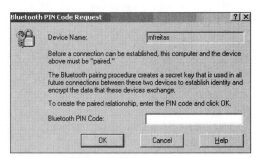

Figure 10.18 Enter a PIN in the dialog box on your computer's screen.

Figure 10.19 The Connectivity icon shows some connection details.

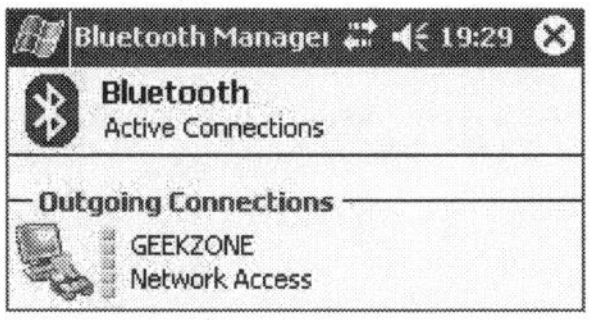

Figure 10.20 Bluetooth Manager shows more connection details.

Figure 10.21 The proof is in the pudding—see if you can view Web sites.

11. Click the Bluetooth icon in the system tray at the bottom right-hand corner of your computer screen.

The Bluetooth PIN Code Request dialog box appears (**Figure 10.18**).

12. Enter a four-digit number in the dialog box as your PIN and click OK.

13. On your Pocket PC, enter the same PIN in the Authentication screen that appears and tap OK.

The connection begins.

✔ Tips

- Tap the 📶 Connectivity icon to display the connection information (**Figure 10.19**).

- In Bluetooth Manager, tap the Active Connections tab to see more connection information (**Figure 10.20**). Right-click the name of the connection and tap Disconnect to disconnect or Status to display more connection details.

- Launch Pocket Internet Explorer to test the connection (**Figure 10.21**).

CONNECTING A BLUETOOTH-ENABLED COMPUTER

Connecting to the Internet with Wi-Fi Networking

Surely the best way to connect your device to the Internet is with Wi-Fi networking, using any available wireless network. This option gets better each passing day, too, because wireless networks are popping up faster than Starbucks coffee shops. In fact, many Starbucks now offer wireless Internet to their caffeinated clients, as do growing numbers of cafes, public libraries, universities, hotels, bars, and bookstores.

More and more Pocket PC models are appearing with Wi-Fi capability built in. If yours is thus equipped, rejoice—it's a snap to get online. If not, you can buy a Wi-Fi networking card and plug it into your device's CompactFlash (CF) or Secure Digital Input/Output (SDIO) slot. iPAQ users can buy an expansion pack that accepts PC Wi-Fi network adapter cards, which can also be used in laptops. See Appendix C for some resources on getting your hands on one of these.

In most cases, once the networking card is installed and set up, connecting to an available wireless network is as easy as doing nothing. The Pocket PC 2003 operating system proudly boasts of its "zero-config" feature. But once in a while there does seem to be some config necessary, and there are a few variables and settings you should be aware of.

To connect to the nearest wireless network automatically:

1. Turn on your Pocket PC.

2. Make sure your Wi-Fi networking is on and enabled.

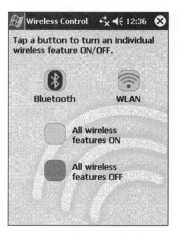

Figure 10.22 Make sure the wireless features are turned on.

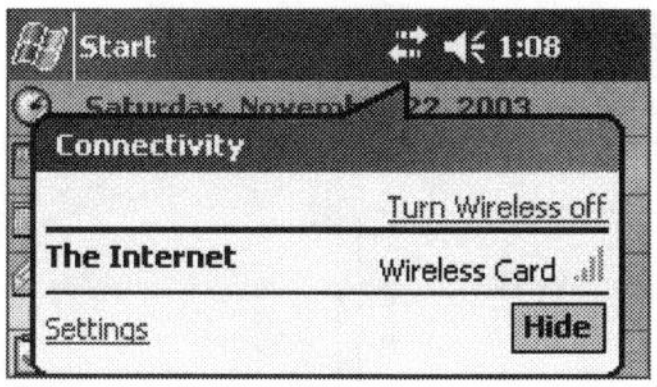

Figure 10.23 Tap the Connectivity icon to display the Connectivity balloon.

3. Wait for the device to detect and connect to the nearest, strongest wireless network.

This could take some time. We've had to wait up to five minutes for the device to settle on a connection it likes.

When it's connected, the ▓ Connectivity icon becomes the ▓ Connectivity icon.

✔ Tip

■ If it never connects, or if you're not happy with the connection choices it offers you, try the manual method, discussed next.

To connect to the nearest wireless network manually:

1. If Wi-Fi networking is not built into your device, install a Wi-Fi networking card along with the software that came with it.

2. Position yourself and your Pocket PC near a Wi-Fi access point.

By near, we mean the closer the better—within dozens of yards certainly—and with as few physical obstructions (walls, trees, appliances) as possible between your device and the access point.

3. Enable your Pocket PC's wireless features.

The exact steps to do this will vary among the wireless software setups. On an iPAQ with built-in Wi-Fi, tap Start > iPAQ Wireless to launch Wireless Control, then tap WLAN to make it match the color of "All wireless features on" (**Figure 10.22**).

4. Tap the ▓ Connectivity icon at the top of the screen to drop down the Connectivity balloon (**Figure 10.23**).

continues on next page

5. In the balloon, tap Settings to display the Connections screen, Tasks tab.

6. Tap the Advanced tab (**Figure 10.24**).

7. Tap the Network Card button.

The Configure Wireless Networks screen appears, with the Wireless tab selected (**Figure 10.25**).

If you're lucky, at least one wireless network will be listed as available in the Wireless Networks box. If not, wait a few minutes before giving up.

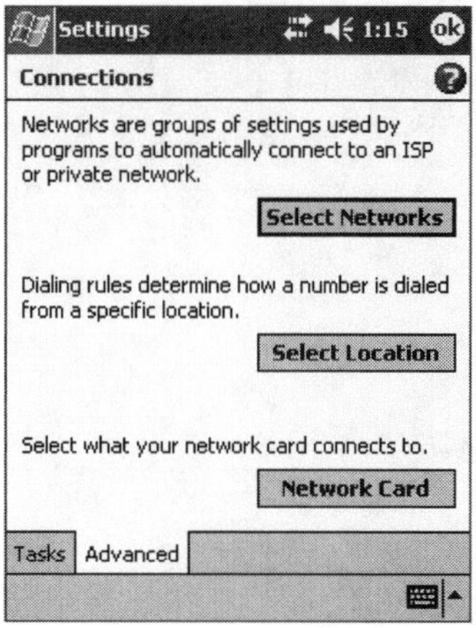

Figure 10.24 The Advanced tab is where most of the Wi-Fi action is.

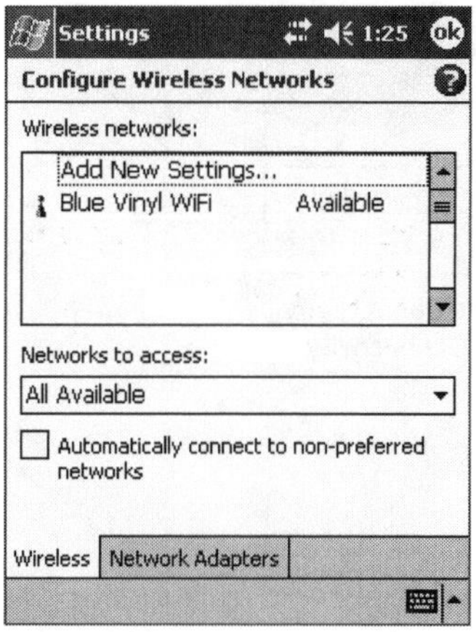

Figure 10.25 Available wireless networks appear in the Configure Wireless Networks screen.

Pocket PC modems

There are modems made to fit the expansion slots for Pocket PCs, but they are awfully slow, and the future of the modem itself is unclear. To learn how to get one of these, see Appendix C.

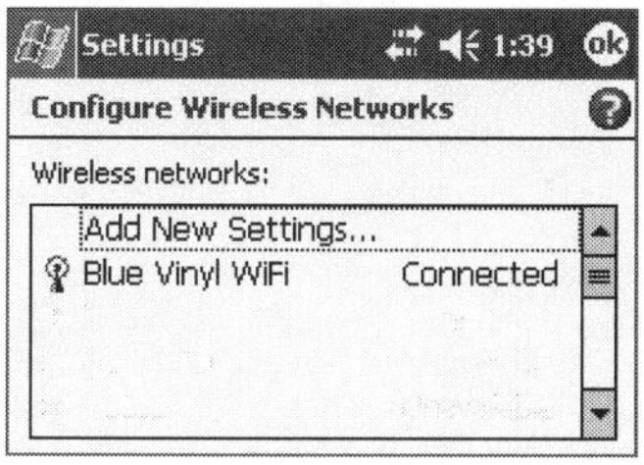

Figure 10.26 The device is connected to a wireless network.

8. Press and hold the tip of the stylus on an available wireless network and tap Connect.

The Pocket PC will attempt to connect with the network. If a Wireless Encryption Protocol (WEP) key is required by the network, you will be asked for it. After you enter it, connection will proceed (if you don't know the key, ask someone involved with running the network).

When the connection succeeds, the status of the network will change from Available to Connected (**Figure 10.26**) and the ![icon] Connectivity icon will change to ![icon].

Your device is now on the Internet—test it by checking email or calling up a Web site.

continues on next page

Creating your own wireless network

If you have one or more computers at home, you can make a wireless network of your own. All you need in most cases is a wireless router, such as the Linksys Wireless-B Broadband router. You can find a basic router for under $100 at Best Buy or CompUSA or other computer stores. Talk to the salesperson about what you want to do. A router can take the connection from your DSL or cable modem, for example, and broadcast it from its antenna. Once you get it up and running, you can access the Internet with your Pocket PC from most places in your house (or yard, even). If you get a wireless network adapter for your laptop, you can get wireless Internet on it, too.

CONNECTING WITH WI-FI NETWORKING

✔ Tips

- Remember, if your wireless features are turned on, the device looks for available networks and will automatically connect to them if it can. Make sure to check the "Automatically connect to non-preferred networks" in the Configure Wireless Networks screen. You can always tell by the ⊞ indicator whether you are connected or not.

- Your device will keep a record of each wireless network it ever connects to, so the Wireless Networks box tends to fill up with old connections that you many never encounter again. To delete one, press and hold the stylus on it and tap Remove Settings in the pop-up menu that appears.

- You can also connect your Pocket PC to a private network, such as at your workplace. See your network administrator for how.

Exploring your network from your Pocket PC

When you are connected to a network, tapping the ⊞ Network Shares icon in File Explorer opens a text box asking for a network path. In that box, type in the name of the computer on the network—the Netbios name, the one used in network settings, usually a single word—and tap OK. The Pocket PC will connect to that PC on the network and show you all the shared drives on that computer. It might prompt you for a username and password, but if the drives/folders are shared, you can just leave the fields blank and it will connect. Unfortunately, you can't open files directly using Network Shares, but you can copy and paste files to and from your device or memory card. And over Wi-Fi, this is very fast, much faster than ActiveSync.

EMAILING WITH INBOX

You can use your Pocket PC to send and receive email using several different methods, depending on whether you're in the office, at home, or at the airport. If your Pocket PC does not have an independent connection to the Internet, then you will be using ActiveSync to synchronize your Pocket PC's Inbox program with Outlook on your computer. This way, the emails you receive on your computer are also stored on your device—meaning you can take your email with you in your Pocket PC. You can write replies to email anywhere, and they will be sent from Outlook the next time you synchronize.

You can also connect directly to the Internet to send and receive email on your device using the pass-through method, in which the Pocket PC, while connected to your computer, passes through ActiveSync to the network your computer is connected to.

If your device is able to connect to the Internet by itself using built-in Wi-Fi, a networking card, a modem card, or Bluetooth, then you can use the Pocket PC's Inbox program to send and receive email independently of your computer. Even if you don't use Outlook on your computer, being able to send and receive email directly with your device can end up the same as synchronizing with, say, Eudora—if you don't have the computer's email program set to delete messages from the server after downloading them.

Synchronizing Email with Outlook

By synchronizing your device's Inbox program with Outlook on your computer, your messages are available both on your device and your computer. And while your device is connected to your computer, when you get a message in Outlook, it is immediately and automatically copied to your device. Synchronizing email does not require that your device have an independent connection to the Internet.

To synchronize your email:

1. In ActiveSync on your computer, click the 🖳 Options icon.

2. In the Sync Options tab, click to put a check mark next to Inbox and click OK (**Figure 11.1**).

    The next time you synchronize with ActiveSync, all the email in Outlook on your computer will be transferred to the Inbox program on your device.

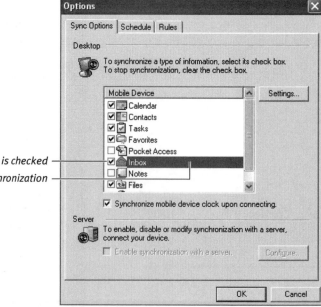

Make sure Inbox is checked ——

Double-click the Inbox item for Mail Synchronization ——

Figure 11.1 The Inbox item must be have a check mark for email to be synchronized.

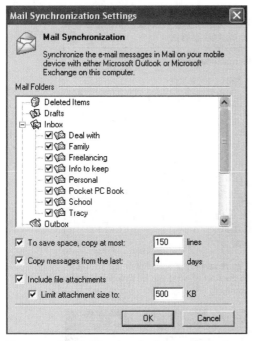

Figure 11.2 The Mail Synchronizations screen is where you control how email synchronization will work.

To change synchronization settings:

1. In ActiveSync on your computer, double-click the Inbox item to display the Mail Synchronization screen (**Figure 11.2**).

2. Put a check mark next to folders you want to synchronize with your Pocket PC.

3. To limit the number of lines you want copied to your device, put a check mark beside "To save space, copy at most:" and enter the maximum number of lines of text.

4. To control how far back you want your Pocket PC to synchronize email, put a check mark next to "Copy messages from the last:" and enter the number of days.

5. To accept file attachments, check "Include file attachments."

6. To limit attachment size, check "Limit attachment size." Enter a size in the KB box.

7. Click OK when you're finished.

✔ Tip

■ We find it's better to decrease how far back your email synchronizes and expand the number of text lines that are synchronized.

Web mail on your Pocket PC

If you use a Web-based email service such as Yahoo Mail or Hotmail, you can check your email using Pocket Internet Explorer in your Pocket PC—but this is often frustrating.

For Yahoo Mail, if you upgrade to Yahoo Mail Plus, you can check Yahoo Mail in Outlook on your computer and then synchronize it to your device.

Hotmail users can check mail at a special site formatted for Pocket PCs at:

www.mobile.msn.com/pocketpc

There are also third-party programs, such as IzyMail, that enable you to synchronize your Pocket PC with Web mail services. Others, such as SyncExpress, let you synchronize with Outlook Express. See Appendix A for more on third-party software programs.

Setting up Your Inbox

As with email programs on your computer, you have to go through a few setup steps in order to configure Inbox for your particular email account. You will need the same kind of server, username, and password information that you needed when you set up email on your computer—in fact, you should just use the same settings that your computer's email program uses.

To create a new email account:

1. Tap Start > Inbox.

   or

   Press the Inbox program button on your device.

   The Inbox screen appears.

2. Tap Accounts > New Account... to display the "E-mail address" screen (**Figure 11.3**).

3. Enter your email address and tap Next.

4. In the "Auto configuration" screen, tap Next when the Status field reads Completed.

5. In the "User information" screen, enter your name, user name, and password (**Figure 11.4**).

   Your name should be entered exactly as you would like it to appear in the From: field in your emails. Your user name and password are the same ones used in your computer's email program.

6. If you want your Pocket PC to remember your password so that you don't have to enter it every time, tap to put a check mark next to "Save password."

Figure 11.3 Enter your full email address in the first of what will be five email setup screens.

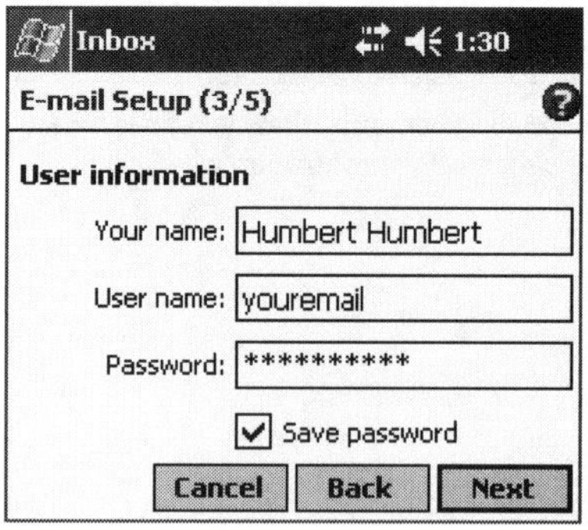

Figure 11.4 Enter your real name, email user name, and password. (Unlike Nabokov's anti-hero, your first and last names probably differ.)

Viewing different email accounts

You can use Inbox to send and receive email from different email accounts. Just go through the setup steps for each account, giving each one a different name. To change accounts while using Inbox on your Pocket PC, tap the Accounts menu and tap the account you want to use for your email session. The menu displays all email accounts on your device.

See your computer's email program settings if you're not sure of your account type

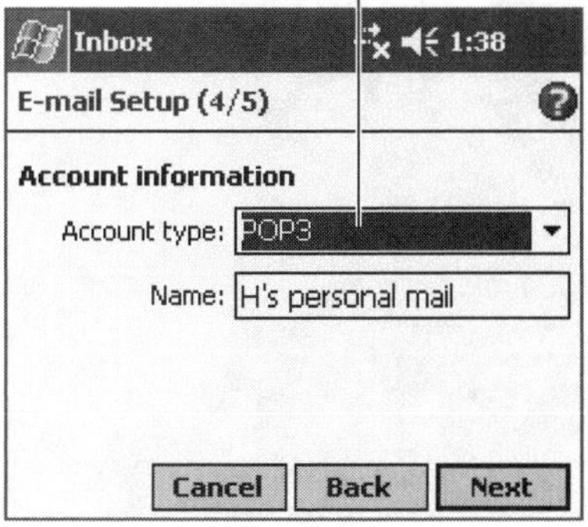

Figure 11.5 Choose your email account type and enter a friendly name for this account.

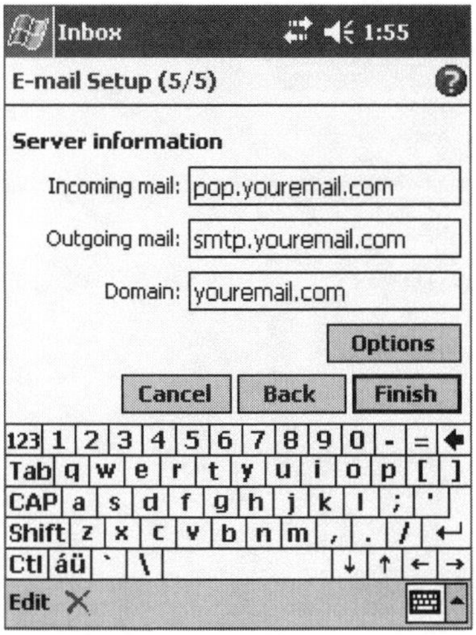

Figure 11.6 Enter the names of your email servers (and domain, if necessary).

7. Tap Next to display the "Account information" screen (**Figure 11.5**).

8. Choose between POP3 and IMAP4 in the "Account type" field.

Most email accounts are POP3, but a growing number of email servers support IMAP4. Again, your choice should be the same as the account type found in your email software on your computer.

9. In the Name: field, give your email account a name and tap Next.

The default name is POP3 for a POP3 account (and IMAP4 for an IMAP account). This is fine if you only have the one account, but if you plan to check multiple email accounts on your device, giving the account a more descriptive name is a good idea.

10. In the "Server information" screen that appears, enter the names of your email servers—and the domain, if required by your ISP (**Figure 11.6**).

You can get these server names and domain from your Internet Service Provider's (ISP) setup instructions or Web site—or from your computer's email program, most likely under an Options menu (in Outlook, it's under Tools > Accounts > Properties > Servers tab).

✔ Tip

■ In the "Server information" screen in step 10, you can set up further options for the account by tapping the Options button (you can also do this later after the account is set up, under Tools > Options in the Inbox screen). The options you can set include how often your device checks for new email, whether your server requires authentication or a SSL connections (check with your ISP or computer email settings), and how much of each email you want the device to grab.

Sending and Receiving Email with Your Pocket PC

Whenever your Pocket PC is disconnected from your computer, you can still compose and read synchronized email with your device. If your device is not connected independently to the Internet, you won't receive any new messages—and the ones you "send" won't actually be sent—until the next time you synchronize.

If you can connect your device to the Internet with a networking card, modem, or Bluetooth (see Chapter 10 for more), then you can send and receive email directly. It's very exciting (and nearly magical) to do this, particularly with a Wi-Fi connection, because you may often find yourself within range of an available wireless network, meaning you can suddenly check and send email without expending any effort to connect.

To read email:

1. Tap Start > Inbox.

   or

   Press the Inbox program button.

   The Inbox screen appears, displaying two-line summary information for each of your email messages, including sender, date, size, and subject heading (**Figure 11.7**).

2. Tap a summary item to display the email's contents (**Figure 11.8**).

✔ Tip

- Depending on how much of each email message your device is set to download, the message you see is probably not the entire message. To get the rest of a message, tap Edit > Mark for Download. The next time you receive new email or synchronize, the entire message will be transferred to your device.

Figure 11.7 The Inbox screen is where you see clickable summary items for your email messages.

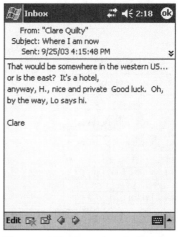

Figure 11.8 Clicking an item in the Inbox screen displays the email message.

Sorting your messages

By default, email messages in your inbox are sorted by Received Date, but you can also sort them alphabetically by sender or the Subject line. Tap the up-arrow next to the Received Date column in the Inbox screen and tap your choice of what to sort by.

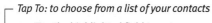
Tap To: to choose from a list of your contacts

Tap the highlighted field to enter an email address

Figure 11.9 The email composition screen is where you begin creating your email.

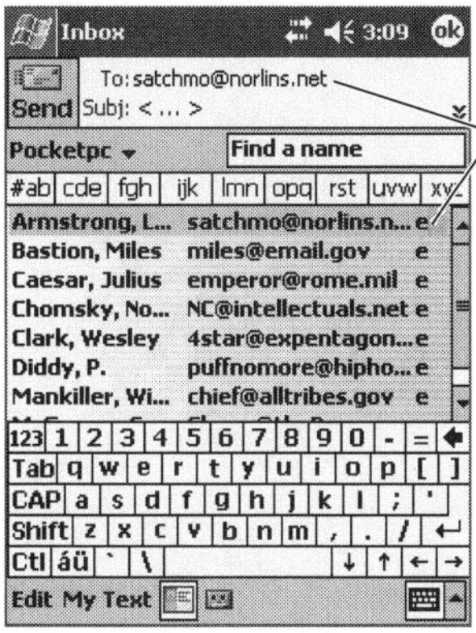

Figure 11.10 Choose a contact from the list that pops up.

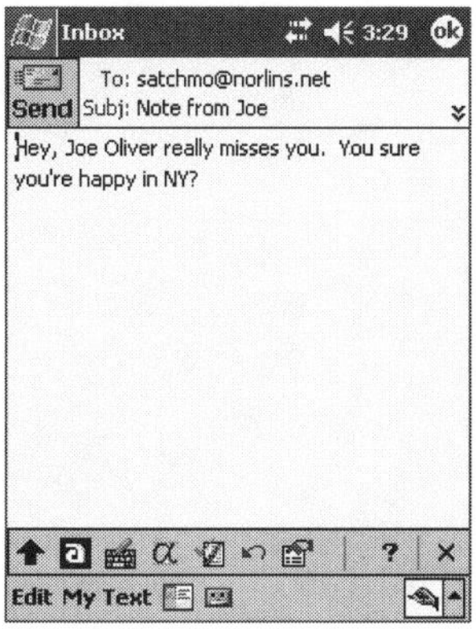

Tap a contact to enter its email address in the To: field

Figure 11.11 Compose your email just as you do in your computer's email program.

To read the next message:

◆ Tap the [→] Next email icon.

The next email message in your inbox is displayed.

To read the previous email:

◆ Tap the [←] Previous email icon.

The previous email message in your inbox is displayed.

To receive new email:

◆ With your device connected to the Internet, tap the [icon] icon to retrieve new email.

If your device is not connected to the Internet, when you synchronize, the email in your Pocket PCs Outbox gets transferred to the Outbox on the desktop Outlook client, and from there it's sent to the recipient.

To create a new email message:

1. In Inbox, tap the New menu to display the email composition screen (**Figure 11.9**).

2. Tap in the highlighted To: < ... > field to enter the email address of the person you want to email.

   or

   Tap To: to display your contacts and tap a contact to enter its email address in the To: field (**Figure 11.10**).

3. Tap the Subj: < ... > field to enter a subject heading for your email.

4. Tap anywhere in the blank body area to begin composing your email (**Figure 11.11**).

5. When you're finished, tap the [icon] Send icon.

continues on next page

SENDING AND RECEIVING EMAIL WITH POCKET PC

✔ Tips

■ You can also begin composing an email by pressing and holding the tip of the stylus on a contact in the Contacts program and tapping Send Email in the pop-up menu that appears. Inbox is opened, and a new email is created in the composition screen with the recipient's email address already filled in.

■ Tapping the Send icon does *not* actually send your email at that instant. If your Pocket PC is connected to the Internet, your email will only be sent when you tap the 📇 Send/Receive icon. If your device is not connected, your email will be sent the next time you synchronize.

■ You can choose whether to keep copies of messages you send in the Send folder by tapping Tools > Options > Message tab and putting or deleting a check mark next to "Keep copy of sent mail in Sent folder."

To delete email:

◆ Tap the 🗙 Delete email icon.

or

Press and hold the stylus on a message's summary line in the Inbox screen and tap Delete in the pop-up menu that appears.

✔ Tips

■ As in Windows email programs, when you delete a message, it is not really destroyed but merely moved to the Deleted Items folder. From there, you can move it to another folder to retain it after all or really delete it for good by tapping Tools > Empty Deleted Items.

■ Deleting an email message on your device will also delete it from Outlook on your computer.

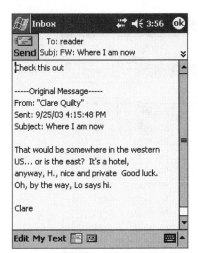

Figure 11.12 When you forward a message, the original is appended at the bottom.

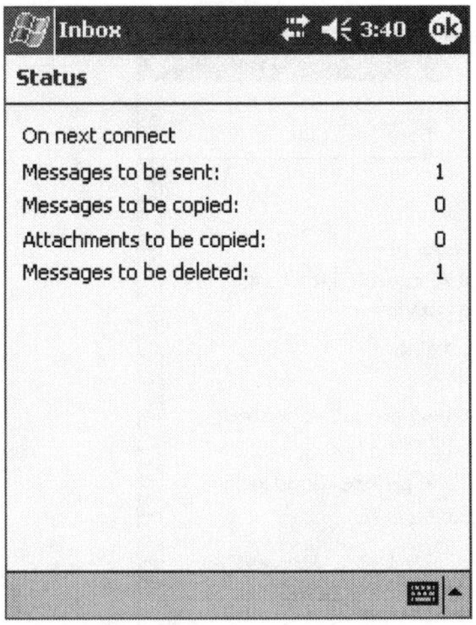

Figure 11.13 The Status screen tells you how many messages and attachments are waiting to be sent, copied (to Outlook), and deleted.

To reply to email:

1. Tap the [icon] Respond icon and from the pop-up menu choose Reply (to reply to the sender only) or Reply All (to reply to everyone the email was sent to).

A new reply email message is created, pre-addressed to the sender of the original message and containing the original email in quoted text.

2. Tap the [icon] Send icon when you are finished composing your reply.

✔ Tip

■ Change how much of the original message is included in your reply and how it is presented by tapping Tools > Options > Message tab. In this Options screen, you decide whether to include the body of the original message, whether to indent it, and whether to add a leading character in the quoted text.

To forward email:

1. Tap the [icon] Respond icon and choose Forward from the pop-up menu.

A new reply email message is created containing the original email in quoted text (**Figure 11.12**).

2. Tap the [icon] Send icon when you are finished composing your message.

✔ Tips

■ You can also reply to and forward messages by pressing and holding the tip of the stylus on the message in the Inbox screen and choosing Reply, Reply All, or Forward from the pop-up menu that appears.

■ You can check how many email messages are waiting to be sent by tapping Tools > Status (**Figure 11.13**).

Attaching Files

Just as with email on your computer, you can send and receive images, documents, and other files with your device. You can also choose to store these on a storage card.

To send a file attachment:

1. Compose your message, but don't click the ![Send] Send icon yet.

2. Tap Edit > Add Attachment... to display the Open file attachment screen (**Figure 11.14**).

3. Navigate to the folder where your file is by tapping the Folder: drop-down box.

4. Tap the filename of the file you want to attach to your email message.

   You return to the composition screen, and your file is attached, shown by an icon at the bottom of the screen (**Figure 11.15**).

5. Tap the ![Send] Send icon when you're ready to send the message and attachment.

Figure 11.14 You choose which file to attach in the Open screen.

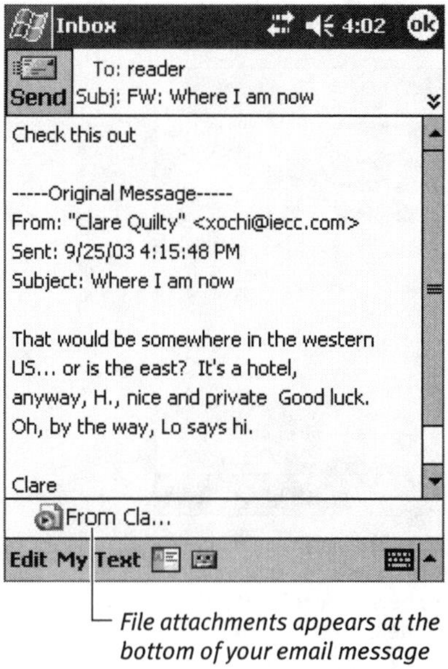

File attachments appears at the bottom of your email message

Figure 11.15 The file is attached.

To open a file attachment:

1. In Inbox, tap a message that contains a file attachment to display the message.

You can tell if an email message has a file attachment by looking at the envelope icon in the Inbox summary screen. A message with a file attachment has a little paperclip 📎 icon.

2. Tap the file attachment's icon at the bottom of the screen to open it.

The program associated with the file attachment automatically opens the file.

✔ Tip

■ If the filename and paperclip are grayed out, it means that the attachment was not downloaded. If you tap the file attachment the next time you sync, then it will download the attachment.

Storing attachments on a storage card

File attachments can balloon to occupy a significant amount of space on your device, which makes the ability to store them on a storage card attractive. First make sure the card is inserted and set up when you receive file attachments.

In Inbox, tap Options > Storage tab and put a check mark in the box next to "Store attachments on storage card."

Warning: Only use this option on a storage card that you rarely or never remove. If the Pocket PC needs a Wi-Fi Compact-Flash card to get online, for example, you wouldn't want to choose this option and have the attachments stored on that card!

ATTACHING FILES

Organizing Messages in Folders

Email has a tendency to pile up in your inbox, and there never seems to be a good time to organize it. Nevertheless, it's a good idea to make at least a few folders within your Inbox folder that represent categories that help organize your messages according to the way you work (and play) with email. This may sound like a chore, and it is, but if you don't, the messages that keep accumulating in your Inbox may become unwieldy and overwhelming.

It's almost always easier and faster to create and manage email folders in Outlook on your computer than it is on your device. Remember: whatever you do in your Inbox folder on your computer is automatically done in Inbox on your device the next time you synchronize, and vice versa. (You can choose to synchronize other folders besides Inbox, but if you don't, anything you do in those folders in Outlook will not be transferred to your device.) That said, Inbox allows you to organize email messages into folders on your device.

To create a new folder:

1. In the Inbox screen, tap Tools > Manage Folders... to bring up the Manage Folders screen (**Figure 11.16**).

2. Tap an existing email folder, such as Inbox, to select it as the one under which you will create the new folder.

3. Tap New to display the New Folder screen.

4. Enter the name of the new folder you want to create (**Figure 11.17**).

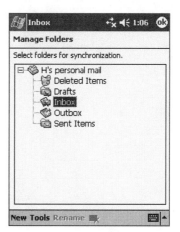

Figure 11.16 The Manage Folders screen is where you create folders.

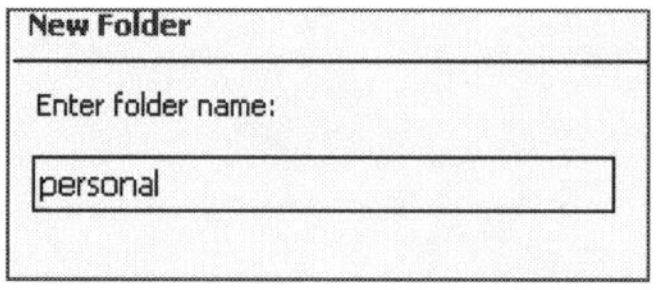

Figure 11.17 Name the folder whatever you want.

ORGANIZING MESSAGES IN FOLDERS

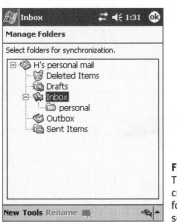

Figure 11.18
The subfolder is created in the folder you selected.

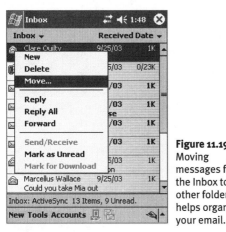

Figure 11.19
Moving messages from the Inbox to other folders helps organize your email.

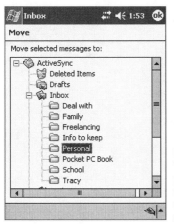

Figure 11.20
Tapping the plus (+) sign next to a folder reveals its subfolders.

5. Tap OK to return to the Manage Folders screen.

The folder you chose in step 2 becomes highlighted, and a plus sign (+) appears next to it, indicating the existence of subfolders. As with clicking Windows folders on your computer, tapping the plus sign turns it to a minus and reveals the subfolder(s) (**Figure 11.18**).

6. Tap OK to return to the Inbox screen.

To move an email to a folder:

1. In the Inbox screen, press and hold the tip of the stylus on the summary line of the email message you want to move and tap Move... in the pop-up window that appears (**Figure 11.19**).

The Move screen appears.

2. Navigate to the folder you want to move the message to by tapping the plus sign (+) to open up subfolders, if necessary (**Figure 11.20**).

3. Tap the folder you want to move the message to.

The folder becomes highlighted.

4. Tap OK to move the selected message to the folder.

✔ Tip

■ You can move several messages at once by dragging through their summary lines in the Inbox screen to select them. With your messages highlighted, press and hold anywhere within them and choose Move... from the pop-up menu that appears. All the messages will be moved.

ORGANIZING MESSAGES IN FOLDERS

To rename a folder:

1. In the Inbox screen, tap Tools > Manage Folders... to bring up the Manage Folders screen.

2. Tap the plus (+) sign beside a folder to reveal a subfolder that you created and that you want to rename.

   You can only rename folders that you have created yourself. You cannot rename any of the original folders that the Inbox program came with (Deleted Items, Drafts, Inbox, Outbox, or Sent Items).

3. Tap the folder that you want to rename. The folder becomes highlighted.

4. Tap Rename in the menu bar to display the Rename Folder screen with the folder to be renamed highlighted (**Figure 11.21**).

5. Enter the new name of the folder.

6. Tap OK to return to the Manage Folders screen.

7. Tap OK again to return to the Inbox screen.

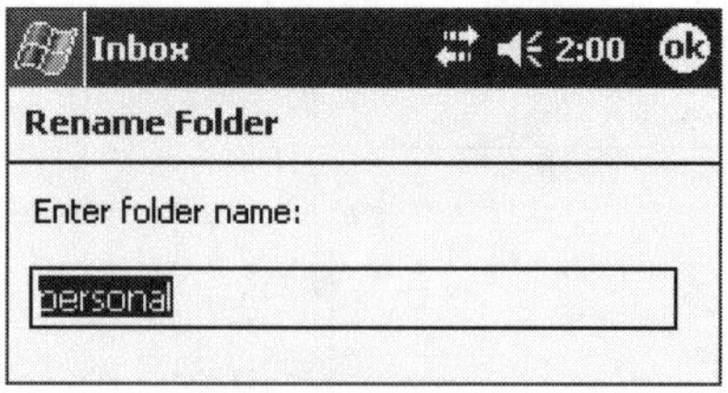

✔ Tip

- As with moving a folder, you can only rename folders that you have created.

Figure 11.21 The current folder name is highlighted—text you enter will replace the highlighted text.

To delete a folder:

1. In the Inbox screen, tap Tools > Manage Folders... to bring up the Manage Folders screen.

2. Tap a plus sign beside a folder to reveal a subfolder that you created and that you want to delete.

3. Tap the folder you want to delete.

4. Tap the [icon] Delete folder icon.
   The folder is deleted.

5. Tap OK to return to the Inbox screen.

✔ Tips

■ As with moving and renaming folders, you can only delete folders that you have created.

■ When you delete a folder containing messages, the folder and the messages are deleted. But as you know by now, deleted messages aren't really deleted until you empty the Deleted Items folder.

Inserting Pre-created Text

If you find yourself constantly writing the same thing over and over, such as "What are you doing for lunch?" or, "Believe it or not, I'm emailing you from my Pocket PC," you can save time by entering these things once in a feature called My Text Messages. From then on, they will be available to you in a pop-up menu called My Text.

You can also create signatures for yourself. Signatures are most typically used to include your sign-off message, such as, "Best regards, [your name]," along with such info as your company affiliation, email address, phone or fax number, a pithy quote, or whatever you want.

To create a My Text message:

1. In the Inbox screen, tap Tools > Edit My Text Messages... to display the My Text Messages screen (**Figure 11.22**).

2. As the screen says, tap a message to select it and then edit it in the text field.

3. Tap OK when you're finished editing My Text messages.

   From now on, when you are composing, replying to, or forwarding an email message, tapping the My Text menu pops up all of your My Text messages (**Figure 11.23**).

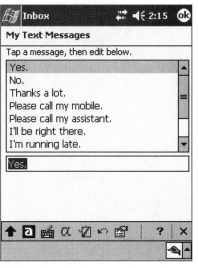

Figure 11.22 Edit the preexisting My Text messages to create your own.

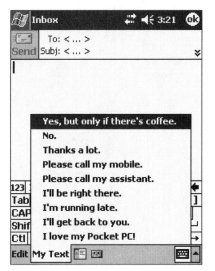

Figure 11.23 My Text messages are customizable and only a tap away.

INSERTING PRE-CREATED TEXT

To insert a My Text message:

1. As you compose an email, with the cursor at the point where you would like to insert your my Text message, tap My Text in the menu bar.

The My Text menu appears.

2. Tap the My Text message you want.

The text appears in your message.

✔ Tip

- My Text comes with nine pre-made messages that you can edit to say whatever you want. There is also a blank one at the end of the list that you can create from scratch, for a total of ten.

Email alternatives: WebIS Mail, riteMail, and nPop

Just because your Pocket PC came with the Inbox email program doesn't mean you have to use it. There are third-party email programs that you may prefer.

WebIS Mail may be the best one. It has several features not found in Inbox, such as enhanced folder structures, ability to read HTML messages, different ways of viewing your messages, and a Find feature to let you search your email for particular text strings. At the time of publication, WebIS Mail costs $25.

NPop and riteMail are two other popular email programs. NPop is free, whereas RiteMail, like WebIS Mail, costs $25. See Appendix A for more on third-party programs for your Pocket PC.

INSERTING PRE-CREATED TEXT

To create a signature:

1. Tap Tools > Options... and make sure the Message tab is selected.

2. Tap the Signatures... button to display the Signatures screen (**Figure 11.24**).

3. Choose the account for which you want to create a signature from the "Select an account:" dialog box.

4. Tap to put a check mark in the box next to "Use signature with this account."

5. Tap to put a check mark in the box next to "Use when replying and forwarding," if you want that option.

   Checking this option will append your signature to email messages that you reply to or forward, in addition to ones you compose from scratch.

6. In the large middle text box, enter your signature.

   There is a character limit of roughly eight full lines.

7. When your signature is ready, tap OK.

   Your signature will be automatically appended to your email messages from now on.

Figure 11.24 A signature can save you a lot of redundant tapping.

✔ Tips

- You can create different signatures for different accounts. For example, if you use your device for work and personal email accounts, your work one can be more formal, and your personal one more relaxed or zany.

- To stop using a signature, clear the "Use signature with this account" check box. The signature remains as you wrote it, but it will not be appended to your emails. To re-enable it, put a check mark in the box again.

INSERTING PRE-CREATED TEXT

POCKET INTERNET EXPLORER

The power and allure of holding the Web in the palm of one's had was brought home this summer when, sitting on the porch, we used the device to bid on eBay for a painting of a monkey smoking. In our excitement, we also bought a CD before forcing ourselves to shut the thing off.

Although it is amazing to cruise the Web on a Pocket PC, once the novelty wears off, ultimately the experience may leave you dissatisfied. True, some sites are optimized for the device, but compared to a computer, the screen is tiny, the download slower, and filling in forms and entering URLs is more difficult. Yet any Web is better than none. For those times when you can only access the Web with your Pocket PC, Pocket Internet Explorer suddenly becomes a marvel of usefulness.

You can use Pocket Internet Explorer in one of two ways: by connecting our device directly to the Internet or by connecting through your computer while the device is attached via ActiveSync (see Chapter 10).

Adjusting the small screen

Tap View > Text Size to select a new size for the text that appears in Web pages. Your choices are Largest, Larger, Medium, Smaller, Smallest. The larger you make the text, though, the less text will fit on the screen and the more you'll have to scroll (the navigation button is ideal for scrolling).

Tap View > Fit to screen to force the Pocket PC to try and fit as much text as possible on the screen to minimize scrolling.

Visiting Web Sites

There's not much difference in basic Web browsing activities between the real Internet Explorer and Pocket Internet Explorer, other than the latter feeling understandably stripped down. You can enter URLs, set a "home page" to automatically display when you open Pocket Internet Explorer, turn images on and off, email links to friends and colleagues, and copy text and images to the clipboard, where they become available for pasting into other programs.

To go to a Web site:

1. Connect your device to the Internet.

2. Tap Start > Internet Explorer to open Pocket Internet Explorer (**Figure 12.1**).

   The home page that opens by default is very likely a local page placed in the device by the manufacturer. For example, on the iPAQ the home page is set to a page showing four links to various HP or Microsoft sites.

3. Tap the address bar to highlight the current URL.

   The address bar is what Microsoft calls the field near the top of the screen where URLs are entered.

4. Enter a new URL into the address bar (**Figure 12.2**).

   The existing URL is replaced by the one you enter.

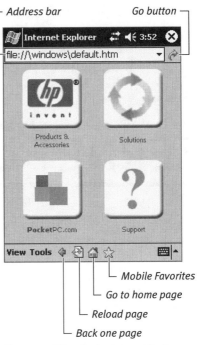

Address bar   Go button

Mobile Favorites
Go to home page
Reload page
Back one page

Figure 12.1 When Pocket Internet Explorer starts, it automatically opens the home page.

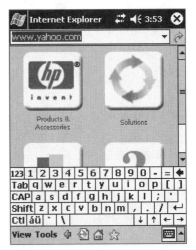

Figure 12.2 Enter the URL of a Web site in the address bar.

Figure 12.3 The new Web site appears when you tap the Go button or the Enter key.

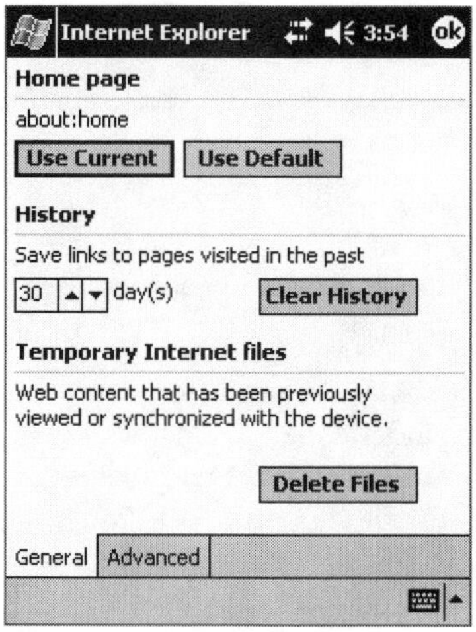

Figure 12.4 The Options screen is where you set your home page.

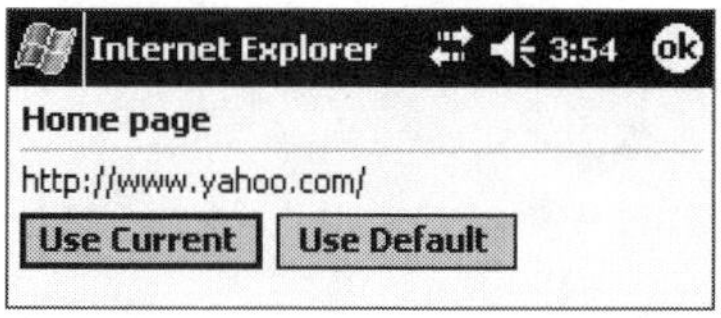

Figure 12.5 Your home page URL shows up in the Options page.

5. Tap the 🔄 Go button.

The new URL is loaded, and the new Web site appears (**Figure 12.3**).

✔ Tips

- You can also tap the Enter key on the soft (onscreen) keyboard to load the Web page.

- Entering a URL is one task for which you'll want to use the soft keyboard. The soft keyboard is more accurate than Transcriber, and most URLs are so short that hunting and pecking for the letters does not turn into a squint-a-thon.

To set a home page:

1. In Pocket Internet Explorer, go to the Web site that you want to set as your home page.

2. Tap Tools > Options to open the Options screen (**Figure 12.4**).

3. Tap the Use Current button.

The URL for the site you chose appears above the Use Current button, making it easy to see what your current home page is (**Figure 12.5**).

4. Tap OK.

The Options screen closes, and you return to Web browsing, with the new home page still visible.

✔ Tip

- You can use a "local" page—an HTML file on your device—as your home page. To do so, create the page on your computer, fill it with your favorite links, and synchronize it to your My Documents folder. Tap it in File Explorer, and Pocket Internet Explorer will launch and open it. Then follow the steps here beginning with step 2.

VISITING WEB SITES

To turn images on and off:

1. In Pocket Internet Explorer, tap View to open the View menu (**Figure 12.6**).

2. Tap Show Images to remove or add the check mark.

✔ Tips

■ No check mark next to Show Images means the device will now only download text, not images, when it displays Web sites. This vastly speeds up loading Web pages, but may make them uglier and harder to navigate. A check mark beside Show Images means images will be downloaded.

■ If images aren't showing, but there's one you'd like to see, press and hold the Web page's ⊠ image placeholder and tap Show Picture from the pop-up menu. The image is automatically fetched and displayed.

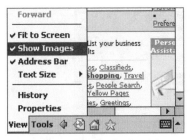

Figure 12.6 The View menu is where you choose to show or not show images in your Web pages.

Security and cookies

Pocket Internet Explorer offers very few security features, at least in comparison with the real Internet Explorer program on your computer.

You can choose whether to accept cookies. Cookies are files that some Web sites store on your device in order to facilitate transactions and maintain data and preferences, instead of your having to input these every time you visit. Depending on your level of paranoia, cookies can be seen as benign and beneficial or as a dubious and murky invasion of your data. You can choose to disallow cookies by tapping Tools > Options... > Advanced tab and then tapping to remove the check mark next to "Allow cookies." Clear the cookies that are already stored on your device by tapping the Clear Cookies button. Be advised, however, that some Web sites will not be accessible unless you allow cookies.

The other Web security setting you can control on the Pocket PC is whether you want to be warned when you about to visit a Web page that is not secure, presumably so that you can abort your mission at that point. Pocket Internet Explorer supports Secure Sockets Layer (SSL), a method of securely communicating sensitive information over the Internet, such as your bank or credit card information. You can disable this warning by tapping Tools > Options... > Advanced tab and tapping to remove the check mark next to "Warn when changing to a page that is not secure." We don't see any advantage to removing this warning, but hey, you can do it if you want to.

Figure 12.7 You can send a link to the current Web page as an email from the Tools menu.

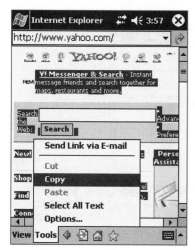

Figure 12.8 The Inbox program opens and creates an email for you.

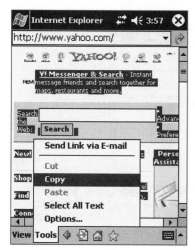

Figure 12.9 Copy text from a Web page to paste into another document on your Pocket PC.

To email a link:

1. In Pocket Internet Explorer, go to the Web page whose URL you would like to send via email as a link.

2. Tap Tools > Send Link via E-mail (**Figure 12.7**).

   The Inbox program opens and creates a new email message, with the To: field highlighted and the Web page's URL entered in the body of the message (**Figure 12.8**).

3. In the To: and Subject: fields, enter the email address of the person you want to email and the subject of the message.

4. Add any text necessary to the body of the email.

5. Tap Send to send the email.

6. Tap OK to return to Pocket Internet Explorer.

To copy text from a Web page:

1. In Pocket Internet Explorer, go to the Web site that has the text you want to copy.

2. Using the stylus, drag through text to select it.

   or

   Tap Tools > Select All Text to select all the text on the Web page.

3. Press and hold the tip of the stylus on the highlighted text and tap Copy in the pop-up menu that appears (**Figure 12.9**).

   The text is copied to the clipboard and is available to paste into other programs, such as Notes or Pocket Word.

VISITING WEB SITES

Organizing Favorite Web Sites

Just as you can with Internet Explorer on your computer, you can build a list of favorite Web sites on your Pocket PC. You can also transfer favorites from your computer. The Pocket PC keeps these in a special place, called Mobile Favorites.

To view your Mobile Favorites:

1. In Pocket Internet Explorer, tap the ☆ Mobile Favorites icon.

   The Favorites screen (with the Open tab selected) appears, showing your current favorite Web sites (**Figure 12.10**).

   You device will probably come with a few "favorite" sites already in the list.

2. Tap a Web site to open it in Pocket Internet Explorer.

To add a favorite Web site:

1. In Pocket Internet Explorer, go to the Web page you want to add as a favorite.

2. Tap the ☆ Mobile Favorites icon to display the Favorites screen.

3. Tap the Add/Delete tab to display the Add... button (**Figure 12.11**).

4. Tap the Add... button to display the Add Favorite screen (**Figure 12.12**).

   The fields are automatically filled in with data from the Web page that is currently loaded in Pocket Internet Explorer.

5. Tap Add to add the site to your Mobile Favorites.

✔ Tips

- Delete favorites with the Delete button.

- If you're careful, you can also press and hold the tip of the stylus on any blank space on the Web page—anywhere that is not a link—and tap Add to Favorites from the pop-up menu that appears.

Figure 12.10 Your device probably comes with a few predetermined "favorites."

Figure 12.11 The Add/Delete tab is where you add (or delete) favorites.

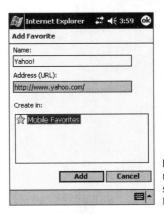

Figure 12.12 Add a new favorite Web site in the Add Favorite screen.

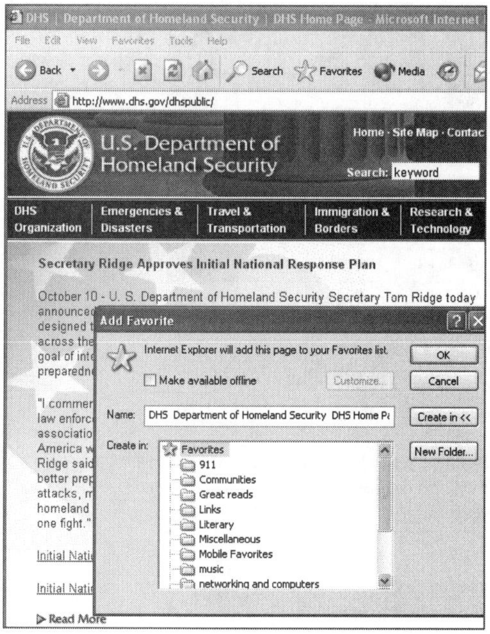

Figure 12.13 On your computer, adding a favorite to your Mobile Favorites folder will automatically add it to your device's favorites when you synchronize.

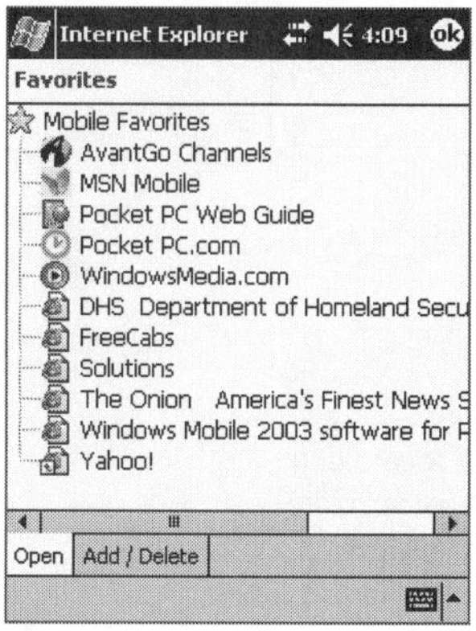

Figure 12.14 ActiveSync places a link to the new favorite on your device.

To transfer a favorite Web site from your computer:

1. In Internet Explorer on your computer, go to the Web site you want to add to your Mobile Favorites.

2. Click Favorites > Add to Favorites... to display the Add Favorite dialog box (**Figure 12.13**).

3. In the "Create in:" list, double-click the Mobile Favorites to select it.

4. If you want to be able to view the site on your device when it is not connected, click to put a check mark next to "Make available offline."

5. Click OK.

   The next time you synchronize with ActiveSync, the site will be added to your Pocket PC Favorites (**Figure 12.14**).

✔ Tip

■ Making the site available offline means you can read the Web page you added at any time on your Pocket PC, without being connected to anything. Note that all parts of the Web page are added, including image files. These files take up memory on your device, so if available memory is an issue, choose carefully which sites to make available offline.

ORGANIZING FAVORITE WEB SITES

Managing Your Web Surfing History

Pocket Internet Explorer keeps track of the sites you visit, calling them "history." You can use history to revisit recently viewed sites, adjust how much of your Web-surfing history you want your device to keep, or delete your history to remove evidence of which sites you have visited.

To view recent Web sites:

1. In Pocket Internet Explorer, tap the down-arrow on the right-hand side of the address bar (**Figure 12.15**).

2. Scroll through the list of recent sites if necessary and tap the one you want.

To view your Web surfing history:

1. In Pocket Internet Explorer, tap View > History to display the History screen (**Figure 12.16**).

2. Scroll through the history list of sites and tap the one you want.

✔ Tip

■ By default, the History screen displays links to all the Web pages you have visited in the last 30 days. This is a wonderful feature because it's automatic. You don't have to do anything to store or remember the links to these sites.

Tap the down-arrow to reveal recent pages

Figure 12.15 The address bar drops down to reveal recently visited Web pages.

Figure 12.16 For better or worse, your Pocket PC keeps a record of all the sites you visit within a specified period of time.

Increase or decrease the number of days to keep in your history

Figure 12.17 You control how much history to keep in the Options screen.

To change your Web surfing history settings:

1. In Pocket Internet Explorer, tap Tools > Options... to display the Options screen (**Figure 12.17**).

2. Tap the up or down arrows in the History area to increase or decrease the number of days you want to keep in your history.

3. Tap OK to save your changes.

To clear your Web surfing history:

1. In Pocket Internet Explorer, tap Tools > Options... to display the Options screen.

2. Tap the Clear History button to remove links to your history of Web pages.

3. Tap the Delete Files button to delete temporary Internet files that have been stored on your device to speed up Web browsing.

4. Tap OK to save your changes.

   All record of the Web sites you have ever visited is now erased.

MANAGING YOUR WEB SURFING HISTORY

Browsing offline with AvantGo

AvantGo is a free online service that allows you to obtain updated information on a variety of topics (called "channels"), all viewable in Pocket Internet Explorer. The AvantGo software is already installed on all Pocket PCs running Pocket PC 2003. To activate it, go to Options in ActiveSync on your computer and check the box next to AvantGo in the drop-down list. Then go to www.avantgo.com to choose your areas of interest and create an account. You will be offered a range of channels to choose from, for example, *The New York Times*, CNET, *Forbes*, and *Rolling Stone*.

After a lot of configuration, when you next synchronize, your selected channels will be downloaded to your device. You can then view them in Internet Explorer by tapping Start > Programs > AvantGo. Each channel is like a mini-Web site, except the information has been synchronized with your device already, so you don't have to be connected to view it, which means it's much faster than the Web to boot. You can go back to the AvantGo Web site at any time to add or delete channels. How can AvantGo be so cool and remain free to use? Be prepared for lots of ads. And at 100K to 200K per channel, keep an eye on memory.

Chapter 12

Some Pocket PC-friendly Web sites

To get you started on your surfing, here are just a few choice Web sites that either cater to the Pocket PC enthusiast or are formatted to be easily viewed on a Pocket PC. Many of these have lists of links to other sites.

mobile.yahoo.com A version of Yahoo designed to be read on a Pocket PC

mobile.alltheweb.com A good search engine that's easy to read on your device

www.pocketpc.com Microsoft's site for and about the Pocket PC

www.pocketpcthoughts.com A good all-around site with news, reviews, forums, and all types of Pocket PC information

www.brighthand.com Another good all-around site with articles, news, and rumors about handheld computers

www.pocketpcmag.com The online version of the only magazine dedicated to the Pocket PC

www.handango.com A great source for third-party Pocket PC programs

And last, but not least...

mobile.theonion.com In-depth articles and thoughtful commentary from "America's Finest New Source"

INSTANT MESSAGING

MSN Messenger is the instant messaging (IM) program that comes installed on your Pocket PC. Unfortunately, Microsoft recently changed its technology because of security issues, issuing a small update to the program. If you find MSN Messenger doesn't work, download the patch at:

```
http://www.microsoft.com/windowsmobile/
resources/msnmessenger/pocketpc.mspx
```

MSN Messenger lets you "talk" (type) in real time with people on the Internet. With email, you have to wait for the other person to reply, but IM is nearly instantaneous. The biggest IM headache is compatibility. Email programs let you read any email—whether it was sent with Outlook or Eudora or a Web browser. But as of this writing, somebody using AOL Instant Messenger can't chat with a friend who uses MSN Messenger or Yahoo Messenger. (We'll look at how to get around this at the end of the chapter.)

About MSN Messenger and Passport Accounts

With MSN Messenger, you can chat with friends and coworkers who use MSN Messenger or Windows Messenger on PCs, Macs, set-top TV boxes, or mobile phones. Remember: If you bought your Pocket PC before December 2003, you may have to download the MSN Messenger upgrade in order to use the service.

Aside from that, and an Internet connection, you need only one more thing to start messaging: a .NET Passport account, which you must use to log in to MSN's messaging servers. You may already have one: Hotmail and MSN email addresses are valid Passports accounts.

If you don't already have a Passport account, you can get one for one for free at www.passport.com (**Figure 13.1**). You can use a computer or your Pocket PC to sign up—it only takes a minute. The email address you use to sign up for a Passport becomes your Passport ID. Some people use a Web-based email address—such as a Yahoo email address—as their Passport ID. This is a good idea, because by not broadcasting your main email address on the Internet, you'll ward off spam—and have an added layer of anonymity.

MSN Messenger also works with Microsoft's Exchange Instant Messaging, which is intended for use within a private corporate network. If this is how you plan to use IM, you'll need to use your Exchange email account and password to sign in. Check with your company's IS department if you have questions about Exchange. (If you're like most people, and you just want to send instant messages to friends on the Internet, you can ignore this Exchange stuff. Just log in with a Passport email address.)

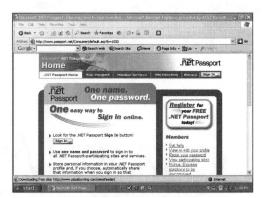

Figure 13.1 You'll need to sign up for a .NET Passport account if you want to start using MSN Messenger.

Figure 13.2 The MSN Messenger sign-in screen invites you to sign in. Don't do it yet.

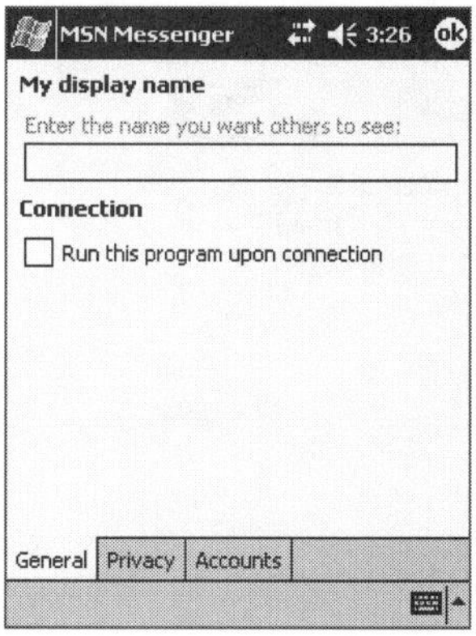

Figure 13.3 The General tab of the Options screen asks you to enter a display name (wait on this for now) and whether you want the program to automatically launch every time your Pocket PC connects to the Internet.

Figure 13.4 The Accounts tab is where you enter your Passport account information that you set up when you applied for a Passport account.

The first thing to do is go get the MSN Messenger program upgrade, if applicable (you'll know for sure that you need it if you try and use the service and get an error message). You must download it and install it using your computer, not your Pocket PC, and then get a Passport account. After you create the account, it's time to start messaging.

To launch MSN Messenger:

◆ On your Pocket PC, tap Start > Programs > MSN Messenger.

 The MSN Messenger sign-in screen appears (**Figure 13.2**).

To enter your account information:

1. In MSN Messenger, tap Tools > Options.

 The General tab of the MSN Messenger Options screen appears (**Figure 13.3**).

2. Ignore the box marked "My display name" for now. (We'll set this later.)

3. If you want MSN Messenger to open every time you go online, check the checkbox "Run this program upon connection."

4. Tap the Accounts tab (**Figure 13.4**).

5. In the "Sign in name" field, enter your Passport or Exchange Server account name. Use the whole email address for the account, including the @ sign.

6. In the Password field, enter your password.

 Your password is optional here, but providing it will spare you from having to enter it each time you sign in to MSN Messenger.

7. Select which Account to use first, Passport or Exchange. If you signed up for a Passport account, choose Passport. (To choose Exchange, you'll have to check the Enable Exchange Instant Messaging box first).

continues on next page

8. Tap OK.

You are returned to the MSN Messenger sign-in screen. Your account information is now stored on your device, so you won't have to go through this setup process again unless you want to change your information.

✔ Tip

- If you want a little privacy, leave the "Run this program upon connection" box unchecked to go online incognito. If it's checked, your contacts will see that you're online, even if you just check your email.

To sign in to MSN Messenger:

1. Connect your Pocket PC to the Internet.

or

Connect your Pocket PC to your computer and connect your computer to the Internet.

2. If it's not already running, tap Start > Programs > MSN Messenger to open MSN Messenger and display the sign-in screen.

3. Tap anywhere on the sign-in screen to begin signing in (**Figure 13.5**).

If you've already entered your account information as described in the preceding task, your sign-in name should already be filled in for you. If not, enter it now. Remember to use your entire email address.

Figure 13.5 Once your information is entered correctly, tapping Sign In will connect your Pocket PC to the MSN Messenger service.

Figure 13.6 The MSN Messenger screen shows that you're signed in, which of your contacts are online, and which are not. If it's your first time, as shown here, you won't have contacts yet.

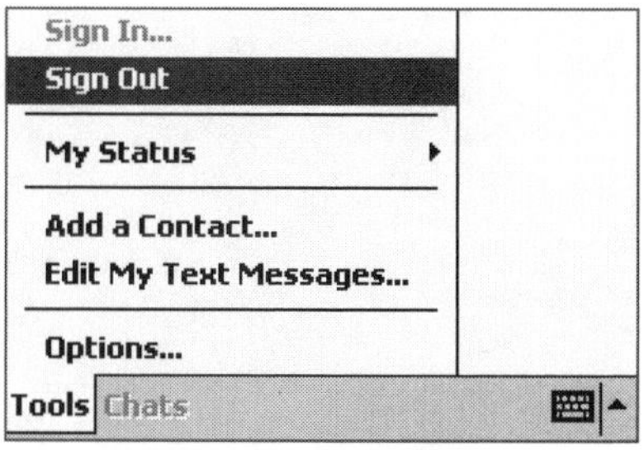

Figure 13.7 When you're finished using MSN Messenger, be sure to sign out—otherwise your contacts will think you're still available to chat (you'll still be online, just not that they can see).

4. Enter your password if it's not already entered on the screen.

(For security reasons, your password appears as asterisks as you type.)

5. Check the Save Password check box if you don't want to reenter your password each time you sign in to MSN Messenger.

6. Tap the Sign In button.

After a second or two, you should see the MSN Messenger screen, displaying your contacts (you may not have any yet) and indicating that you're online (**Figure 13.6**). An error message appears if you entered the wrong information or if you're not online.

✔ Tips

■ You can't log into MSN Messenger from two locations at once. If you're logged into Windows Messenger on your computer and then sign into MSN Messenger from your Pocket PC, you'll automatically be signed out of your computer's connection.

■ When a Pocket PC or Smartphone user logs in, the icon indicates a mobile device.

To sign out of MSN Messenger:

◆ Tap Tools > Sign Out (**Figure 13.7**). You are returned to the sign-in screen.

MSN MESSENGER AND PASSPORT ACCOUNTS

Adding Contacts

The people you plan to chat with are known as your *contacts* in MSN Messenger. If you've used other instant messaging programs, you may be familiar with other terms for contacts, such as AOL Instant Messenger's: *buddies*.

Calling them contacts was an unfortunate choice, because MSN Messenger contacts are completely different from your contacts in the Contacts program. Your IM contacts are stored on MSN's servers, not on your device. That means you can't view or manage your MSN Messenger contacts unless you're online and signed in. On the other hand, your contacts list will follow you when you sign in to MSN Messenger from any computer or device.

You can't send an instant message to someone until you've added that person as a contact in MSN Messenger. Once you enter a contact, you'll be able to see when the person is online and signed in to MSN Messenger. When that happens, you can exchange short messages back and forth.

When you enter a contact, MSN's servers will check to make sure that person has a Passport account. (The program will immediately let you know whether they do or don't.)

To add a contact:

1. Sign in to MSN Messenger on your Pocket PC.

2. Tap Tools > Add a Contact.
   The "Add a Contact" screen appears (**Figure 13.8**).

3. In the Sign-in Name field, enter the contact's Passport (or Exchange) full email address.

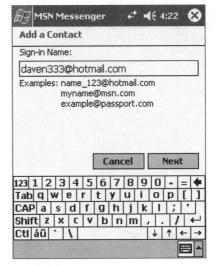

Figure 13.8 Even if a contact is stored in other Pocket PC programs, you have to reenter it here to store it on the MSN Messenger servers.

MSN Messenger
4:23
ok
Success!
daven333@hotmail.com has been successfully added to your contacts list.

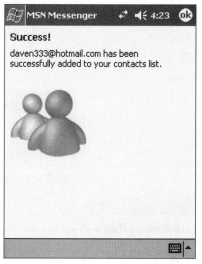

Figure 13.9 Success means your contact does have a valid Passport account and has been stored in the MSN Messenger servers for you.

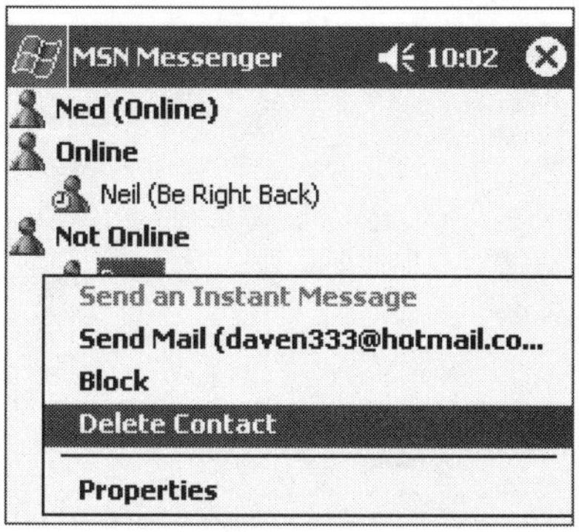
MSN Messenger
10:02
Ned (Online)
Online
Neil (Be Right Back)
Not Online
Send an Instant Message
Send Mail (daven333@hotmail.co...
Block
Delete Contact
Properties

Figure 13.10 If you delete a contact, you can always enter it again later.

4. Tap Next.

   You should see a "Success!" message (**Figure 13.9**). You'll see a failure message if you mistyped the email address or if your contact doesn't have a valid Passport account.

5. Tap OK.

   Your contact will now appear on the main MSN Messenger screen (as either Online or Not Online) whenever you sign in to the service.

To delete a contact:

1. After signing in, in the main MSN Messenger screen, press and hold the tip of the stylus on the contact's name.

2. Tap Delete Contact from the pop-up menu that appears (**Figure 13.10**).

   You'll see a dialog box that reads, "Contact will be permanently deleted. Continue?"

3. Tap Yes to delete the contact.

   The contact's name disappears from the contact list.

Sending and Receiving Messages

IM is all about instant gratification. When you send an instant message, you can be pretty sure that your friend or co-worker is going to see it right away, or at least the next time she looks at her screen.

Some people get carried away and pepper their friends with instant messages day and night. If you engage in this kind of behavior, you might begin to wonder why all your contacts appear to be offline. They've probably *blocked* you (see "Managing Your Privacy" later in this chapter).

Take the lead from your contacts. If your friends don't send a lot of instant messages, they probably don't want to receive 25 messages a day from you. But if they join in the fun and reply to all your jokes and random musings, then by all means, message them all you like.

Before you can send a message, you must first sign in to MSN Messenger (see "To sign in to MSN Messenger" earlier in this chapter.)

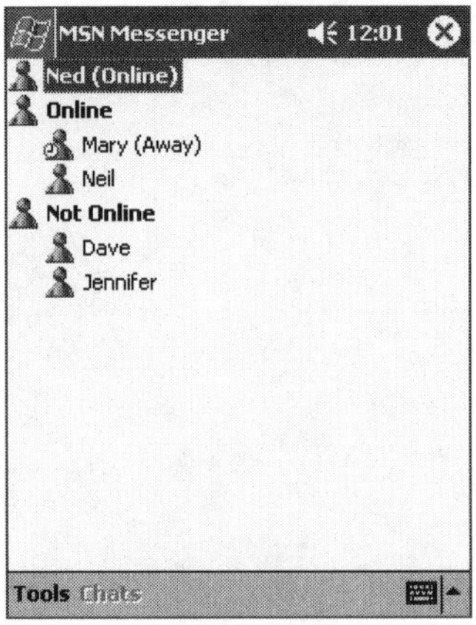

To see which contacts are online:

- If you're wondering whether a particular contact is available to chat, check the main screen of MSN Messenger (**Figure 13.11**), which you'll see after signing in.

  If the strange little bubbleman icon next to a name is blue/green, and it's in the Online group, that means the contact is online and taking messages.

  If the icon is red and the contact is in the Not Online group, you can't send that contact an instant message, because he or she is not signed in to MSN Messenger.

Figure 13.11 In this screen, Mary is online but away from her computer. You can send her messages, but don't expect an instant reply.

Figure 13.12
Let's bother Dave. He has to be online in order for us to be able to send him an instant message.

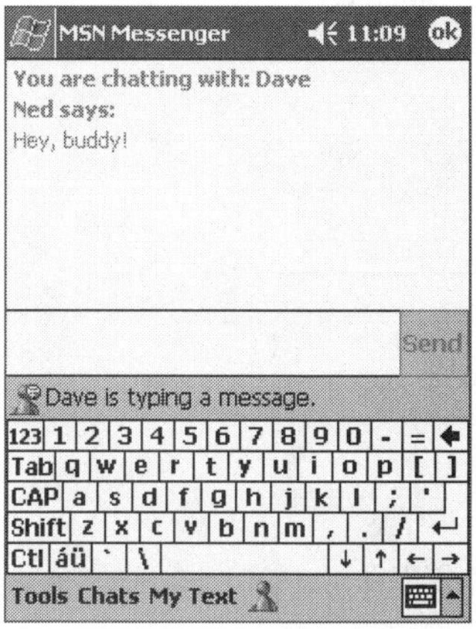

Figure 13.13 Type your message in the center part of the screen and tap Send to send it.

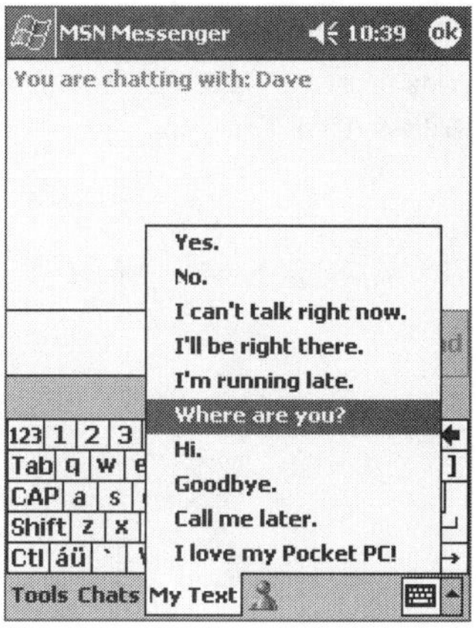

Figure 13.14
Choosing preset messages in the My Text menu saves you from having to type all those letters.

✔ Tip

■ Depending on the device you're using, these colors may vary slightly. On a Dell Axim, for example, an online contact may appear more blue than green.

To send a message:

1. In the main MSN Messenger screen, tap an online contact's name to start a chat.

   The "You are chatting with:" screen appears (**Figure 13.12**). You must be signed in to see this screen, and to send a message.

2. Enter your message in the field next to the Send button.

3. When you've finished your message, tap Send or tap the Enter key on the soft (onscreen) keyboard.

   Your text will now appear in the upper half of the screen. As your contact replies to your message, you'll see a note above the keyboard indicating that your contact is typing a message (**Figure 13.13**).

4. If you don't get a reply after a few seconds, tap OK to return to the main screen.

   There's no point in sitting around waiting for a response. MSN Messenger will notify you when your contact replies, even if you're in another program on your device.

To send a My Text message:

1. In the main MSN Messenger screen, tap an online contact's name to initiate a chat.

2. Tap My Text and tap a preset message (**Figure 13.14**).

3. Tap Send or the Enter key to send the message.

continues on next page

SENDING AND RECEIVING MESSAGES

✔ Tip

■ The My Text feature is useful when you'd rather not painstakingly tap out a standard "I'm running late" or "Call me later" message to a friend. Your wrists will thank you.

To create your own preset messages:

1. Tap Tools > Edit My Text Messages (**Figure 13.15**).

   The My Text Messages screen appears.

2. Select a message to edit by tapping it.

   My Text comes with ten preset messages. You can't add more messages, but you can change the ten existing messages as often as you like.

3. Enter new text in the text box over the keyboard (**Figure 13.16**).

4. Tap OK to exit, or tap another message to edit it.

   Your new preset message will now appear when you tap the My Text menu during a chat.

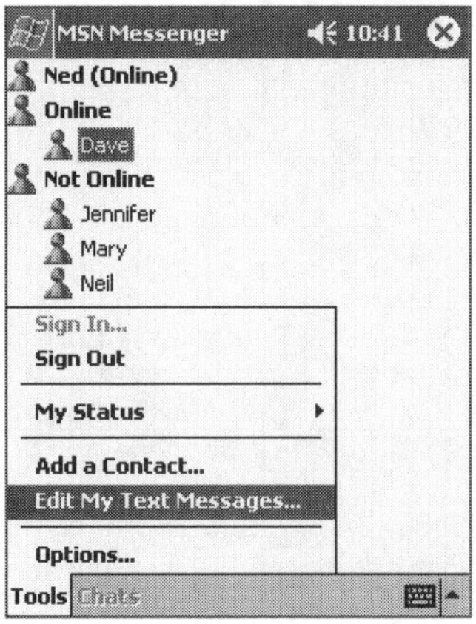

Figure 13.15 You can edit the My Text messages to say whatever you want.

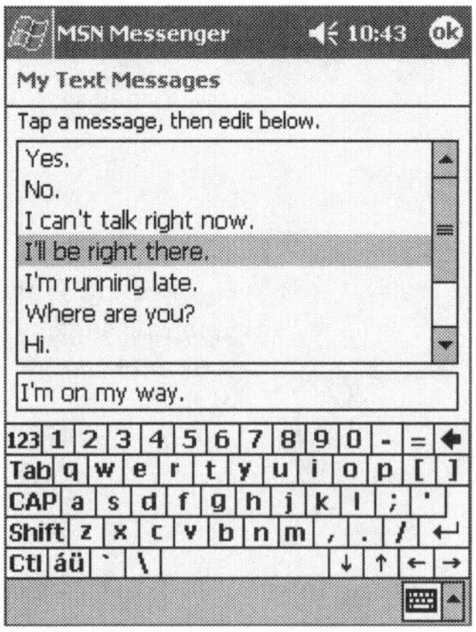

Figure 13.16 To edit a My Text message, tap it and type to replace the old text.

Table 13.1

Emoticons in MSN Messenger	
TO SEND THIS:	TYPE THIS:
😊	:-) or :)
😃	:-D or :d
😉	;-) or ;)
😮	:-O or :o
😛	:-P or :p
😎	(H) or (h)
😠	:-@ or :@
😕	:-S or :s
😳	:$ or :-$
🙁	:-(or :(
😢	:'(
😐	:-| or :|
🐻	(})
👥	(M) or (m)
😺	(@)
🐶	(&)
🌙	(S)
⭐	(*)
🎵	(8)
📧	(E) or (e)
🌹	(F) or (f)
🥀	(W) or (w)
🕐	(O) or (o)
💋	(K) or (k)
🎁	(G) or (g)
🎂	(^)
📷	(P) or (p)
💡	(I) or (i)
☕	(C) or (c)
📞	(T) or (t)

Table 13.1 In chats, emoticons are used for emotional shorthand, like sticking your tongue out at somebody. This is only a partial list of MSN Messenger emoticons. To find help pages that will show you more, do a Google search on "msn messenger emoticons."

✔ Tips

■ Your My Text messages are also available when you're creating email messages in Inbox.

■ You can also add *emoticons* to your messages. Emoticons is a fancy word for those little smileys that attempt to make up for the lack of facial expressions in textual communications. **Table 13.1** lists the available emoticons in MSN Messenger. Note that the Pocket PC doesn't support displaying the graphic emoticons in the left-hand column—it only shows the text versions. But if your contact is signed in on a bona fide computer, he or she will see the graphic ones, even if you type the text versions.

To receive messages:

◆ No matter what program you're using when a friend sends you an instant message, as long as you're connected and signed in, a dialog box appears at the top of your screen when the message arrives (**Figure 13.17**). Tap the Chat button to reply, or tap Ignore to not.

If you tap the Ignore button (or don't tap anything), the dialog bubble vanishes after a few seconds, but you'll still see an icon of a little bubble-headed guy at the top of your screen (**Figure 13.18**).

✔ Tip

■ Instant messaging uses a lot of short-hand jargon, such as LOL (laughing out loud), ROTFL (rolling on the floor laughing), and IMHO (in my humble opinion). For more on IM, chat, and email jargon, visit www.netlingo.com.

Figure 13.17 No matter what program you're using (here we're reading an eBook), a dialog box appears when somebody sends you a message. Click Chat to reply or Ignore if you don't want to be bothered.

Bubbleman means someone attempted to chat with you— click him to see what he or she said

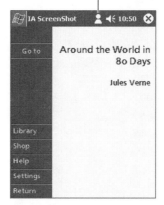

Figure 13.18 We clicked Ignore at the top of the screen, but Dave's message is still waiting for us. Tap the bubbleman icon to make the message appear.

Figure 13.19 Looks like Mary is the only one available to invite.

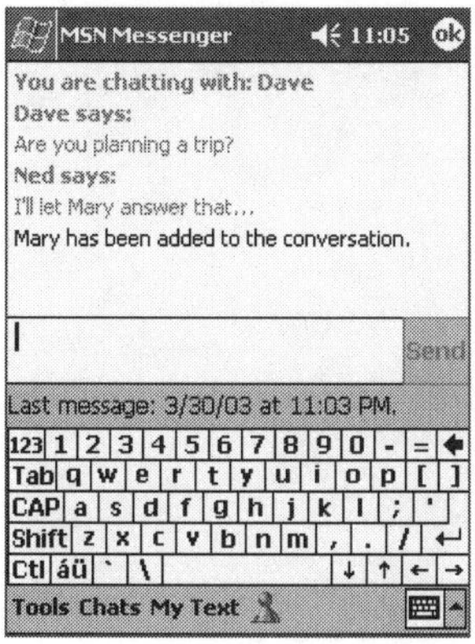

Figure 13.20 We've added Mary to the conversation, but she won't know it until we type another message.

Figure 13.21 Now we have three people in the chat.

Expanding Your Chats

Perhaps the person you're chatting with has become tiresome. Or hilarious. Or controversial. In such cases, you may be glad you can invite another contact to join in. You can also run multiple chat sessions at the same time.

To invite somebody else into a chat:

1. In MSN Messenger on your Pocket PC, tap Tools > Invite.

   A box appears, displaying list of contacts who are available to join the chat (**Figure 13.19**). If the box is empty, that means you're already chatting with the only available contact.

2. Tap a contact to invite him or her, then tap OK.

   In the MSN Messenger screen, you'll see a note that this person has been added to the conversation (**Figure 13.20**).

3. Send a message welcoming the new person—otherwise she won't know she's been invited to join you (**Figure 13.21**).

✔ Tip

- If you want to make your IM account name available to other MSN members who share your interests, set up a public profile in the MSN Member Directory at http://members.msn.com. Be careful, however: If you post your IM account name here, you can expect a lot of messages, because your public profile can be seen by anyone on the Internet.

To juggle multiple chats:

- Simply start another conversation by tapping the contact's name. When you have more than one chat going and want to switch among them, tap the Chats menu at the bottom of the screen and tap a contact's name.

   The Chats menu appears only when you have active chats going.

EXPANDING YOUR CHATS

251

Managing Your Privacy

As annoying as spam emails are, imagine getting spam instant messages. Or being pestered by unwanted messages from someone who can't take a hint. This is where blocking comes in handy. MSN Messenger can notify you when other users add you to their contact lists, and the program lets you block their messages and prevent them from viewing your online status. Blocking gives you control over your inner circle of messaging contacts and helps you prevent unwanted interactions.

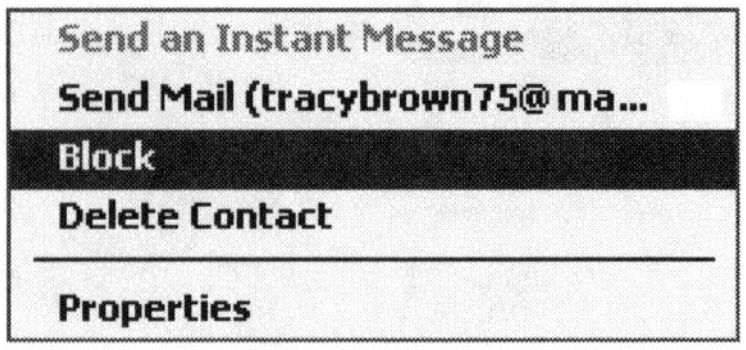

Figure 13.22 When you block contacts, you appear always offline to them, and they won't be able to send you messages.

To block a contact:

1. In the main MSN Messenger screen, press and hold the stylus on a contact's name.

2. Tap Block in the pop-up menu that appears (**Figure 13.22**).

   On MSN Messenger's main screen, you'll see a red slash through the icon next to this contact's name. Blocked contacts don't know they are being blocked. To them, your online status will always appear to be "not online" and they won't be able to send you messages.

To unblock a contact:

1. In the main MSN Messenger screen, press and hold the stylus on the name of a blocked contact.

2. Choose Unblock from the pop-up menu.

   On the main MSN Messenger screen, the red slash will disappear from the icon next to the contacts name. He or she is now unblocked.

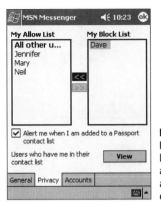

Figure 13.23 The Privacy screen lets you receive alerts when people add you to their contact lists.

Figure 13.24 When somebody first adds you to their contact list, you can choose to block that person from sending you messages.

Figure 13.25 Your display name is what appears on other people's screens, and you can make it anything you want.

To be notified when people add you to their contact lists:

1. Tap Tools > Options > Privacy tab.

2. Check the box marked "Alert me when I am added to a Passport contact list" (**Figure 13.23**).

   Now when somebody adds you to their contact list, a dialog box will appear on your device that lets you block them right away if you choose (**Figure 13.24**).

✔ Tip

- To see users who have you in their contact lists, tap the View button in the Privacy tab.

To change your display name:

1. Tap Tools > Options.

2. Enter a new name or nickname as your display name (**Figure 13.25**).

3. Tap OK.

   Your new nickname is now instantly updated on your friends' contact lists.

✔ Tip

- Some people change their display name to let contacts know where they are, such as "In meeting" or "Studying for finals." Others make up nicknames to keep friends on their toes. We suggest using your real name so people know who is trying to contact them. Some people block messages from people they don't know, so if you use a nickname, don't be surprised if your messages don't get through all the time.

MANAGING YOUR PRIVACY

To change your status appearance:

1. Tap Tools > My Status (**Figure 13.26**).

2. Select your new status from the pop-up menu that appears.

✔ Tips

■ When you're signed in but unable (or unwilling) to reply to messages, you should change My Status to something like "Away" or "Busy" to let your contacts know that they shouldn't expect a reply anytime soon.

■ If you're feeling shy, choose "Appear Offline." That way, you can see your contacts even though it will appear to them that you're not signed in. MSN Messenger won't let you send instant messages to people while you're in this mode, which is just as well. That would be akin to jumping out at them from behind a tree.

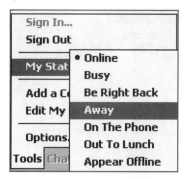

Figure 13.26 The My Status setting enables you to let others know why you may not be answering right away.

MSN Alerts message service

MSN Alerts is a free service that sends you automated instant messages notifying you about time-sensitive events and information.

Think of this alert service as a robot assistant that will send you messages about news, stock prices, sports scores, local traffic jams, and so on.

There are hundreds of possible alerts you can receive, and you can customize them to arrive at certain times of the day. Sign up for alerts at http://alerts.msn.com.

MANAGING YOUR PRIVACY

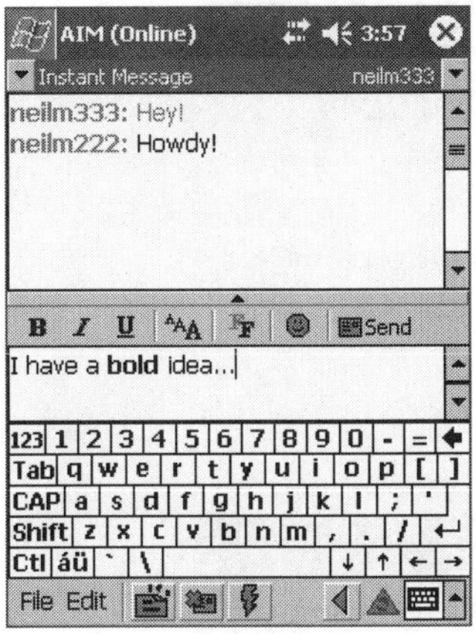

Figure 13.27 AOL Instant Messenger lets you change the style of text in your messages.

Using Other Instant Messengers

Imagine that you have three colored phones on your desk. You must use the green phone to call some of your friends, the blue phone to call others, and the yellow phone to call the rest of them. That's the ridiculous state of instant messaging: The most popular IM programs aren't compatible with each other.

It's quite likely that some of your friends use AOL Instant Messenger (the most popular service), while others use Yahoo Messenger or MSN Messenger (or Windows Messenger, its computer counterpart).

To make things even more challenging for Pocket PC users, AOL and Yahoo seem to be taking ambivalent stances to the Pocket PC platform.

AOL Instant Messenger

You can buy AOL Instant Messenger 2.0 For Pocket PC 2002 for about $20 at www.handango.com. This version reportedly works with Pocket PC 2003 devices. It's strange that Pocket PC (and Palm PDA) users have to pay for the program while it's free for PC and Mac users.

We were able to download a free Windows CE version of AOL Instant Messenger at www.aol.co.uk/aim/wince/ (**Figure 13.27**). It worked just fine, allowing us to chat with other AIM users all over the world. One possible dark cloud looms: At the time of this writing, AOL spokespeople weren't commenting on whether or not the company would keep developing for the Pocket PC platform.

Yahoo Messenger

The situation is even bleaker on the Yahoo side. If you poke around online, you can probably find an old version of Yahoo Messenger for Windows CE. However, at the time of this writing, this program no longer works with Yahoo Messenger servers, and it can neither send nor receive instant messages.

iMov

You can still send instant messages to AOL Instant Messenger and Yahoo Messenger users through a Windows CE program called iMov (**Figure 13.28**), which you can download at www.movsoftware.com. This program is approved by the Jabber Software Foundation, which oversees an open-source standard called *extensible messaging protocol*, which makes it possible for users to log in to AOL, MSN, and Yahoo instant messaging services all at once. Using Jabber is a bit clunky, however, because you have to log in to a Jabber server, which in turn logs you in to each of the big instant messaging services. As a result, when you set it up, you have to enter all your separate account names and passwords. But by doing so, you're able to exchange messages with all your instant messaging pals, no matter what IM services they're using.

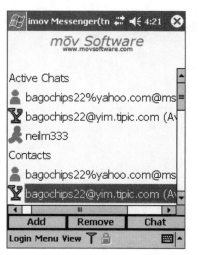

Figure 13.28 With the versatile iMov Messenger, you can use Yahoo, MSN, and AOL instant messaging services at the same time.

MUSIC & VIDEO WITH WINDOWS MEDIA PLAYER

14

The Pocket PC's ability to play music and video is a lucky bonus when you consider that the device is supposed to *increase* productivity by allowing you to continue working while you're away from your computer. Yet the thing is also a portable stereo and video player. It's quite wonderful to whip out a futuristic gadget and listen to downloaded music or tunes you ripped from CDs—not to mention show off video of the dog or kids or UFO that landed in the yard.

The program that makes all this happen is Windows Media Player. All devices running the Windows Mobile 2003 operating system come equipped with Windows Media Player 9. It simplifies your audio and visual entertainment by playing both music and video files in the same program. That's important to grasp: Your Pocket PC regards audio and video as two different aspects of the same thing, and, in a way, they are—a song is a movie that just happens to not have a visual track yet, and what comes out of your digital camera could easily be enhanced by some music.

And with Windows Movie Maker, Microsoft's free digital video editing application, you can indeed combine digital pictures, video, and audio into full-blown films, music videos, and multimedia presentations.

Converting Media Files to Play on Your Pocket PC

Windows Media Player plays audio files on your Pocket PC that are in Windows Media format (extensions .wma or .asf) or MP3 format (extension .mp3). The program plays video files, too, but only if they are in Windows Media format (extension .wmv). If you have media files stored on your computer that are already in Windows Media format, you can play them on your Pocket PC without a hitch.

But if you have audio and video files in other formats, such as .wav, .avi, or .mpeg, you can play them on your device, but you must first convert them to Windows Media format with a third-party conversion program or with Windows Movie Maker, which is available free for download from Microsoft: www.microsoft.com/windowsxp/moviemaker/

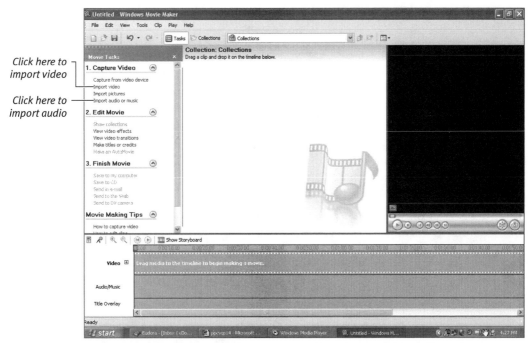

Click here to import video

Click here to import audio

Figure 14.1 Windows Movie Maker lets you import video, pictures, and music files and outputs them as Windows Media files, which you can play on your Pocket PC.

Figure 14.2 Choose a file to import into Movie Maker.

To convert a media file to play on your Pocket PC:

1. On your computer, download, install, and launch Windows Movie Maker.

   Windows Movie Maker's Movie Tasks pane appears on the screen (**Figure 14.1**).

2. In the Movie Tasks pane, do one of the following:

   ▲ To import an audio file, click "Import audio or music" in the Capture Video portion of the Movie Tasks pane.

   ▲ To import a video file, click Import Video.

   The Import File dialog box appears (**Figure 14.2**).

continues on next page

3. Navigate to where the media file resides.

Supported audio file types include: aif, .aifc, .aiff .asf, .au, .mp2, .mp3, .mpa, .snd, .wav.

Supported video file types include: .asf, .avi, .m1v, .mp2, .mp2v, .mpe, .mpeg, .mpg, .mpv2.

4. Double-click the file you want to convert.

An audio file appears as an icon in the Collections window (**Figure 14.3**). A video file appears as one or more frames of the movie (**Figure 14.4**).

5. Drag the file's icon or frame(s) to the timeline at the bottom of the screen by doing one of the following:

▲ Drag the audio file icon to the Audio/Music timeline.

▲ Drag video files (all at once—select them by holding down Shift as you click) to the Video timeline.

When you drag the audio file, the Audio/Music timeline fills up with a squiggly waveform, similar to a lie-detector print-out (**Figure 14.5**). Video files may be split into "clips" or remain as one frame.

6. In the Finish Movie section of the Movie Tasks pane, click "Save to My Computer" to start the Save Movie Wizard (**Figure 14.6**).

Windows Media Player calls your file a "movie," but, in fact, it can be any Windows Media file containing video, video and audio, or just audio.

7. In the Wizard's first text field, name your file.

Figure 14.3 When you import a music file into Windows Movie Maker, it appears in the Collections window as a musical note icon.

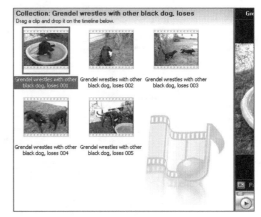

Figure 14.4 When you import a video file, it may be split into "clips."

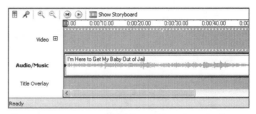

Figure 14.5 Drag a song to the 0:00 mark at the far left-hand side of the Audio/Music timeline.

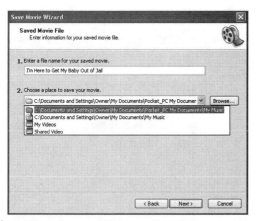
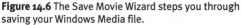

Figure 14.6 The Save Movie Wizard steps you through saving your Windows Media file.

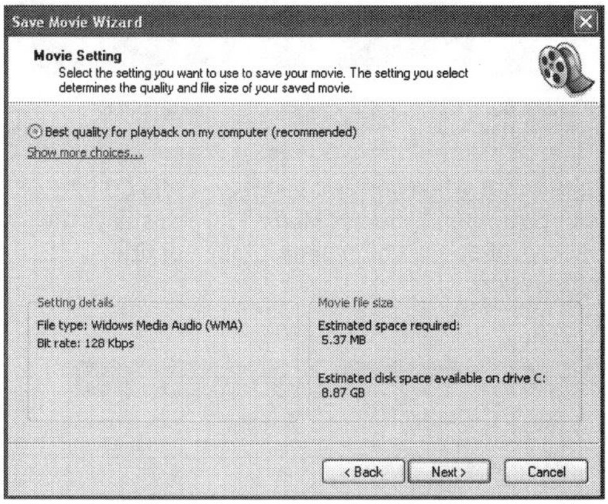

Figure 14.7 Name your file and pick a place to save it.

■ An alternative to Movie Maker is Windows Media Encoder 9 Series, another free download from Microsoft (www.microsoft.com). This is a more advanced tool, but it's good for converting a bunch of files at once. It converts avi, .wav, .mpg, .mp3, .bmp, and .jpg files to Windows Media format.

8. Choose a place to save your file in the second field.

If you choose the Pocket_PC My Documents folder, and you have chosen to synchronize files (see Chapter 4), the file will be automatically copied to your device the next time you synchronize.

9. Click Next to display the Movie Setting dialog box (**Figure 14.7**).

10. Make any changes to playback quality by clicking "Show more choices" or accept the default choice of quality (recommended).

The default choice copies music at 128 Kbps (kilobits per second), which sounds good enough most of the time. For slightly better quality, choose 160 Kbps (but keep in mind that the file will be bigger).

11. Click Next.

A Saving Movie dialog box displays Movie Maker's progress in converting the file.

12. When saving is finished, uncheck the "Play movie when I finish" check box if you don't want the file to play right now.

13. Click Finish.

The file is saved as .wma format, and can now be played on your Pocket PC. If you saved it somewhere other than in your Pocket_PC My Documents folder, you will have to place it in that folder to transfer it to your device during ActiveSync.

✔ Tips

■ Movie Maker is a full-featured, powerful program. Describing its capabilities is beyond the scope of this book, but you can check out *Windows Movie Maker 2 for Windows: Visual QuickStart Guide* published by Peachpit Press (ISBN: 0-321-19954-5) to find out how to combine video, audio, pictures, and titles into your own multimedia extravaganzas.

Getting Music and Video onto Your Pocket PC

There's a version of Windows Media Player for your computer, and you probably already have it. To find out whether you do, click Start > All Programs > Accessories > Entertainment and see if there's an icon for Windows Media Player. If you don't have it, or if you have a version earlier than version 9, download the latest version by entering the following URL into Internet Explorer: www.windowsmedia.com/9series/Download/download.asp

Once you have Windows Media Player installed on your computer, you've made the first step to turning your Pocket PC into a mobile entertainment station. With the player, you can copy music and video files to your device.

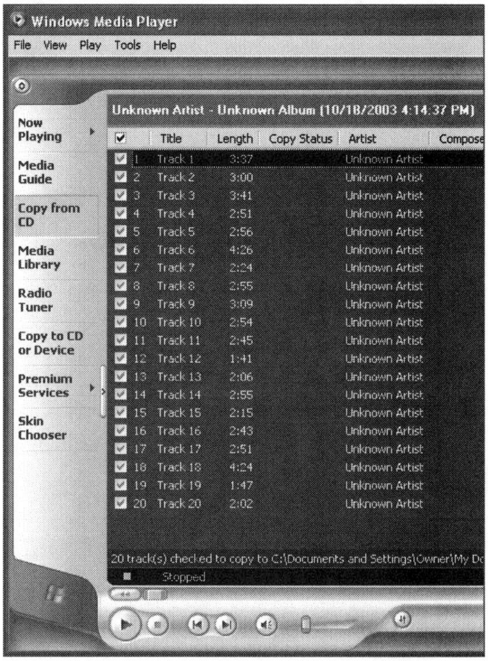

To retrieve song and title information for your CD:

1. Connect your computer to the Internet.

2. On your computer, launch Windows Media Player.

3. Insert an audio CD into your CD-ROM drive.

4. In Windows Media Player, click the "Copy from CD" button.

   The CD's tracks appear in a list, but note that most of the information appears to be unknown (**Figure 14.8**).

5. Click the Find Album Info button below the All Music tab in the upper right-hand corner of the screen.

   A warning will likely appear, asking you to change your privacy options. If you don't see the warning, skip to step 7.

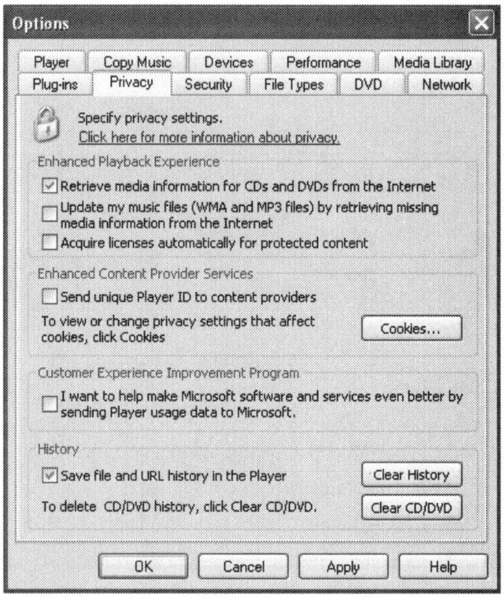

Figure 14.8 When you first insert an audio CD into your computer, Windows Media Player displays the tracks, but doesn't offer song, album, or title information.

Figure 14.9 Change your privacy options to enable Windows Media Player to retrieve information about your CD from the Internet.

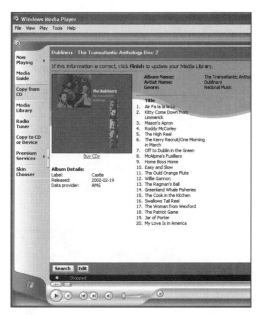

Figure 14.10 When you click Find Album Info, Windows Media Player automatically connects to an online database and retrieves song, album, and artist information for your audio CD.

Figure 14.11 After retrieving song and artist information, Windows Media Player displays your audio files, ready to copy.

6. Click Tools > Options > Privacy tab, check the box next to "Retrieve media information for CDs and DVDs from the Internet" (**Figure 14.9**), click OK, and click Find Album Info in the upper right-hand corner of Windows Media Player (you may have to click it twice).

After a few seconds, the album cover magically appears in the Windows Media Player screen, along with the names of the tracks on your CD and additional album information (**Figure 14.10**).

7. If the information is correct, click Finish.

If the information is incorrect, click Search to search a different database for the information, or Edit to edit the info by hand.

The correct track titles and artist information are now registered in Windows Media Player and displayed (**Figure 14.11**).

To copy music files from a CD to your computer:

1. On your computer, launch Windows Media Player.

2. Insert an audio CD into your computer's CD-ROM drive.

3. Import the album information as described in the previous task, if necessary.

4. Click the "Copy from CD" button.

All the tracks on the CD appear in a list, as shown back in Figure 14.11.

5. Keep the preset check mark next to each track that you want to copy from the CD.

continues on next page

GETTING MUSIC AND VIDEO ONTO POCKET PC

6. Click the Copy Music button in the upper right-hand corner of the screen.

Copying music can take a long time, as much as a couple minutes per song—it depends on the speed of your computer and CD drive.

The status of each track is shown in the Copy Status column. When a track is finished copying, the status will read "Copied to Library."

As you import your audio files, they're copied in Windows Media format (.wma) and placed in the Media Library.

7. Still in Windows Media Player, click the Media Library button and click All Music in the left-hand pane to see your audio files (**Figure 14.12**).

✔ Tips

■ You can also buy and download music and movies from Internet services such as Napster, Rhapsody, MusicNow, CinemaNow, and dozens of others. To find them, search your favorite search engine for "download music" or "download video." Always be mindful of copyright infringement.

■ It is relatively difficult and possibly illegal to copy DVDs to your hard disk, where you could burn them as new DVDs. That said—and bearing in mind recent media industry file-sharing and copyright-infringement crackdowns, and after somber reflection upon the very understandable financial reasons why artists and entertainment companies want to protect what they work so hard to create, and after preparing yourself for a labyrinth of disclaimers, winks, and nods—one might be interested, from a purely educational perspective, in visiting a Web site such as www.doom9.org.

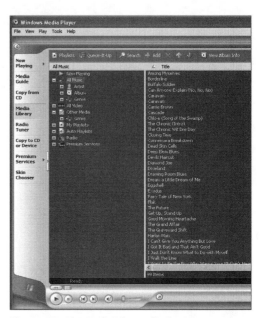

Figure 14.12 The Media Library displays your music files. Tap column headings to sort files by different criteria.

To copy music and video files from your computer to your Pocket PC:

1. Connect your Pocket PC to your computer.

2. On your computer, go to the My Documents folder or a subfolder of it, where your media files are stored (**Figure 14.13**).

continues on next page

My Music folder, which we created to store music files in

My Documents folder   Music files stored in My Documents /My Music folder

Name	Size	Type	Date Modified
Louis13	3,606 KB	Mpeg Audio	10/18/2003 3:47 PM
Louis14	3,485 KB	Mpeg Audio	10/18/2003 3:47 PM
Louis15	3,868 KB	Mpeg Audio	10/18/2003 3:47 PM
Louis16	3,541 KB	Mpeg Audio	10/18/2003 3:58 PM
Louis17	3,994 KB	Mpeg Audio	10/18/2003 4:01 PM
Louis18	3,257 KB	Mpeg Audio	10/18/2003 3:55 PM
Louis19	3,778 KB	Mpeg Audio	10/18/2003 4:09 PM
Lover Man (Ellington)	3,152 KB	Mpeg Audio	10/17/2003 11:26 AM
Mood Indigo (Ellington)	2,973 KB	Mpeg Audio	10/17/2003 11:30 AM
Oh the Wind and the Rain	4,371 KB	Mpeg Audio	10/17/2003 11:30 AM
One Piece at a Time	3,745 KB	Mpeg Audio	10/17/2003 11:30 AM
Panama	6,001 KB	Mpeg Audio	10/18/2003 3:41 PM
Perdido (Ellington)	3,034 KB	Mpeg Audio	10/17/2003 11:30 AM
Prelude to a Kiss (Ellington)	2,908 KB	Mpeg Audio	10/17/2003 11:28 AM
Ring of Fire	2,466 KB	Mpeg Audio	10/17/2003 11:30 AM
Sample Music	1 KB	Shortcut	9/25/2001 5:46 PM
Sophisticated Lady (Ellington)	2,597 KB	Mpeg Audio	10/17/2003 3:55 PM
Sunday Morning Coming Down	3,864 KB	Mpeg Audio	10/17/2003 4:05 PM
Sweethearts	4,475 KB	Mpeg Audio	10/17/2003 4:10 PM
Swing Low, Sweet Chariot	3,274 KB	Mpeg Audio	10/17/2003 4:13 PM
Take the A Train (Ellington)	2,803 KB	Mpeg Audio	10/17/2003 2:29 PM
Thank You (Dido)	3,413 KB	Mpeg Audio	10/17/2003 11:34 AM
Thank You (Tori Amos)	3,591 KB	Mpeg Audio	10/17/2003 11:34 AM
The Chronic (Intro)	1,846 KB	Mpeg Audio	10/18/2003 4:56 PM
The Chronic Wit Dre Day	4,563 KB	Mpeg Audio	10/17/2003 11:27 AM
The Future	6,304 KB	Mpeg Audio	10/17/2003 11:21 AM
The Grand Affair	3,501 KB	Mpeg Audio	10/17/2003 11:27 AM
The Red Rose Cafe	3,792 KB	Mpeg Audio	10/17/2003 11:30 AM
Thousands Are Sailing	5,136 KB	Mpeg Audio	10/17/2003 11:34 AM
Track01	6,000 KB	Mpeg Audio	10/18/2003 3:11 PM
Track02	535 KB	Mpeg Audio	10/18/2003 3:09 PM
Track04	2,602 KB	Mpeg Audio	10/17/2003 11:48 AM
Track05	2,789 KB	Mpeg Audio	10/17/2003 11:48 AM
Track06	3,134 KB	Mpeg Audio	10/17/2003 11:51 AM
Turkish Song of the Damned	3,249 KB	Mpeg Audio	10/17/2003 11:35 AM
Waiting for the Miracle	7,236 KB	Mpeg Audio	10/17/2003 11:37 AM
When I Win the Lottery	3,408 KB	Mpeg Audio	10/17/2003 11:37 AM

Figure 14.13 Keep your music files in a subfolder of your My Documents folder called My Music, and your video files in one called My Videos.

GETTING MUSIC AND VIDEO ONTO POCKET PC

3. Choose the files you want to copy, and then copy them to the Pocket_PC My Documents folder (or, we suggest, a subfolder of it that you create, called My Music).

ActiveSync synchronizes the files onto your device.

or

1. On your computer, start Windows Media Player.

2. Click the "Copy to CD or Device" button.

All the available media files on your computer will be displayed in a list in the left-hand pane (**Figure 14.14**).

3. Keep the check mark next to each track you want to copy to your Pocket PC (all files are automatically checked for you).

4. In the Items on Device drop-down list (not shown in Figure 14.14) in the upper right-hand corner of the screen, click to choose your Pocket PC's icon.

5. Click the Copy button in the upper right-hand corner of the screen.

The files are copied to your Pocket PC and placed in its My Documents folder.

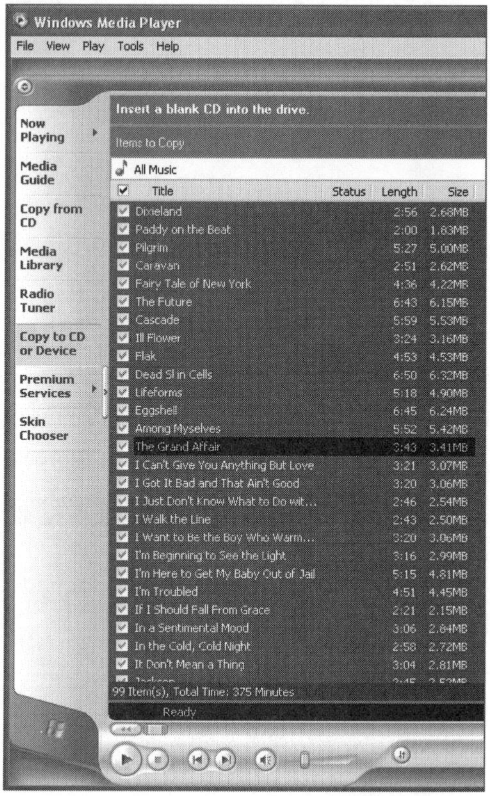

✔ Tips

■ It's a good idea to create My Music and My Video subfolders in your Pocket PC's My Documents folder and move media files to them. That way, they stay organized—and will still be recognized by Windows Media Player on your device, because they're still in the My Documents folder. However, you can't then store music in subfolders of the My Music subfolder (you can, but Windows Media won't find them). The alternate is to create a subfolder for each artist instead of a My Music subfolder.

Figure 14.14 Media files available to copy appear in Windows Media Player's Items to Copy pane.

■ Media files are large—a minute of video weighs in at 8–10MB, and a song typically ranges 2–6MB in size. Ten long songs, therefore, could consume up to 60MB of space. So it's not practical to think you can store your media library on your device. Instead, store your songs and videos on your computer and refresh them on your device before heading out for the day. Or buy an SD or CompactFlash storage card—for $50–100 USD, you can get one big enough (256MB or more) to store a lot of media.

Figure 14.15 The Local Content folder in your playlist shows all the media files available to play on your device.

Figure 14.16 A Windows Media video, as it appears on the Pocket PC. (That's our dog, Grendel, barking at a squirrel.)

Playing Music and Video Files

Playing music and video in Windows Media Player works much like it does on your computer. The program turns your device into a portable MP3 and video player, though with much more limited storage space than, say, an iPod. Files that are stored on your device are called *local content*.

You can also use your device to play Windows Media files straight off the Web—known as *streaming media*—provided you can connect your Pocket PC to the Internet. And if you've used digital music programs (such as Music-Match or WinAmp) before, you'll be pleased to know that you can mix and match your music collection into organized playlists, depending on your mood.

To play a music or video file:

1. On your Pocket PC, tap Start > Windows Media to launch Windows Media Player on your Pocket PC (see nearby sidebar "Using Windows Media Player's controls" for a full description of the Windows Media Player screen and controls).

2. In Windows Media Player, tap Playlist to display the files available for playing (**Figure 14.15**).

   Make sure the Local Content folder is selected, so that every playable music and video file on your device is displayed.

3. Tap a file to select it, and then tap the Play icon to play the file.

   or

   Press and hold the stylus on a file and tap "Play selection" in the pop-up menu that appears.

   The music or video file is played (**Figure 14.16**).

continues on page 13

PLAYING MUSIC AND VIDEO FILES

267

Using Windows Media Player's controls

Windows Media Player is fairly studded with icons, menus, and buttons whose functions may not be immediately clear. Here is a visual guide to the main screen:

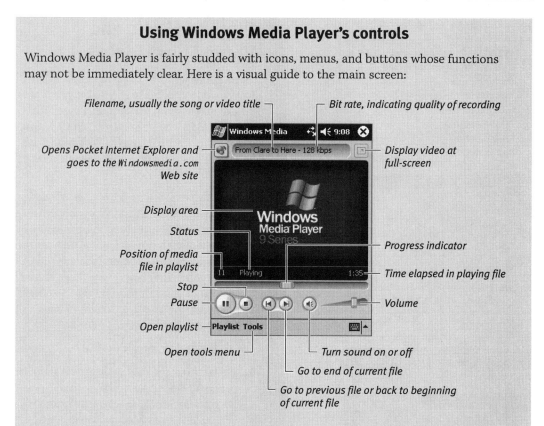

Tapping the Playlist menu opens the Playlist screen, which displays the media files available for play and offers more controls, as shown here:

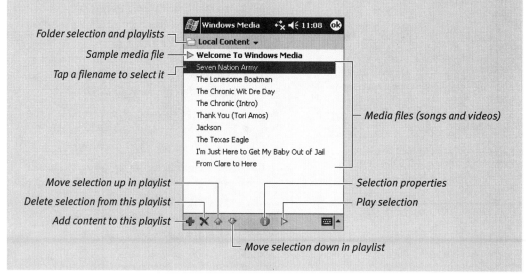

Figure 14.17 Full-screen mode fills up your device's entire screen with the video image.

✔ Tips

■ Always use headphones to listen to music on your device (the headphone jack is probably along its top or bottom). Playing songs through the built-in speaker is like listening to a 1960s transistor shortwave radio. For video, if you're watching it by yourself, headphones still make for a better experience. But if you're showing your video to someone else, the built-in speaker will probably have to do.

■ Some video files are at a larger resolution than the device's little window finds comfortable—they display beyond the edges of the Windows Media Player screen. You can display the whole video image by tapping the Full screen button in the upper right-hand corner of the Windows Media Player screen. When you do, the Pocket PC's entire screen will be filled with your video, which will play "sideways"—taking advantage of the more natural landscape orientation of the device's shape (**Figure 14.17**). To return to normal view, tap anywhere on the screen, and the Player will appear again.

■ Adjust the volume by dragging the Volume control right for louder, left for softer. Or use the physical volume button if your device has one (they are independent of each other).

■ Tap the Pause button to pause play and the Stop button to stop.

■ Tap the left arrow button to rewind and the right-arrow to skip to the end of the song or video.

■ Tap Mute to mute the sound. Tap it again to turn Mute off and make the sound come back again.

■ Drag the Progress indicator left and right to begin playing the song or video at any desired point.

- It's easy to find additional information about a music or video file. In the file list screen, accessible by tapping Playlist, tap a file to select it, and then tap the Selection properties button. The file list screen splits, and the bottom part displays information about the file, including the file's duration, filename, location on your device, file size, bit rate (quality), codec (format), video size (in pixels), audio sampling rate (in kHz), and protected status (whether it's copyrighted and unavailable for sharing with others).

To change audio and video settings:

1. In Windows Media Player on your Pocket PC, tap Tools > Settings > Audio & Video.

   The Audio Video screen appears (**Figure 14.18**).

   ▲ Tap the "While using another program" drop-down list and tap "Pause playback" if you want Windows Media Player to pause files when you switch to another program, or tap "Continue playback" to let media—music, presumably—keep playing while you work in other programs.

   ▲ Tap the "Play video in full screen" drop-down list. Tap Never to disable the full-screen video playback feature; tap "Only when oversized" to only allow full-screen video playback if the video doesn't fit on the normal Windows Media Player screen; tap Always to always play videos in full screen mode.

   ▲ Put a check next to "Shrink to fit in window" to force all videos to fit in the normal Windows Media Player screen.

   ▲ Put a check by "Rotate 180 degrees in full screen" to make full-screen video appear oriented 90 degrees clockwise on the screen, instead of the 90 degrees counter-clockwise (the default).

Figure 14.18 You can change aspects of how your audio and video files play in the Audio Video screen.

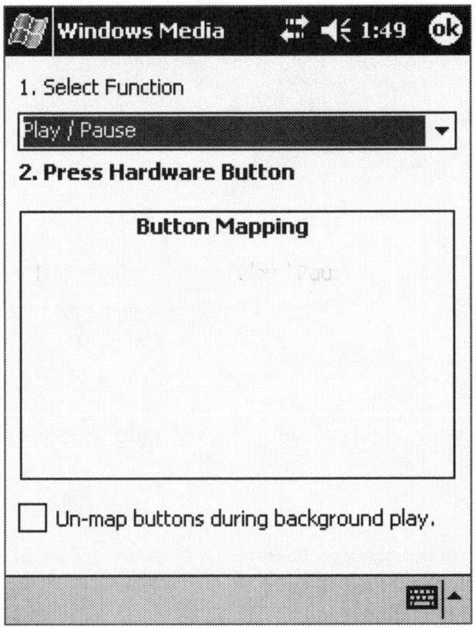

Figure 14.19 Reprogram the Program buttons in the Button Mapping screen.

Figure 14.20 After selecting the function, press the button you want to reprogram.

To reset program buttons to play media files:

1. In Windows Media Player on your Pocket PC, tap Tools > Settings > Buttons.

The Button Mapping screen appears (**Figure 14.19**).

2. Tap the Select Function drop-down list and tap the function you want the button to control—for example, Play/Pause, which lets you play a file and then pause it by pressing the same button again.

3. Press the physical program button on your Pocket PC that you want to execute that function.

The button is entered in the Button Mapping area (**Figure 14.20**).

4. Repeat for each button you want to reprogram.

✔ Tips

■ Mapping a button to the Screen Toggle function lets you turn off the screen during play, which greatly increases battery life.

■ You can only program four buttons because there are only four program buttons on the face of your Pocket PC.

■ Check the box next to "Un-Map buttons during background play" to retain the original functions of the program buttons while Windows Media Player is playing in the background—that is, while you're listening to music but working in another program.

■ Undo your button reprogramming by tapping Un-Map in the Select Function drop-down list and pressing the button.

To play a streaming audio or video file on the Web:

1. Connect your Pocket PC to the Internet.

or

Connect your Pocket PC to your computer and connect your computer to the Internet.

2. In Pocket Internet Explorer on your Pocket PC, go to a Web site with streaming audio or video, such as `mobile.windowsmedia.com` (**Figure 14.21**).

3. Tap the link you want to play.

If it's a playable streaming Windows Media file, Windows Media Player will open and play the file (**Figure 14.22**).

To add a Web Favorite:

1. Play a streaming audio or video file on your Pocket PC, as described in the preceding task.

2. Tap Tools > Add Web Favorite.

The Favorite Name screen appears (**Figure 14.23**).

3. Change to the name in the highlighted field if you want.

The name should be descriptive enough that you can recognize it days or weeks later.

4. When the name of the Web Favorite appears as you want it, tap OK.

The online file is added to your Web Favorites (**Figure 14.24**).

Figure 14.21 On your Pocket PC, go to a Web site that offers streaming Windows Media files.

Figure 14.22 When you click on a Windows Media link, Windows Media Player launches and plays the media file.

Figure 14.23 Add a favorite Windows Media Web site to Web Favorites so you can access it in the future.

Figure 14.24 A Web Favorite appears in the list of Web Favorites.

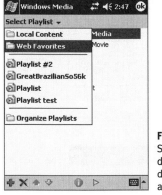

Figure 14.25 The Select Playlist drop-down menu displays the folders available.

Figure 14.26 Open a URL for a Windows Media file directly in Windows Media Player.

To play a Web Favorite:

1. Connect your Pocket PC to the Internet.

   or

   Connect your Pocket PC to your computer and connect your computer to the Internet.

2. In Windows Media Player on your Pocket PC, tap Playlist to display the file list screen.

3. Tap the drop-down list box in the upper left-hand corner of the screen to display the available folders (**Figure 14.25**).

4. Tap Web Favorites.

5. Tap a Web favorite to select it.

6. Tap the Play button to play the Web Favorite.

   Windows Media Player connects and plays the file.

✔ Tip

■ If you know the URL of a Windows Media file, you can open it directly in Windows Media Player by tapping Tools > Open URL and entering the URL in the Location to Open box (**Figure 14.26**).

Using Playlists

It's all well and good to have several songs available to play on your device, but in what order should they play? And which ones? That's where playlists come in. They let you turn the jumble of music files on your Pocket PC into the equivalent of party tapes. Each playlist can evoke a certain sustained mood, build intensity, orchestrate your emotions according to a plan, or what have you.

To create a playlist:

1. In Windows Media Player on your Pocket PC, tap Playlists to display the file list screen.

2. Tap the drop-down list box and tap Organize Playlists in the box that drops down.

   The Organize playlists screen appears (**Figure 14.27**).

3. Tap the New button to display the Save As screen (**Figure 14.28**).

4. Enter a name for your playlist in the Name box.

5. Tap the Folder box and tap a folder in the drop-down list to store your playlist there.

   Don't bother tapping the Type box because you only have one type of playlist to choose from: Windows Media Playlist.

6. In the Location box, tap to select in which area of memory to store the playlist: Main memory, some type of file store, or a storage card (if you have one).

7. Tap OK.

   The "Select files to add:" screen appears (**Figure 14.29**).

Figure 14.27 Organize Playlists lets you create, rename, and delete playlists.

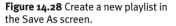

Figure 14.28 Create a new playlist in the Save As screen.

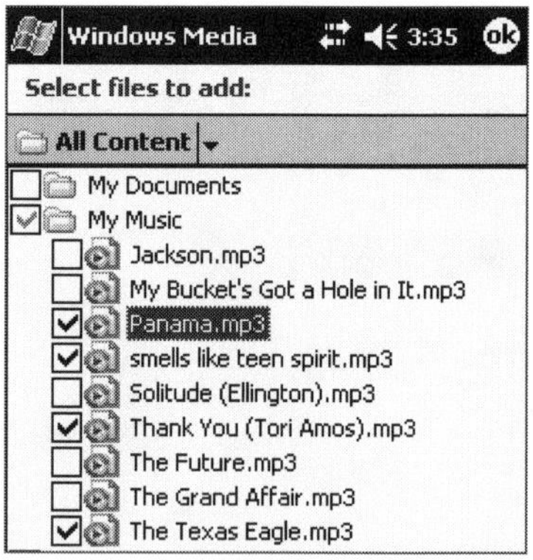

Figure 14.29 Choose files to add to your playlist.

Figure 14.30 The playlist is added to your other playlists.

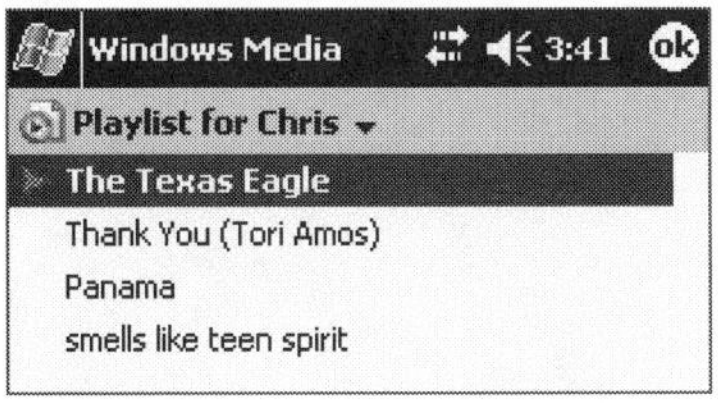

Figure 14.31 Choose a playlist to play.

Figure 14.32 Tap Shuffle and/or Repeat to play media in random order and/or to repeat them.

8. Put check marks next to each song (and/or video) you want in your playlist.

9. Tap OK when you're done.

The playlist appears in the file list screen (**Figure 14.30**).

✔ Tips

■ The playlist plays in the order showing on the screen. Move selections up and down the list by tapping to select them and tapping the up or down arrows. Tap the X to delete an entry and + to add one.

■ You can create as many playlists as you like.

To play a playlist:

1. In the file list screen, tap the drop-down list box to display your playlists.

2. Tap the playlist you want to select (**Figure 14.31**).

3. Tap the Play button to begin playing the playlist.

✔ Tips

■ You can play your playlist in random order by tapping Tools > Shuffle (**Figure 14.32**).

■ To repeat your playlist ad infinitum, tap Tools > Repeat.

■ Delete a playlist by tapping Playlist, tapping the drop-down list, and tapping Organize Playlists. In the Organize Playlists screen, tap to select the playlist and then tap Delete.

USING PLAYLISTS

Customizing Windows Media Player

Apparently it's not enough to be able to play music on your Pocket PC—you have to have the coolest "skin" as well. Skins are like different clothes that Windows Media Player can change into. They add color and variety to the display of the player while retaining the same functionality. If you get bored with the generic look of Windows Media Player, try giving it some skin.

To change the appearance of Windows Media Player:

1. Connect your device to your computer.

2. On your computer, go to the Microsoft Powertoys for Pocket PC page at www.microsoft.com/windowsmobile/ resources/downloads/pocketpc/ powertoys.mspx, scroll down, and click the Download Now link for "Windows Media Skin Chooser for Pocket PCs" (**Figure 14.33**).

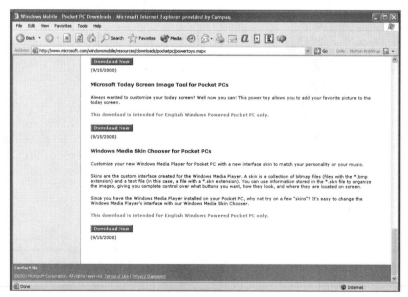

Figure 14.33 You can download Windows Media Skin Chooser for Pocket PC to customize the look and feel of the program.

3. Click to accept the license agreement.

4. In the dialog box that appears, click Open to download the Skin Chooser Powertoy.

5. When the download is finished, exit all Windows programs except ActiveSync.

6. In the Welcome dialog box that appears, click Next.

7. Click Next again to begin installing the Skin Chooser Powertoy.

8. Follow the instructions until you finish installing. (You may have to soft reset your device to get the Skin Chooser to work.)

continues on next page

Other media players

If you're a music freak and really want the best, try **PocketMusic Player**, which makes Windows Media Player seem like a Fisher-Price turntable. It plays .wma, .ogg, .mp1, .mp2, and .mp3 files, has a ten-band equalizer, a bookmarks feature for audio books, an "extra bass" setting, playlist organizer—the list goes on and on. Download it for free by searching for "PocketMusic" at: www.pocketgear.com

Another one is **Pocket Player** by Conduits (www.conduits.com), a superb player and very powerful.

Real Networks, which makes the **RealOne Player** for computers, has a version for the Pocket PC. You can download it for free at: http://www.realnetworks.com/mobile/player/ppc/index.html

This player allows you to play the popular RealAudio and RealVideo file formats.

Macromedia Flash is another popular media format. There is a Flash player for the Pocket PC available for free download from Microsoft at: www.microsoft.com/windowsmobile/resources/downloads/pocketpc/default.mspx

Scroll down and click on the Macromedia Flash Player link.

CUSTOMIZING WINDOWS MEDIA PLAYER

9. On your Pocket PC, tap Start > Programs > Windows Media Skin Chooser to see the skins available (**Figures 14.34** and **14.35** show two examples).

10. In Windows Media Player, tap Tools > Settings > Skin Chooser to choose a different skin for your player.

Figure 14.34 The skin "Silver" is a mild update of the default look and feel of Windows Media Player.

Figure 14.35 "Tech Purple" is a little more radical, but wearing it, Windows Media Player functions exactly the same as always.

Turning your Pocket PC into a universal remote control

You can use your Pocket PC's infrared capability to run your TV, VCR, CD player, DVD player, cable, and satellite—up to 30 different devices—with a remarkable piece of software called **TV Remote Controller**. It can "learn" about your devices and then set them up. It costs around $15. Go to www.handango.com and search for "TV Remote Controller."

There are other remote control programs for the Pocket PC, but this one won a People's Choice Award.

Some Pocket PC's, such as the iPAQ 2215, have this remarkable capability built in.

VIEWING PHOTOS IN PICTURES

As if it's not enough that your Pocket PC provides you with the means to check email, listen to music, update spreadsheets, read books, and surf the Web, it is also a photo album. It solves the problem of how to fit your favorite photos of your dog/child/ spouse into your wallet for viewing and sharing: store them on your Pocket PC and view them in Pictures, the photo viewing program that comes installed on it.

Pictures shows off your photos as they are, sure—but it also enables you to crop, adjust brightness and contrast, zoom in and out of photos, and then save your adjustments. You can share photos by emailing or beaming. Perhaps best of all, you can now view the photos of your last vacation from the confines of your cubicle and still seem, from a distance anyway, as if you're hard at work.

Looking at Photos in Pictures

After you synchronize digital photographs from your computer to your Pocket PC, the Pictures program displays them with surprising clarity and brightness. If you have an iPAQ, you can also view your photos with the iPAQ Image Viewer (but you can't edit them—see the sidebar later in this chapter). The first thing you'll need to get started, though, is to get some photographs saved on your Pocket PC.

To get photos onto your Pocket PC:

1. Connect your device to your computer with ActiveSync.

2. On your computer, using Windows Explorer (right-click My Computer and click Explore), drag photos from their folder to the Pocket_PC My Documents folder (**Figure 15.1**).

In Windows Explorer, drag photos from your hard drive to your device's My Pictures folder

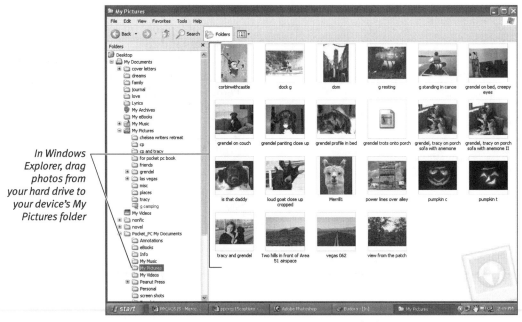

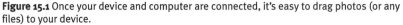

Figure 15.1 Once your device and computer are connected, it's easy to drag photos (or any files) to your device.

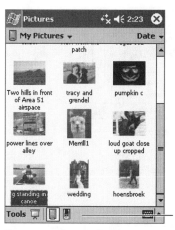

— Menu bar

Figure 15.2 Pictures displays your photos as thumbnails, so it's easy to see which ones you might want to tap on to view.

Figure 15.3 Tapping a thumbnail displays the photo at a larger size for viewing.

✔ Tips

- Tap OK to close the photo and return to thumbnail view.

- Tap Tools > Options > General tab to view the Options screen. Here, you can choose to enable dithering, a kind of "color smoothing," and you can also set the Pictures program to open automatically when your device detects a digital camera storage card.

Actually, we recommend creating a My Pictures subfolder within the My Documents folder and placing your photos there.

or

▲ Drag the photos to your device's storage card icon (if you have one).

or

▲ Email photos to yourself and synchronize your email.

or

▲ Beam photos from another device.

ActiveSync copies the files to the My Pictures folder (or a subfolder) on your device, and now they can be opened.

✔ Tip

- Pictures can display files in either .bmp (Windows bitmap) or .jpg formats. If you have photos in other formats, you'll need to convert them to one of these two first with an image-editing program on your computer.

To open a photo:

1. Tap Start > Programs > Pictures.

   You will see thumbnails (small "thumb-size" photo images) of all the viewable photos currently in the My Pictures folder (**Figure 15.2**).

   If you don't see the thumbnails, tap the ▢ Pocket PC icon on the menu bar (if your photos are stored in My Pictures) or the ▢ storage card icon if your photos are on a storage card.

2. Tap a thumbnail to open the photo (**Figure 15.3**).

LOOKING AT PHOTOS IN PICTURES

281

To delete a photo:

1. Press and hold the stylus on the thumbnail of a photo and tap Delete from the pop-up menu that appears (**Figure 15.4**).

2. Confirm your choice when prompted to. The photo will be deleted from the Pictures thumbnail screen as well as from the My Documents folder.

✔ Tip

■ Due to a programming bug, to delete photos that have been edited in Pictures, you have to close the program and reopen it.

To send a photo via beam or email:

◆ Press and hold the stylus on a thumbnail and, in the pop-up menu that appears, tap either "Beam Picture..." to prompt beaming or "Send via Email..." to send the photo in an email (**Figure 15.5**).

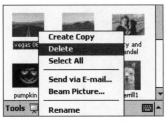

Figure 15.4 Delete a photo in Pictures just as you would any other file you see on your Pocket PC—by pressing and holding and tapping Delete.

Figure 15.5 Press and hold on a thumbnail and select whether you want to beam or email a photo to someone.

LOOKING AT PHOTOS IN PICTURES

Viewing photos in iPAQ Image Viewer

With some iPAQ models, you can view individual photos and create and view slide shows with iPAQ Image Viewer, a program that comes pre-installed. To access the program, tap Start > Programs > iPAQ Image Viewer.

The first time you open Image Viewer, you won't have any images stored there. Tap File > Look In and navigate your way to My Pictures (assuming you have copied images to that folder). You can also use the Location bar at the top of the screen to navigate to your photo files. Tap OK and you return to Image Viewer and see thumbnails of all your images, as shown here:

On the menu bar, tap Edit > Sort Images and choose to sort images by name, file type, size, or date. Tap View > Information Window and a window appears just above the menu bar, giving you information about the photo thumbnail you have selected (file size, image type, and the date it was modified).

continues on next page

Viewing photos in iPAQ Image Viewer *(continued)*

Tap View > Full Screen and your photo image is blown up to fill your screen. Tap anywhere on the image to move automatically to the next image. Tap the triangle icon in the lower left-hand corner to see a menu offering the following options: Next, Previous, Go to... (then tap a photo file from the menu that appears), and End Show.

Finally, with the Show menu you can set up a photo slide show. Tap View Show to see a show of all the photos on your device (you can choose to advance from one image to another manually or to have your device advance them automatically). Tap Set Up Show to choose photos to be included and to choose other preferences such as orientation and transition effect. When viewing a show, tap the triangle icon in the lower left-hand corner to see a the menu commands Next, Previous, Go to... (then tap a photo file from the menu that appears), and End Show, as shown here:

Tap Hide Image to hide an image in a slide show. When you have set up your show, save it by tapping File > Save Show Settings As... and choosing a name for it.

You can also use the View and Show icons at the top of the screen to change viewing options.

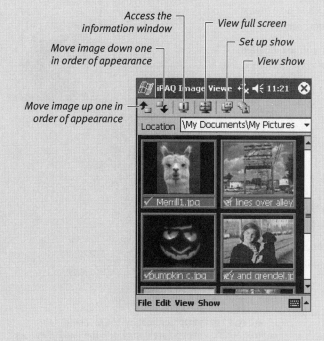

(4100 and 4300 series iPAQs have an app called iPAQ Image Zone instead.)

Editing Photos in Pictures

The Pictures program is more than just a fancy, electronic photo album—although it is that, and that in itself is pretty cool. With Pictures, you can also edit your photos. Although not anywhere near a top-of-the-line photo-editing program, Pictures does let you do the basics: cropping, zooming, and adjusting brightness and contrast.

To edit photos in Pictures:

1. Tap a thumbnail to open a photo.

2. From the menu bar, select from the following editing options:

   ▲ Tap Edit > Brightness and Contrast. A new menu appears. Tap the Up Contrast icon to increase contrast (**Figure 15.6**) and Down Contrast to decrease it.

   Tap the Up Brightness icon to increase brightness and Down Brightness to decrease it.

   Tap Done when you are done or Cancel to cancel the changes.

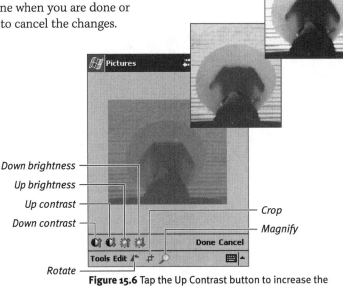

Down brightness
Up brightness
Up contrast
Down contrast
Crop
Magnify
Rotate

Figure 15.6 Tap the Up Contrast button to increase the contrast—hold until you are happy with the result. Tap Down Contrast if you go too far, as we may have done with our lonesome, post-surgery dog here.

Tap the Crop button and drag your stylus across the area of the photo you wish to be preserved–everything outside the box will be cropped

— *Crop button*

Figure 15.7 Just who is this handsome pair? It's hard to tell from so far away... but cropping can help.

Figure 15.8 Cropping photos is a good way to focus in on details, but beware that the quality of the image suffers for it.

Tap to arrange for best fit

Tap to zoom in

Tap to zoom out

Figure 15.9 Here we are zooming in on a happy dog in a canoe.

▲ Tap the Rotate icon on the menu bar to rotate your image. Tap OK when you are done. When prompted to save changes, tap Yes, No, or Cancel.

▲ Tap the Crop icon and then drag your stylus diagonally across the screen to select the area of the image you want to crop (**Figure 15.7**). Tap inside the box when prompted, and your image will be cropped (**Figure 15.8**).

▲ Tap the Magnify icon, and a smaller version of the screen appears in the lower right-hand side. Tap the Zoom In icon to zoom in (**Figure 15.9**), and the Zoom Out icon to zoom out.

Tapping the Best Fit icon displays the whole photo as large as possible within the screen again.

3. Tap OK to close the image.

You will be asked whether you want to save changes. Tap Yes, No, or Cancel. Note that saying Yes will overwrite the original version of the photo with the edited version—and resaving a .jpg image can result in loss of quality. Better to tap Cancel, then tap Tools > Save Picture As, and enter a new name for the photo.

continues on next page

EDITING PHOTOS IN PICTURES

✔ Tips

■ Tap Edit > Undo to undo an edit.

■ The safest way to ensure that you don't accidentally copy over a valued original photo with an edited version is to edit a renamed copy of the photo. Press and hold the photo you wish to edit and tap Create Copy from the pop-up menu that appears (**Figure 15.10**). Scroll down the copy (it will have the same filename as the original but with "(1)" (if it's the first copy after it). Tap and hold on the copy and tap Rename from the pop-up menu that appears. Rename the file something different from the original version. If you do attempt to save an edited photo, Pictures warns you before allowing the save (**Figure 15.11**).

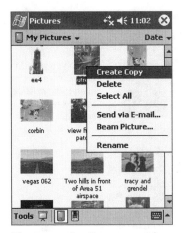

Figure 15.10 Creating a copy makes sure you don't save over the original.

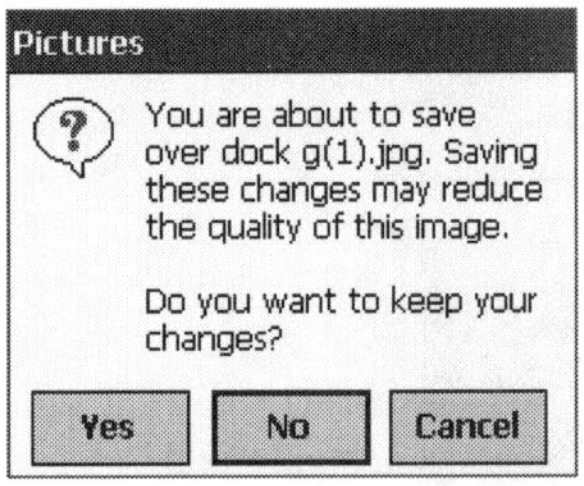

Figure 15.11 Pictures reminds you that you are saving over the original photo.

Taking pictures with your Pocket PC

The ViewSonic V36 was among the first Pocket PCs with a built-in digital camera to be available in the United States. Its camera can capture photos and small videos. Though it has no flash, and its photo-taking capabilities are somewhat limited, it's hard to not be intrigued by a Pocket PC that is also a camera.

But you don't have to have this flashy new device to take photos with your Pocket PC. You can buy a digital camera card that attaches to your device and enables you to take still photos. See Appendix C for more.

EDITING PHOTOS IN PICTURES

Figure 15.12 It's hard to show a slide show in a single still photo, but this is how you'll feel when you get your own slide show to work.

Pause ─┐   ┌─ Previous
Play ─┐ │   │ ┌─ Next
Flip View ─┐ │ │   │ │ ┌─ Close

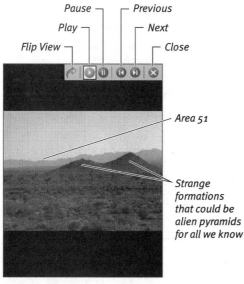

─ Area 51

Strange formations that could be alien pyramids for all we know

Figure 15.13 Is that an alien spacecraft looming over the hills of Area 51? Alas no, it's just the Slide show toolbar.

Displaying Photos as Slide Shows

Many of us have fond childhood memories of our dads whipping out the slide projector, setting up a screen (or removing pictures from a white wall), and our families gathering around to view slides of vacations, holidays, and other special events while chomping on popcorn. With Pictures, you can take your slide show with you wherever you go—and you don't have to fuss with the screen.

To view a slide show:

1. Tap the 🖳 Slide show icon in the menu bar.

   Your photos display in Slide show mode, appearing for about five seconds at a time, one after the other, and taking up the whole screen (**Figure 15.12**).

2. Tap anywhere on the screen.

   The Slide show toolbar appears at the top of the screen (**Figure 15.13**).

   ▲ Tap the Flip View button to switch to landscape view (tap it again to switch back).

   ▲ Tap the Play button to resume "playing" your slide show if you've paused it.

   ▲ Tap the Pause button to pause your slide show.

   ▲ Tap the Previous button to return to the previous photo.

   ▲ Tap the Next button to skip to the next photo.

   ▲ Tap the Close button to close your slide show and return to the main Pictures screen.

   continues on next page

✔ Tip

■ The Pictures program displays all of your photos with its slide show feature. If your device is an iPAQ, you may prefer the iPAQ Image Viewer's slide show, which lets you select the photos you want in a slide show and save different series of photos in separate slide shows. See the sidebar earlier in this chapter for more information.

To set slide show options:

1. Tap Tools > Options > Slide Show.
   The Slide Show Options screen appears (**Figure 15.14**).

2. In the "Delay between slides" field, set the amount of time you want to each photo in your slide show to display before moving on to the next. Enter a number in the box or use the up and down arrows to lengthen or shorten viewing time.

✔ Tip

■ You can choose to have your slide show appear as a screensaver when your device is in its cradle by checking the box next to "Play a screen saver when docked." Beneath that, select the amount of time you want your device to be idle before the screensaver appears.

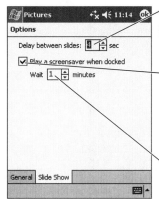

Select how long you want each photo to appear onscreen

Select whether you want your slide show to play as a screensaver when the device is in its cradle

Set how much time you want your device to wait before the screensaver appears

Figure 15.14 The Slide show Options screen lets you adjust how the slide show will display.

If you like Pictures, you'll love almost any other photo viewer

Photo viewing applications are usually among the top ten most popular downloads from places like Handango.com. Pictures, when compared to some of them, is less than impressive. Here are just a few that blow it out of the water.

Resco Picture Viewer is a very popular and highly functional program with a great desktop component to help prepare the photos. Get it for $19.95 from www.resco-net.com.

Picture Perfect is a fast viewer with nice slide show functionality. Available for $19.95 at www.applian.com.

Imageer is in beta at the time of this writing, but it should be released by the time this book is in your hands. It can open and view 11-megapixel images and anti-alias them so they look good on the Pocket PC. Also included are red eye reduction, brightness and contrast adjustments, auto-levels, RGB level adjustment, and more. Get it from www.spbsoftwarehouse.com.

READING eBOOKS

If you're like most people, you probably prefer reading an actual book to an electronic one—otherwise known as an *eBook*. After a day of sitting upright and staring at a computer screen, nothing beats curling up with a good book and getting absorbed in the printed word.

Of course, the problem with bound books arises when you aren't home on your couch, but waiting at a bus stop, standing in a subway, or in the middle of a dull lecture or long meeting. Most books are too big or bulky to carry around in your pocket, and they take up precious space in your bag. Few people would dream of whipping one out in the middle of a meeting. But with your Pocket PC, you can take stories with you without the burden of the printed book. You don't have to lug books around—you can summon them at will.

You can load your device with dozens of eBooks in every genre, including crime thrillers, self-help best-sellers, pocket dictionaries, calculus study guides, poetry, historical biographies, and classic novels. Once loaded on your Pocket PC, these eBooks are always there if you have a few minutes to kill. And if you want to give your eyes a rest—perhaps while you're driving to work—your Pocket PC can even read eBooks aloud to you.

Getting Started with Microsoft Reader

Microsoft Reader comes preloaded on your Pocket PC. Not only does it display eBooks in beautifully rendered type, it also lets you bookmark pages and annotate them with text notes, drawings, and an onscreen highlighter.

Microsoft also offers free versions of Reader for PCs and Tablet PCs, so you can read your eBooks on those platforms as well. But Reader makes the most sense on the Pocket PC, which is small enough that you can hold it like a book.

If you want to read commercial, copy-protected eBooks—and many of the eBooks you'll find online are copy protected—you must first activate your Pocket PC by registering at Microsoft's Web site. Activation enables your computer and Pocket PC to read secure content and ties your Pocket PC to your .NET Passport account. (You might already have a .NET Passport: Hotmail email addresses and MSN member names are valid Passports, so you can use one of those if you have one. If you don't have a .NET Passport account, you'll have to sign up for one during the activation process.)

Once you've activated your Pocket PC, only you can read the commercial eBook you've downloaded. You can't share the eBook with friends, nor can you post it on the Internet for friends and strangers to download (well, you can, but they won't be able to read it).

Activation is controversial among Pocket PC users. Some say it's a pain and an invasion of privacy. Others shrug and ask, what's the big deal? Love it or hate it, one good thing about activation is that you only have to do it once.

Figure 16.1 Microsoft's Pocket PC Activation Web page has a link to a FAQ that addresses technical and privacy questions.

To activate your Pocket PC:

1. Connect your Pocket PC to your computer.

2. Connect your computer to the Internet.

3. In Internet Explorer on your computer go to `http://das.microsoft.com/activate/en/default.asp`.

   The Microsoft Reader Update Web page appears (**Figure 16.1**).

   This is the English language page. You can click on another language at the bottom of the page if you wish to activate in, say, Dutch or Italian.

4. If you already have a .NET Passport, clicking Sign In will take you to a page where you can log on to the site.

   If you don't have a .NET Passport, clicking No will produce a prompt for you to get a free Passport ID if you don't already have one.

5. After signing in, click the button labeled Activate your Pocket PC.

   Wait until you see the confirmation message "Activation components have been successfully downloaded to your device and installed." This may take a few minutes.

   Once you've activated your Pocket PC, you're done. If you decide to purchase and download commercial, copy-protected eBooks, you'll now be able to read them on your device.

✔ Tips

■ If you're prompted to sign up for a .NET Passport, you can use any email address, including one from a Web-based service such as Yahoo! Mail.

■ If you're worried about your privacy, click the Privacy link on the site for more info. But there's no need for alarm—the sign-up process is approximately as invasive as buying something on eBay, for example.

Installing eBooks

All files for Microsoft Reader eBooks have a .lit suffix, and installing them is as easy as copying .lit files over to the Pocket PC. You'll find thousands of free eBooks online. You can also buy eBooks from Amazon.com.

To install eBooks from the Pocket PC companion CD-ROM:

1. Connect your Pocket PC to your computer using ActiveSync (see Chapter 4).

2. Insert the Pocket PC companion CD-ROM into your computer's CD-ROM drive and navigate to the directory that contains the eBooks.

3. On your PC's desktop, open your Pocket_PC My Documents folder.

4. Drag the desired .lit files from the CD-ROM's folder into your Pocket_PC My Documents folder and wait until ActiveSync automatically copies them to your Pocket PC.

✔ Tip

■ Depending on the model of Pocket PC you have, you may not have books on your companion CD. But don't fret— there are other sources of great electronic reads.

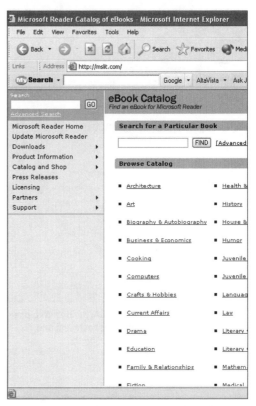

Figure 16.2 Browse for titles at Microsoft's online eBook catalog.

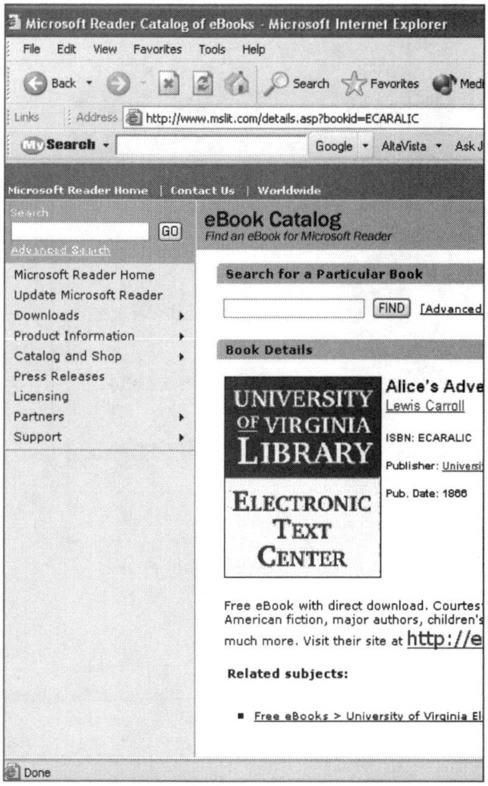

Figure 16.3 The University of Virginia Library Electronic Text Center is one of many Web sites offering free eBooks.

To download an eBook:

1. Go to a Web site that offers eBooks, such as the free area of www.mslit.com (**Figure 16.2**—scroll down the list of genres and click "Free eBooks").

2. Choose an eBook to download by clicking on a title.

You may be directed to another site to actually download the book, such as the University of Virginia Library (**Figure 16.3**).

3. Follow the directions to download the .lit file directly into your Pocket_PC My Documents folder. Each site will give different instructions.

The next time you sync your Pocket PC, ActiveSync will copy the eBook to your device.

✔ Tips

■ Microsoft Reader eBook files can eat up a lot of memory on your Pocket PC, so you might want to store them on an external storage card. (For more information on external storage cards for your Pocket PC, see Appendix C.) Microsoft Reader will find the files on your storage card as long as they're within a folder called My Documents. (If the folder isn't already there, you can create it using File Explorer.)

■ See Appendix A for other sites that offer eBooks for download.

■ If your device is connected to the Internet, tap Shop on the Library screen in Reader to be brought directly to www.mslit.com.

Browsing the Library in Microsoft Reader

Now that you've copied a book or two over to your Pocket PC, why not pause to admire your collection? You can do that in the Microsoft Reader Library. The Library is the home page of Microsoft Reader—it's the first thing you see when you launch the program.

To launch Microsoft Reader:

1. Tap Start > Programs.

   The Programs screen appears.

2. Tap Microsoft Reader.

   The Microsoft Reader Library appears on the screen. (**Figure 16.4**).

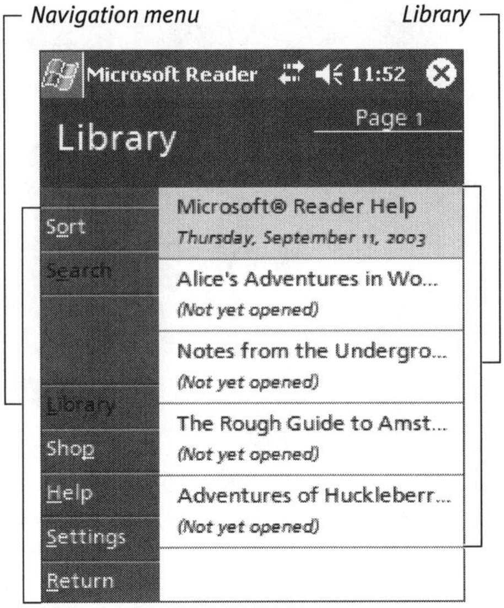

✔ Tips

■ If you see a small right arrow near the upper-right corner of the screen (next to "Page 1"), it means the list of eBooks in your Library extends to two or more pages. Tap the arrow to see more titles.

■ The Sort button in the Library lets you re-sort your books by Title, Author, Last Read, Book Size, or Date Acquired.

Navigation menu   Library

Figure 16.4 You can browse your Pocket PC's Library.

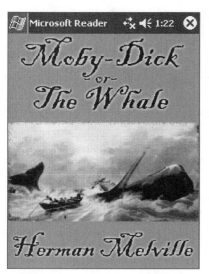

Figure 16.5 Just like paper books, cover images can set the mood for an eBook—or, in this case, give away the ending.

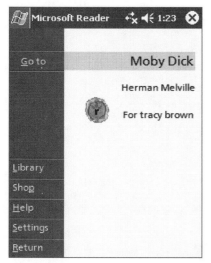

Figure 16.6 Covers pages of eBooks usually aren't much to look at, but they offer access to the handy Go To menu, located in the Navigation menu.

Reading and Navigating eBooks

Microsoft Reader offers a clean, spare interface intended to approximate the experience of reading a bound book. But if you poke around a bit, the program provides many ways of navigating through books and offers several hidden features, including the riffle feature.

Pressing and holding the stylus on the page number opens Riffle Control. Named after the sound that's created when you quickly flip through a paper book—*rrrriffle!*—you'll find riffling useful when you want to navigate quickly through several chapters, jump to a specific page, or just get a better idea of where you are within an eBook. The page number at the bottom right of the Riffle Control tells you how many pages are in the eBook you're reading.

It's time to check out a book from the Library stack and start reading.

To open an eBook:

◆ In the Library, tap a book title.

Depending on the title you choose, you might see a cover image (**Figure 16.5**) before being whisked away to the book's cover page. Unfortunately, not all eBooks have a cover image.

To use the Navigation menu:

◆ Click buttons in the Navigation menu, the red bar along the left-hand side of the screen (**Figure 16.6**).

The Navigation menu appears in most parts of the program, but not inside the pages of eBooks. The menu buttons change depending on what you're doing in Microsoft Reader, but you'll usually see options that let you change settings, get help, and return to the Library.

READING AND NAVIGATING EBOOKS

To start reading:

◆ From the Go To menu, choose Begin Reading (**Figure 16.7**).

This will take you to the first page of the book.

To turn pages:

◆ To go forward one page, tap the right arrow next to the page number (**Figure 16.8**). To go back one page, tap the left arrow.

or

◆ Press the bottom or the right side of the navigation button (**Figure 16.9**) to move forward a page. Press the top or the left side of it to go back a page.

To move quickly forward or backward through the book, press and hold down the right or left side of the navigation button.

✔ Tips

■ The navigation button frees you from having to use the stylus to turn pages, meaning you can read an eBook with one hand.

■ Some Pocket PCs, like the Toshiba e750, have a scroll wheel on the side of the device. Turning this scroll wheel up or down offers another handy way to turn pages.

Figure 16.7 The Go To menu, accessible from the cover page, lets you navigate within an eBook.

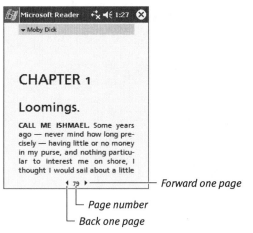

Forward one page

Page number

Back one page

Figure 16.8 The page number of an eBook is at the bottom—tap the little arrows next to it to move forward or back one page.

Navigation button

Figure 16.9 You can also use your Pocket PC's navigation button to move forward or backward through the text.

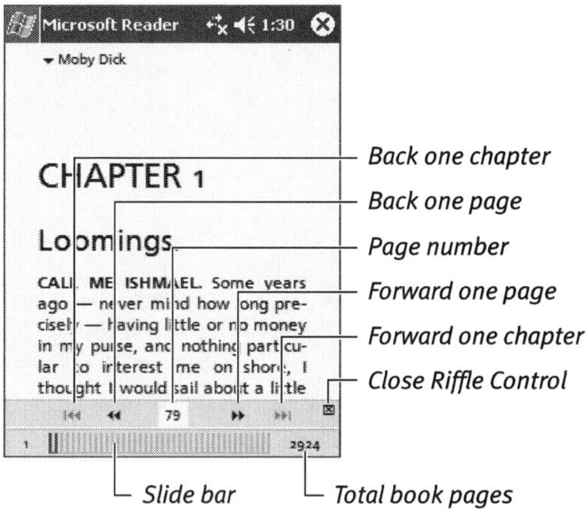

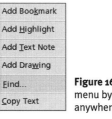

— Back one chapter
— Back one page
— Page number
— Forward one page
— Forward one chapter
— Close Riffle Control

Slide bar   Total book pages

Figure 16.10 The Riffle Control is another way to cruise through an eBook.

Add Book<u>m</u>ark
Add <u>H</u>ighlight
Add <u>T</u>ext Note
Add Dra<u>w</u>ing
<u>F</u>ind...
<u>C</u>opy Text

Figure 16.11 Access this pop-up menu by pressing and holding anywhere in the text.

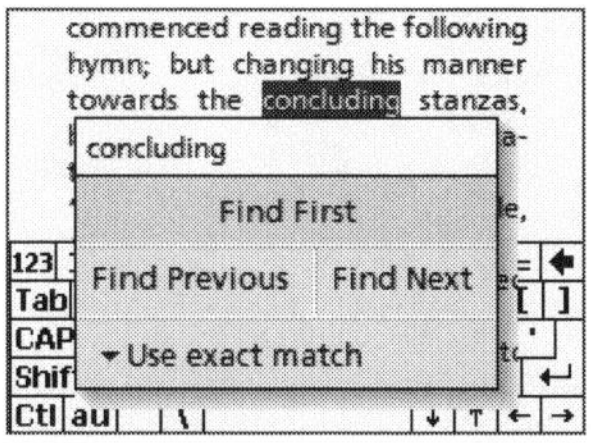

commenced reading the following hymn; but changing his manner towards the concluding stanzas,

concluding

Find First

Find Previous   Find Next

▾ Use exact match

123
Tab
CAP
Shif
Ctl au

Figure 16.12 To find a word (or words), enter text in the Find pop-up menu's white box and tap on one of the Find options.

To riffle through pages:

◆ To access Riffle Control, press and hold a page number at the bottom of a page for a few seconds (**Figure 16.10**). The Riffle Control appears.

◆ To quickly move through pages, drag the stylus along the Slide bar at the bottom of the Riffle Control.

◆ To skip forward and backward a chapter at a time, tap the section arrows located at either end of the Riffle control. (If the eBook has no chapters, the arrows are dimmed.)

◆ To close Riffle Control, tap the ⊗ close button in the upper right-hand corner.

To search for text:

1. Press and hold anywhere within an eBook and tap Find from the pop-up menu that appears (**Figure 16.11**).

2. Enter the text in the Find pop-up menu that appears.

   or

   Tap in the white portion of the Find pop-up menu, and enter the text you want to find (**Figure 16.12**).

   You can search for the first occurrence of the word, the next occurrence (from where you are), or the previous occurrence.

READING AND NAVIGATING EBOOKS

To peruse the table of contents:

1. Tap the eBook's title at the top of the page.

2. Tap Table of Contents in the pop-up menu that appears (**Figure 16.13**). The Table of Contents page appears.

3. Tap on a green underlined chapter title in the Table of Contents to go to that chapter (**Figure 16.14**).

✔ Tips

- Some books don't have a Table of Contents.

- Green underlined type indicates that the words are links, such as links on a Web site—only these links take you elsewhere in the book program.

To close an eBook:

1. Tap the eBook's title at the top of the page. A pop-up menu appears.

2. Choose Library. The eBook closes and returns you to the Library.

| Cover Page |
| Table of Contents |
| Annotations |
| Help |
| Library |
| Settings |
| Return |

Figure 16.13 Tap the book title to display the pop-up menu and then choose Table of Contents.

Table of Contents

"Looking-glass house"

1 ▶

Figure 16.14 In Table of Contents, tap an underlined link to go to that chapter (*Moby-Dick* didn't have these, but *Through the Looking-Glass and What Alice Found There* did).

Looking up words in Microsoft Reader

If you tend to read books with a big dictionary on hand, you may find Reader's Lookup feature to be a big plus. It allows you to tap an unfamiliar word to view its definition, but it doesn't appear as a menu choice until you download and install Microsoft's Encarta Pocket Dictionary on your Pocket PC. This is a free download at www.mslit.com.

Once you install this dictionary, you can look up a definition by tapping on a word in any eBook. Choose Lookup from the resulting pop-up menu, and the definition appears in a small box.

Tap outside the box to close it and get back to your reading.

Old age is always wakeful; as if, the longer linked with life, the less man has to do with aught that

Encarta® Pocket Dictionary

aught   Lookup...

i

aught *pron*
anything

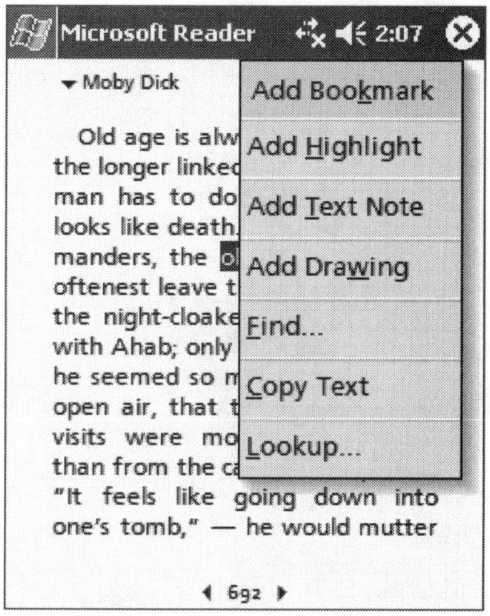

Figure 16.15 A pop-up menu appears when you highlight text and hold the stylus on the screen for a moment.

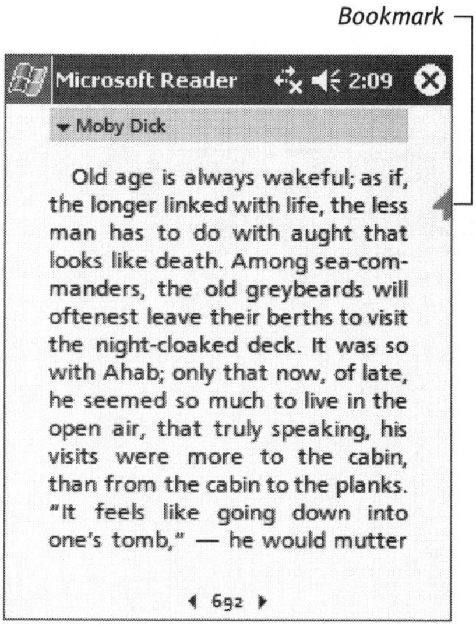

Figure 16.16 Bookmarks appear on the right side of the screen.

Adding Bookmarks and Annotations

With Microsoft Reader, you can add bookmarks, highlight text, add "sticky notes," and scribble doodles in your eBook, just as you would in a paper book (and you can edit and remove these comments, unlike those embarrassingly naïve queries you scribbled in your college texts). This can be helpful if you want to highlight passages to quote in a book report or a speech.

To create a bookmark:

1. Drag your stylus over a word or two at the place you want to bookmark.

2. From the pop-up menu, choose Add Bookmark (**Figure 16.15**).

   When you create a bookmark, it appears as an arrow along the right side of your screen (**Figure 16.16**). If you create multiple bookmarks, they appear in different colors. The colors start repeating after 12 bookmarks.

✔ Tips

- Within an eBook, you can tap and hold a bookmark to bring up a pop-up menu that lets you delete or change the bookmark's color.

- Before you go on a bookmarking binge, keep in mind that when you open an eBook, Microsoft Reader always remembers the most recent page you've visited—so you don't need to add a bookmark for this purpose. From the Go To menu, simply choose Most Recent Page or Furthest Read to navigate back to where you left off.

ADDING BOOKMARKS AND ANNOTATIONS

- To view a list of your bookmarks, tap the heading at the top of a page and tap Annotations from the pop-up menu. From the book title page, you only have to tap Annotations.

- To rename a bookmark, tap the bookmark icon and tap Rename in the pop-up menu that appears. Type the new name in the name field and tap Enter.

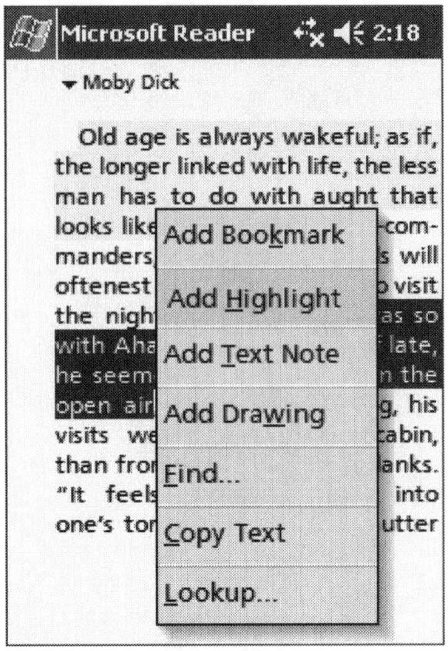

To highlight text:

1. Within an eBook, drag your stylus over the words you want to highlight.

2. Choose Add Highlight from the pop-up menu that appears (**Figure 16.17**).

✔ Tips

- To remove highlighting, drag your stylus back over the highlighted text, hold, and tap Edit Highlight in the resulting pop-up menu.

- To change the color of a highlight, select it by dragging your stylus over it (actually, just a part of it will do) and tap Edit Highlight on the pop-up menu that appears. Change the color of the highlight with the Color Selector pop-up menu.

- Select the highlight you want to delete by dragging your stylus over it. Tap Erase Highlight in the pop-up menu to get rid of it. Or tap and hold the highlighted item in Annotations and tap Delete in the pop-up menu that appears.

- View highlighted text from the cover page of an eBook by tapping Annotations.

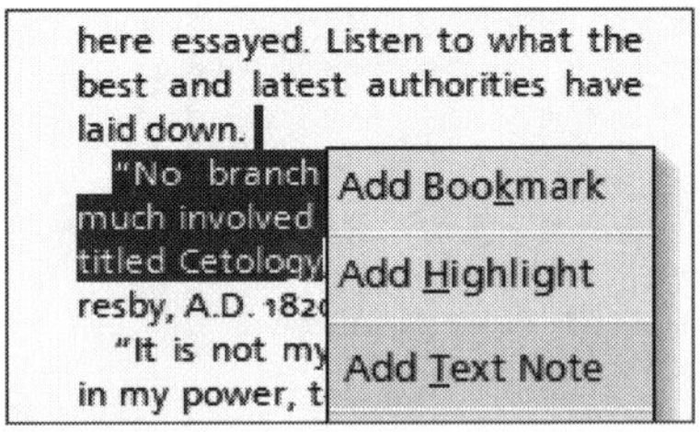

To add a text note:

1. Drag your stylus over the words you want to annotate with a text note.

2. Choose Add Text Note from the pop-up menu that appears (**Figure 16.18**).

Figure 16.17 The first line is now highlighted yellow (trust us). The text further down the screen is a selection that's about to be highlighted.

Figure 16.18 After you select a text block, tap Add Text Note in the pop-up menu.

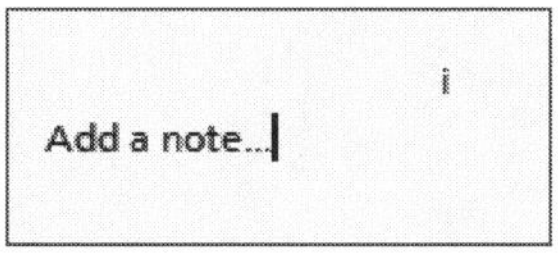

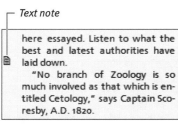

Figure 16.19 Enter the text of your note.

Text note

here essayed. Listen to what the best and latest authorities have laid down.
  "No branch of Zoology is so much involved as that which is entitled Cetology," says Captain Scoresby, A.D. 1820.

Figure 16.20 Text notes appear as teeny-tiny icons on the left side of the screen. Tapping on one of these icons opens the note.

Microsoft Reader   2:41

▼ Moby Dick

CHAPTER 42

The Whiteness of The Whale.

WHAT THE WHITE WHALE was to Ahab, has been hinted; what, at times, he was to me, as yet remains unsaid.

◄ 996 ►

| Done | ■ | Undo |

Figure 16.21 The Draw tool almost begs you to doodle on eBooks.

3. Enter your note using Transcriber or the keyboard (**Figure 16.19**).

4. Tap the note to minimize it (**Figure 16.20**).

✔ Tip

■ To delete a text note, press and hold on a text note icon. When the pop-up menu appears, select Delete.

To add a drawing:

1. Drag your stylus anywhere on the page where you want to add a drawing.

2. Choose Add Drawing from the pop-up menu that appears.

3. Scrawl away (**Figure 16.21**).

4. Tap Done at the bottom of the page when you're finished.

✔ Tip

■ Within an eBook, press and hold on a drawing icon, and a pop-up menu will let you delete or edit the drawing.

To view annotations:

1. Within an eBook, tap the book's title at the top of the page.

2. Choose Annotations from the pop-up menu that appears (**Figure 16.22**).

   The Annotations page appears (**Figure 16.23**).

3. Tap one of the annotations in the list to go to the page on which it appears.

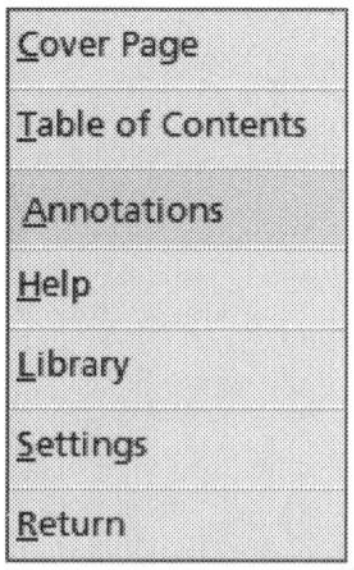

✔ Tips

- If you haven't made any annotations in a book, the annotations choice is grayed out, meaning it is unavailable.

- If you've made more than a few annotations, the Annotations section will spill over into two or more pages.

To rename or delete an annotation:

1. On the Annotations page, tap and hold any bookmark, drawing, or text note in the list.

   A pop-up menu appears (**Figure 16.24**).

2. Choose Rename or Delete from the pop-up menu.

   Rename highlights the name of the bookmark, drawing, or text note so that you can enter the new name.

   Delete deletes the annotation.

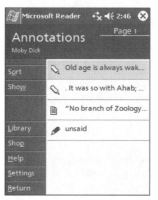

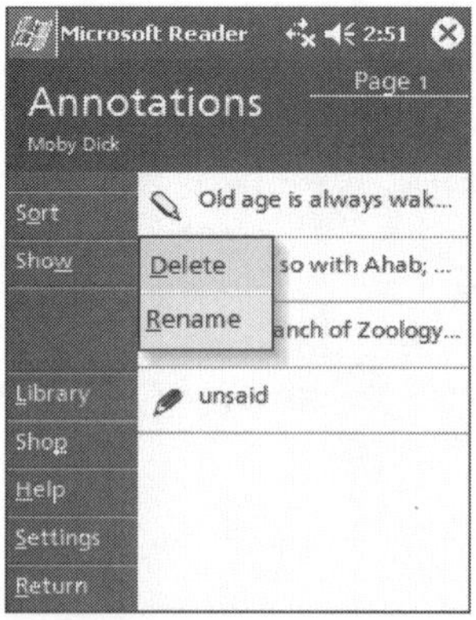

| Cover Page |
| Table of Contents |
| Annotations |
| Help |
| Library |
| Settings |
| Return |

Figure 16.22 Tap the title at the top of the page to access this pop-up menu.

Figure 16.23 The Annotations page is a handy place to see all your bookmarks, highlights, text notes, and drawings. Tapping an item here takes you to that annotation.

Figure 16.24 Pressing and holding on an annotation and choosing the relevant choice from the resulting menu lets you delete or rename it.

Adding Bookmarks and Annotations

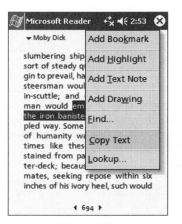

Figure 16.25 Tap Copy Text to copy the selection and paste it into another program. The catch? Reader only lets you select a page at a time.

Copying Text

If you want to copy text from an eBook into another program, there's good news and bad news. The good news is that you can in fact copy text from an eBook from within Microsoft Reader. The bad news is that you can only copy one page at a time.

This means you can't just copy a whole eBook and paste it into a Microsoft Word document, for example. That would defeat the elaborate copy-protection scheme of Reader, including the activation sign-up process that permits only your Pocket PC to read the eBooks you purchase. This limitation is the trade-off you accept when using copyrighted material on your Pocket PC.

To copy text from an eBook:

1. Drag the stylus over the text you want to copy.

(You can only drag down to the bottom of the current page.)

The text is highlighted to show that it's selected.

2. Press and hold the stylus in place on the selected text for a second.

3. Tap Copy Text in the pop-up menu that appears (**Figure 16.25**).

The selected text is copied and placed in the clipboard.

✔ Tip

■ Now if you launch another program, such as Pocket Word, you can paste the text into a file by tapping, holding, and selecting Paste from the pop-up menu that appears.

Changing eBook Settings

All the menus within Microsoft Reader offer to take you to the Settings page (**Figure 16.26**). In Settings you can change of the look and feel of the program (to a limited extent). For example, if you want more text to flow on a page, you may want to remove the navigational arrows that appear on every page. And if you find it difficult to read the small type on your Pocket PC, you can make the text bigger.

You can navigate through all three pages of settings by tapping the directional arrows at the top right of the Settings page. At any point you can use the Navigation menu to return to the screen you were in before you entered Settings.

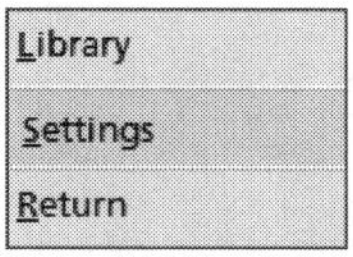

To change text size:

1. From within an eBook, tap the book's title at the top of the page and then tap Settings from the pop-up menu.

The Font Settings page appears (**Figure 16.27**).

2. Tap one of the dots on the Select Font Size bar to choose smallest, small, large, or largest font.

3. Tap Return on the Navigation menu to return to your eBook and see the change.

✔ Tips

■ In the Library, you can get to the Settings pages by tapping Settings in the Navigation menu on the left side of the page.

■ Changing the font size will change the page numbering of your eBook, so if you've added a drawing to a specific page, changing the font size may reflow that drawing to another page.

Figure 16.26 Tap Settings to access your Settings options.

Figure 16.27 The Font Settings page lets you increase or decrease the screen text size. Drag the slider left and right to reduce or enlarge.

CHANGING EBOOK SETTINGS

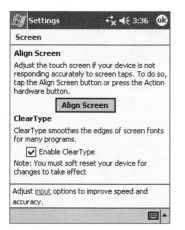

Figure 16.28 Make things a little easier on your eyes by enabling ClearType in the Screen Settings screen.

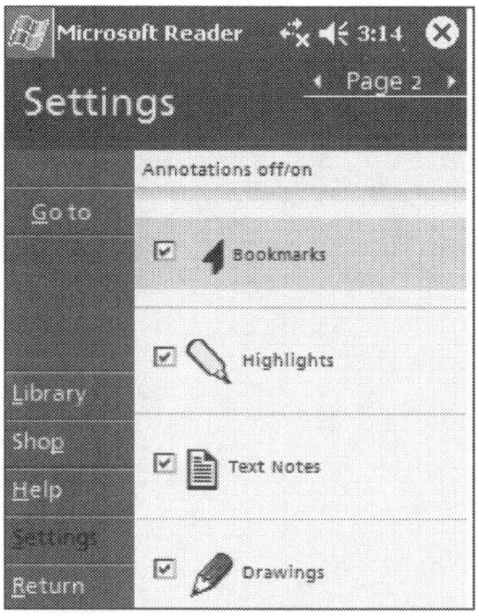

Figure 16.29 Depending on your mood, you can view or hide your annotations by checking or unchecking the options on the Annotations off/on Settings page.

- To turn on ClearType, which makes screen fonts a little gentler on the eyes, tap Today > Settings > System tab > Screen. In the Screen Settings screen that appears, check the box that says Enable ClearType and then tap OK (**Figure 16.28**). Then do a soft reset.

To hide annotations:

1. From within an eBook, tap the book's title in the header at the top of the page and then tap Settings from the pop-up menu.

   The Screen Settings page appears.

2. At the Screen Settings page, tap the top right directional arrow to go to Page 2, the "Annotations off/on" page (**Figure 16.29**).

3. Check or uncheck the check boxes for Bookmarks, Text Notes, Drawings, and Highlights.

   Items with checked boxes will display on the screen; items with unchecked boxes will be hidden.

Turn any Word file into an eBook

Microsoft offers a free add-in utility for Microsoft Word on the PC that lets you save files in the Microsoft Reader format. This offers a handy way to read business reports, memos, or white papers without having to carry a bulky laptop around. For information on how to download and install this utility, visit www.microsoft.com/reader/downloads/ and select "Read in Microsoft Reader add-in," which is found under Tools.

Reading eBooks with Palm Reader and Acrobat

Microsoft Reader isn't the only game in town. You can also install free eBook readers from Palm Digital Media and Adobe Systems.

If you've used a Palm handheld before, you may already be familiar with Palm Reader. Since the Palm Reader's original debut in the mid-1990s, new versions for different platforms have appeared, including Windows, Mac OS, and the Pocket PC. Like Microsoft Reader, Palm Reader has a spare, clean, intuitive interface (**Figure 16.30**). One difference: Palm Reader has a wider column, allowing more text to fit on the screen. This translates to less page flipping, saving wear and tear on stylus and thumb.

Since the Pocket PC comes preloaded with Microsoft Reader, you might wonder why you'd bother installing additional eBook readers. One advantage to installing Palm Reader is that there are more than 10,000 eBook titles available for it. If you can't find a book in Microsoft Reader format, it might well be available for the Palm Reader. (Browse the catalog at www.palmdigitalmedia.com.)

The granddaddy of eBook formats is Adobe Acrobat, Adobe's document-creation and reading software, which has been around for more than a decade. Chances are you already have dozens of Acrobat documents on your PC. (All Acrobat files end with a .pdf suffix. PDF stands for Portable Document Format.) Many software companies no longer offer printed manuals, but provide manuals in PDF format instead. We often end up burning through toner cartridges trying to print them out. (Yes, it's a conspiracy.)

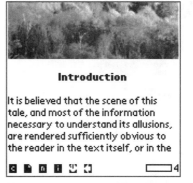

Figure 16.30 In Palm Reader, navigation menus appear at the bottom of the screen. The battery icon tells you how much juice is left in your Pocket PC's battery. The bar in the lower right shows you what page you're on.

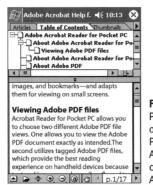

Figure 16.31 The first PDF file you should open on your Pocket PC is the Adobe Acrobat Help file that comes with Adobe Acrobat Reader.

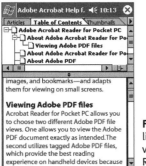

Figure 16.32 Click the link to download a version of Palm Reader that works on your Pocket PC.

Figure 16.33 Download a Pocket PC version of Adobe Acrobat Reader.

Acrobat Reader is available for all the major computing platforms, including Microsoft Windows, Mac OS, Linux, Palm OS, and Pocket PC. The same PDF files can be read on any and all of these platforms. The Pocket PC is a great way to refer to Acrobat files when you're away from your home or office (**Figure 16.31**).

To install Palm Reader:

1. Connect your Pocket PC to your computer.

2. Connect your computer to the Internet.

3. In Internet Explorer on your computer, go to www.palmdigitalmedia.com.

4. At the Palm Digital Media Web site, click the link that promotes the free reader for all platforms (**Figure 16.32**).

5. Download the Reader install program for the Pocket PC. (You may have to unzip it.)

6. Run the installer on your computer. It will copy the correct files to the Pocket PC.

✔ Tips

- eBooks in the Palm Reader format have a .pdb suffix.

- You can download free and premium eBooks online at www.palmdigitalmedia.com.

- See Appendix A for other sites that offer eBooks.

To install Acrobat Reader:

1. Connect your Pocket PC to your computer.

2. Connect your computer to the Internet.

3. In Internet Explorer on your computer, go to http://www.adobe.com/products/acrobat/readermain.html.

4. Click on the link that promotes the free reader for the Pocket PC (**Figure 16.33**).

continues on next page

5. Download the Reader install program for the Pocket PC (you may have to unzip it).

6. Run the installer on your PC. It will copy the correct files to the Pocket PC.

✔ Tips

■ Acrobat Reader for the Pocket PC may be on the CD-ROM that came with your device (see Chapter 4 for how to install it).

■ Acrobat Reader for the Pocket PC has a feature that lets you reflow documents so that they're easier to read on small screens.

■ Repligo is another electronic document/creation system that gives Adobe Acrobat a run for its money. Check out www.cerience.com for more. Repligo is faster than Acrobat and much cheaper than the full-version Adobe document creation tools. It's ideal for taking Web pages and other documents with you.

Listening to Audio Books

The audio book is a fabulous invention. In the car, on the treadmill, or in your home, a well-performed eBook is a wonderful way to pass the time. Now, your Pocket PC can read you stories, with the help of Audible, which you'll find on your companion CD-ROM.

Install Audible and synchronize with your Pocket PC. Then visit www.audible.com for a large selection of downloadable audio books and radio shows. These premium books are nothing to sneeze at.

Audible also offers free software for syncing and playing audio books on the Pocket PC, and you can even play Audible books from within Microsoft Reader.

Audible's books are sold individually, usually for around $15 to $30. You can also subscribe to radio shows. You can use Audible every day to download NPR's "All Things Considered" and sync it to your Pocket PC—then enjoy the show with headphones as you're driving, eating lunch, or walking down the street.

It's incredibly useful to be able to pause (or rewind) a radio show and come back to it later—you don't have to rush home to catch that Terry Gross interview. And if you've forgotten what a pleasure it is to have books read out loud to you, give an audio book a try. Don't underestimate the value of listening to cheesy spy novels or celebrity memoirs while cleaning house or going for a run.

READING WITH PALM READER AND ACROBAT

MORE PROGRAMS

Figure A.1 Your device comes with two games already loaded.

Although the Pocket PC feels a lot like a finished product, if you're willing to put in a little time, attention, and in most cases money, it becomes more of a platform, like the PC itself. You probably wouldn't be satisfied with the default programs that come with Windows XP, and the same becomes true for the Pocket PC when you sample some of the thousands of excellent third-party programs available for it on the Web. This appendix is meant to give you just a taste of what's out there.

Let's start with two programs that are already on your device, but haven't been mentioned much so far: Jawbreaker and Solitaire. Both are available in the Games subfolder of Programs by tapping Start > Programs > Games and tapping an icon (**Figure A.1**).

Jawbreaker

"Easy to learn, difficult to master" is how Microsoft describes it, and we agree. The object of this game is to score the most points by linking up as many horizontally and/or vertically connected, same-colored balls as possible before "popping" them and causing all the balls above them to drop down. The game is over when you can't link any more balls (likely) or all the balls are gone (unlikely).

When you first start the game, the screen is filled with an 11×12 grid of green, blue, red, purple, and white balls that do indeed look like Jawbreakers, those big hard candy gumballs that nearly did break many a jawbone in our youthful years (**Figure A.2**).

Tap any ball that is directly next to another ball of its color (above it or beside it—diagonal doesn't count) to display in a score box the number of points the combination would be worth if you popped it (**Figure A.3**).

If you want those points, and the disappearance of the selected balls will serve your strategic interests, tap anywhere in the score box to complete the move.

If you're not satisfied with that many points, "tap off"—tap anywhere besides the score box—to remove the score balloon. Each successively large combination of balls is worth increasingly more. So, 2 balls = 2 points, 3 balls = 6 points, 4 balls = 12 points, 5 balls = 20 points, and so on. The most we've been able to pop in a single blow was 17 balls for 272 points. Man, does it feel good to pop a bunch at once (**Figure A.4**). When a column becomes empty, the column to its left shifts right—opening up new, last-minute scoring opportunities, if you last that long.

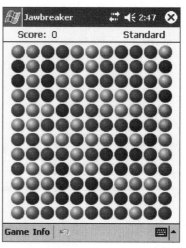

Figure A.2 A screenful of Jawbreakers is ready to go. Unlike as shown here, they really are colorful.

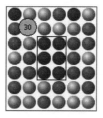

Figure A.3 Thirty points isn't too shabby, but also consider what will happen when the balls vanish.

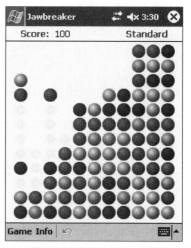

Figure A.4 Popping 13 balls at once for 156 points.

✔ Tips

- When you screw up, tap the Undo icon.

- Pick a color that looks promising—try to find which color has a ball in every column. Then try to pop smaller combinations of different-colored balls underneath your target color in such a way that you end up aligning as many balls of your target color as possible.

- Check out the Options screen in the Game menu, where you can, among other things, change from Standard game style to the more complex styles Continuous (the balls just keep coming), Shifter (balls atop columns shift right whenever there is room), and Megashift (balls loop back from left of the screen toward the end).

- Take a peek at Info > Statistics to see how many games you've played, your high score, and your average score.

JAWBREAKER

Finding more games

There are literally thousands of games for the Pocket PC, ranging from free to pricey. You'll find a bewildering array of action, adventure, board, card, casino, game packs, puzzles, sports, trivia, and word games by going to www.handango.com, clicking the Pocket PC link in the left side panel, and clicking Games in the software category list. At the time of this writing, there were 2225 games at this site ready to download.

Solitaire

If you've spent any time goofing around in Windows when you should have been working, you already know how to play a computerized version of this classic card game (**Figure A.5**).

We don't have time to explain the actual game here, but here are some quick tips if you've yet to play computer Solitaire.

✔ Tips

- When you screw up, tap the Undo icon.

- Using your stylus, drag cards where you want them to go, whether on the seven front stacks or the four back ones.

- Drag a king to a blank space when one opens up.

- Instead of dragging, double-tap an ace to send it automatically to its stack up top, and double-tap any top card showing in the deck to send it to its correct location in the back stacks.

- Tap the face-down deck to draw from it. In Tools > Options you can choose between drawing every third card or cheat and lay them down one at a time (**Figure A.6**).

- Choose from six different card backs (see Figure A.6).

- If the clock makes you nervous, you can turn it off in Options.

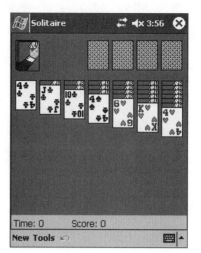

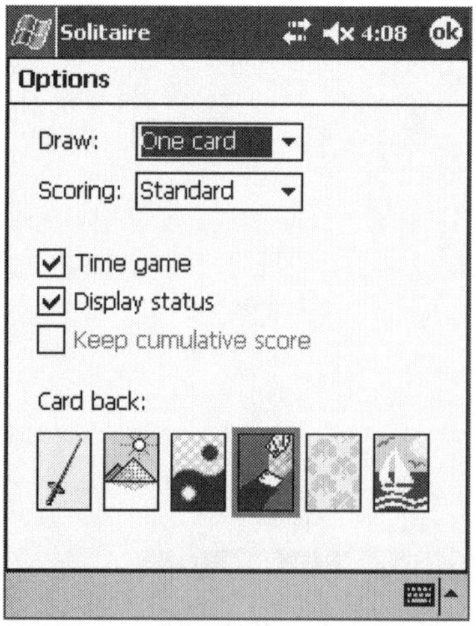

Figure A.5 A brand new Solitaire game, ready to start spending time you probably don't have.

Figure A.6 If you get stuck, you can always draw every card one at a time in the deck. Of course, you'll know in your heart what you have done, and it's still all too easy to lose.

Third-Party Programs

We mention quite a few of these in this book. What we're talking about are not (necessarily) programs produced by the Dixiecrats, the Anti-Masons, or even the Libertarians. These are programs created for the Pocket PC platform by companies which are neither Microsoft nor your device's manufacturer. You probably have a few third-party programs on your computer. Popular Windows software developers include such big and well-known names as Adobe, Macromedia, and Norton, as well as lesser known, smaller companies, and even individuals who make a living by selling and maintaining perhaps a single piece of software.

Often, the best way for software creators to get their wares out into the world is to offer them as *shareware* downloadable from the Web. A shareware program might be a demo, meaning that it is free to try, but will stop working after a certain number of days or weeks. If you like it, you can go get the real version. Some shareware comes partially useable, and if you like what you're using you can pay to obtain a "key" that unlocks its full potential. Still other programs are sustained entirely via the honor system— you download and use the full version, and send the program's author the suggested amount of money only if you choose to.

In this section, we aim to give you a taste of just a few of the programs that are out there for you to download and try on your Pocket PC. This is a mere sampling, of course, and new programs appear all the time.

Where to look for programs to download

Start with the following three sites. Software authors want their programs to reach as large a potential audience as possible. Their distribution will almost always include at least one of the following popular sites.

www.handango.com

www.pocketgear.com

www.pocketpc.com

THIRD-PARTY PROGRAMS

Utilities

These are programs that enhance or add some basic function to the Pocket PC. Generally, they give you extra information about something your device is doing or make something possible that wasn't possible before.

Battery Pack 2004

www.omegaone.com/PocketPC/
BatteryPack.html

Price: $14.99

The Pocket PC doesn't offer much in the way of monitoring exactly how your battery and memory are doing. Battery Pack (**Figure A.7**) does this elaborately and well, plus it adds several other features to your device, such as a battery bar display, a program bar that holds up to 120 icons, powering off from a menu, one-tap access to the Today screen, and more. This useful little bugger has been the number-one selling Pocket PC program for two years running.

Figure A.7 Battery Pack lets you view all kinds of information about your Pocket PC in unprecedented detail.

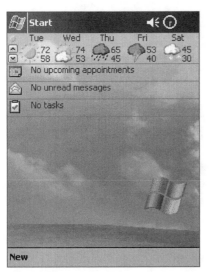

Figure A.8 Journal Bar turns your Pocket PC into something like a customized newspaper.

Figure A.9 Microsoft Voice Command lets you do various things on your device using just your voice.

Journal Bar 2

www.omegaone.com/PocketPC/
JournalBar.html

Price: $14.99

The award-winning Journal Bar gathers information online while your computer is connected. The stuff it finds includes news, weather, movie and TV listings, stock market data, sports scores, horoscopes, and your own custom links. Once it's finished gathering, it displays that information on your Pocket PC so you have it wherever you go (**Figure A.8**).

Microsoft Voice Command

www.handango.com

Price: $39.95

Now you can do more than just yell at your Pocket PC—you can talk to it. And it listens. Use your voice to look up contacts, get calendar information, play and control your music, and launch programs without tapping (**Figure A.9**). It does take some learning, but you can ask it "What can I say?" at any time to get help.

Organizers and Schedulers

These are products that do the work that Tasks and Calendar do in terms of scheduling and keeping track of what you have to do, but they do it with more style, grace, and detail.

SuperCalendar

www.scarybearsoftware.com

Price: $9.95

SuperCalendar synchronizes with Outlook, just like Calendar does, but it uses graphic indicators and icons to show how full current and upcoming days are (**Figure A.10**). Use the navigation button to move through your appointments. Coloring options let you grasp upcoming appointments at a glance. Pop-up balloon windows show attached notes and abbreviated appointments. Other features include word wrap and international calendars.

Figure A.10 SuperCalendar is a lot like Calendar—only more so, in every way.

ORGANIZERS AND SCHEDULERS

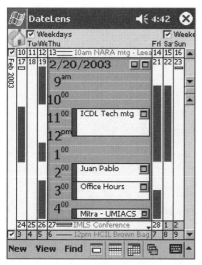

Figure A.11 DateLens allows for unusual ways of viewing your appointments.

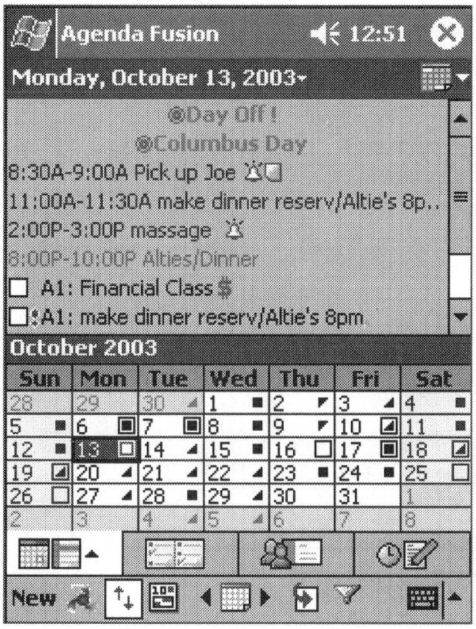

Figure A.12 Agenda Fusion does a lot, and for the price you would expect it to.

DateLens

www.windsorinterfaces.com

Price: $15

DateLens is unusual in that it employs an "organic" interface, meaning all the views are integrated at more intuitive and complex levels, offering great flexibility (**Figure A.11**). You drill down and up through greater and lesser levels of detail, using animated transitions. Synchronizes with Outlook just like Calendar.

Agenda Fusion 5

www.developerone.com

Price: $29.95

The award-winning Agenda Fusion 5 not only handles appointments and tasks, it incorporates your contacts as well into a powerful all-around time-management application (**Figure A.12**). It offers seven ways of viewing your calendar, alarm notes for anything you want, customizable views, and a simple, intuitive interface. It synchronizes with Outlook just like Tasks, Calendar, and Contacts.

ORGANIZERS AND SCHEDULERS

317

Business and Finance

Here are a few choice programs that can turn making and tracking money into having fun on your Pocket PC.

Pocket SlideShow

www.cnetx.com

Price: $19.95

This program lets you display your PowerPoint presentations right on your Pocket PC (**Figure A.13**). You can show full-screen slide shows with animations and all PowerPoint transition effects. Its features allow you to browse, rearrange, and merge your presentations directly on your device.

Pocket Quicken

www.landware.com/pocketquicken/ppc

Price: $39.95

Pocket Quicken is just that—the Pocket PC version of the financial tracking software (**Figure A.14**). It makes it easier to keep track of your financial information by allowing you to input checking, credit card, and cash transactions quickly wherever you go. Synchronizes with Quicken on your computer via ActiveSync.

Mastersoft Money

www.mastersoftmobilesolutions.com

Price: $19.95

This is the best-selling personal finance manager for Pocket PCs (**Figure A.15**). Once called PoQuick, this program sports many new features including icons, budgets, and enriched navigation. Mastersoft Money allows you to run all your finances from your device, and the company notes that getting your finances in order with this program costs about the same as "a single bounced check."

Figure A.13
Pocket SlideShow turns your Pocket PC into a PowerPoint display screen.

Figure A.14
Pocket Quicken lets you track your finances while you're on the go.

Figure A.15
MasterSoft Money is the leading Pocket PC personal finance program.

Figure A.16 Pocket IRC works something like MSN Messenger, but you can send and receive messages with everyone who uses Internet Relay Chat.

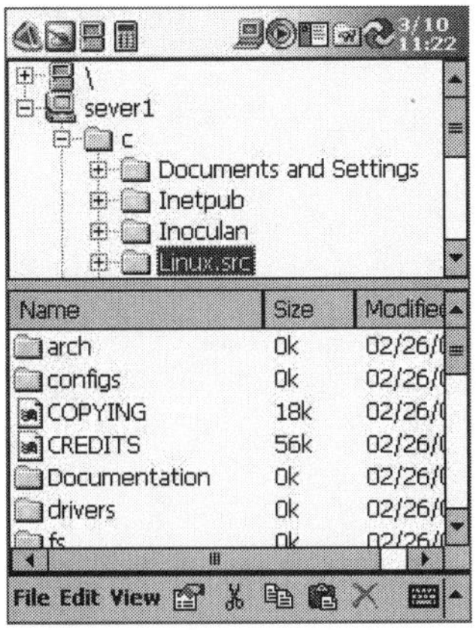

![PE FTP Explorer screen]

Figure A.17 PE FTP Explorer turns the Internet's FTP servers into a file explorer on your Pocket PC.

Communications

In Chapter 11, we mentioned three alternative email programs. Here are a few more Pocket PC applications that can enhance the online experience.

Pocket IRC

www.codenorth.ca

Price: $14.95

This is an Internet Relay Chat client for the Pocket PC, similar to the popular computer program mIRC. IRC is similar to Instant Messaging, though it's an older form of Internet chatting that swept the Internet in the '90s and is still going strong. It supports color coding, custom message formatting, pop-up menus for usernames, channel names, and URLs (**Figure A.16**).

PE FTP Explorer

www.vieka.com

Price: $14.95

FTP stands for File Transfer Protocol, still the most popular way of transferring files over the Internet. This FTP program emulates Windows FTP programs in that it looks just like a file browser while it connects to remote computers (**Figure A.17**). Upload and download files or even whole folders over the Internet with any FTP server.

COMMUNICATIONS

Pocket Phone Tools Pro

www.bvrp.com

Price: $49.90

This clever set of tools lets you send and receive faxes over your mobile phone, send and receive SMS messages to and from any mobile phone and pager, and manage your mobile Internet connection with GPRS, GSM Data, and WAP networks with predefined settings for principal mobile phone operators (**Figure A.18**). It also comes with a phonebook compatible with Contacts.

Figure A.18 Pocket Phone Tools Pro turns your Pocket PC into your cell phone's best friend.

GETTING HELP ONLINE

Luckily, you're not limited to the user manual when you have additional questions and concerns about your device. There are several Web sites whose purpose is to provide assistance and advice in operating and expanding your Pocket PC. Here, we'll take a quick look at some of the more popular ones.

PocketPC.com

www.pocketpc.com

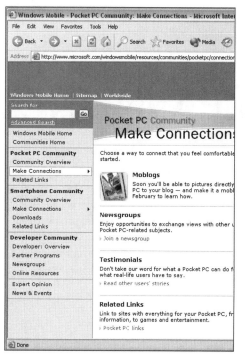

This is the official Microsoft Pocket PC site. It contains extensive information on the different models, the operating system and software, news on what's coming down the road for the devices, and links to the knowledge base and support center. This is where you'll find upgrades to the various Pocket PC programs that came with your device, plus new free downloads that enhance some capabilities. Particularly valuable are the forums and newsgroups devoted to different aspects of the Pocket PC, where users from all over weigh in with gripes, questions, and tips.

Pocket PC Thoughts

`www.pocketpcthoughts.com`

Billing itself as daily "News, Views, Rants & Raves" about the Pocket PC, this site is a treasure trove of up-to-the-minute forums, reviews, and articles crammed with practical advice, plus archives of material dating back two years. You can submit your own news and shop for hardware, software, and accessories.

Pocket PC Magazine

www.pocketpcmag.com

This is the companion Web site to the printed magazine. It offers daily updates, feature articles, a buyer's guide, discussion forums, reviews, device comparisons, new product awards, Tips of the Week (with archives), and something called the Encyclopedia of Software and Accessories, which is searchable and browsable. You can also subscribe to the print version here if you want.

Pocket PC City

www.pocketpccity.com

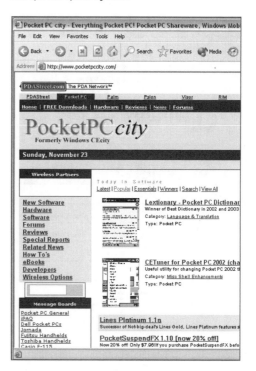

Pocket PC City is part of the larger PDA Street, a family of Web sites devoted to handheld computing. The site lists extensive software, ranked by popularity or release date. The How-To part of the site lists three or four screenfuls of links to articles or support documents that answer specific problems users are having. There are also huge forums organized by brand—the iPAQ forum alone contains more than 11,000 posts from people asking and answering questions.

CE Windows.Net Forums

`http://discuss.cewindows.net`

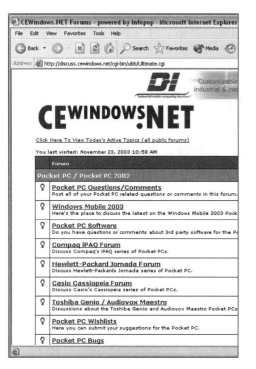

Before the Pocket PC, the old name for Microsoft's handheld device operating system was Windows CE. This site is a survivor from that era, and you can see why. It's an extensive collection of different forums, many with thousands of posts, on the Pocket PC and similar devices, plus links to many other forums on the Web, official and independent.

✔ Tip

- See your product packaging materials for addition support information. Your model's manufacturer probably offers telephone and/or email support as well as Web content (covered next).

GETTING HELP ONLINE

Individual Product Web Sites

HP, Dell, and Toshiba are the big three Pocket PC manufacturers. Each maintains a Web site for its products that offer downloads, advice, troubleshooting help, and product news.

HP iPAQ

```
http://welcome.hp.com/country/us/en/
support.html
```

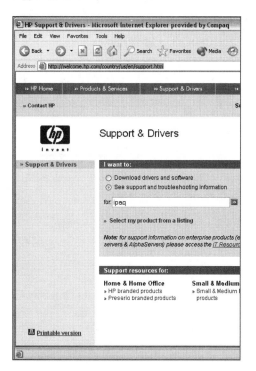

Finding Wi-Fi networks and Wi-Fi help

To find locations of Wi-Fi networks that are close to you, try **WiFinder** at www.wifinder.com. The site asks you to enter your local information, address, state, and/or ZIP code. You can choose to only look for free networks.

WiFiMaps at www.wifimaps.com is another hot-spot locator service. It will show you maps of Wi-Fi network locations when you enter the city and state you want.

For general help with Wi-Fi networking, try **Wi-Fi Planet** at www.wi-fiplanet.com. It's loaded with news, reviews, and information on various other aspects of Wi-Fi, including a tutorial section with how-to and why-to articles.

On this page, you can enter a product to search for, and the site lists what it has to offer. If you search for "iPaq" you'll get a long list of models. Click on your model, and you come to a page that summarizes all of HP's support and additional information for that model, including downloads, setup, configuration, troubleshooting, upgrades and migration, manuals, forums, and ways to contact HP support.

Dell Axim

http://support.dell.com/us/en/
solutions.asp

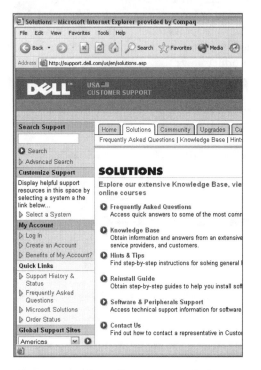

This page on the Dell site is a good place to
go to search for help on your model or browse
the extensive Knowledge Base. To use it,
click the Knowledge Base link and enter your
search criteria in the search page that opens.
Searching for "axim" and "ActiveSync," for
example, resulted in about a dozen links
from all over the Dell site, including one
from a forum.

Toshiba Pocket PC

www.csd.toshiba.com

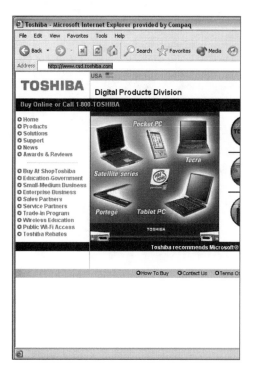

Click on "Pocket PC" to view information about the Pocket PCs Toshiba makes. Click the Support link, then click Ask IRIS to bring up an intelligent question handler—typing in "how do I ActiveSync," for example, resulted in 44 documents offered. Or click the Support link, then click Tech Support Center, and choose PDAs. You will be given a list of models to choose from. Click your model, then click Go to see a list of articles.

POCKET PC ACCESSORIES

As much as the Pocket PC is a platform for a growing body of software, it's also become a magnet for all kinds of add-on doodads and gadgets. Many of them hook into one of the types of expansion slots available on Pocket PCs, such as Secure Digital (SD), Secure Digital Input/Output (SDIO), MultiMediaCard (MMC), and CompactFlash (CF) slots. Some accessories come in the form of PCMCIA (shortened to just PC) cards, which were developed for laptops but which can be fitted to an iPAQ via an expansion pack, available from Hewlett Packard. (See Chapter 1 for more on these slots.) Check your device's documentation to see which kinds of card(s) your device can accept.

Here is a taste of just some of the stuff you can attach to your device to give it some extra capability—or just to make it more fun to use. The prices we quote are rough averages of the street prices we've seen.

Where to buy Pocket PC accessories

You can try checking with your device's manufacturer to see what accessories it offers, but your choice will be (naturally) limited to one brand and the price may be inflated.

Superstores and specialty stores offer better choices and prices. Your local computer or office superstore, such as Best Buy, Staples, OfficeMax, or CompUSA, almost certainly stocks lots of Pocket PC accessories, and it's fun to browse these places and stumble on stuff you suddenly decide you need.

Note: Be absolutely positive that your accessory will fit your exact brand and model of Pocket PC.

If you're not close to a real bricks and mortar computer supply place, or if you prefer to shop online, try searching for what you want on one of the following Web sites:

- www.amazon.com
- www.bestbuy.com
- www.buy.com
- www.cdw.com
- www.compusa.com
- www.ebay.com
- www.egghead.com
- www.newegg.com
- www.officemax.com
- www.onlinemicro.com
- www.overstock.com
- www.shoplet.com
- www.staples.com

Bluetooth cards

Price: $50 to $75

If your device doesn't have Bluetooth built in, not to worry. A Bluetooth card, such as those made by Ambicom or Socket Communications, occupy your CF or SDIO slot and make your Pocket PC Bluetooth-ready.

Bluetooth USB adapters

Price: $40 to $75

A Bluetooth adapter—or *dongle*—is something for your computer, not your Pocket PC. With a dongle, you can use your Bluetooth-enabled Pocket PC to access the Internet via your Bluetooth-enabled computer—and ActiveSync and transfer files. Simply plug the dongle into a USB port on your machine and install the software. Belkin, IoGear, Ambicom, Hawking, and Orange Micro all manufacture Bluetooth USB adapters.

Cameras

Price: $50 to $75

A snap-on camera for Pocket PCs, such as the Veo Photo Traveler, is a digital camera on a stick—you plug the stick into your device's CF or SDIO slot, and poof, you can take digital pictures with your Pocket PC. Note that photos from an add-on camera like this are usually limited to 640×480 pixels, or 1.3 megapixels in a best-case scenario, and the quality is not nearly as good as a full-blown digital camera's.

Cases

Price: $15 to $40

There is a universe of fancy leather and plastic cases out there to protect your Pocket PC. Your device likely came with a case, but you can bet the case that came with it compares poorly to some of the third-party designs by companies such as Vaja, Sena, Fellowes, Belkin, Targus, and Nite Ize. These cases range from wallet-style elegance to zippered belted packs to adjustable stand-up holster cases.

GPS navigators

Price: $125 to $300

The Global Positioning Satellite (GPS) system can calculate to frightening detail where you are on the surface of the planet, and can also tell you how to get to almost any destination from where you are. With a GPS navigator—for example, the Pharos Pocket GPS Navigator—it becomes impossible to get lost. You stick it into one of your slots (or use a Bluetooth version) and then install the accompanying software. Bring your GPS-enabled Pocket PC with you in your car, activate the navigation program, and start driving. Automated voice-prompts instruct you when and where to turn to get to your destination or point of interest. If you make a wrong turn and go "off route," the automated voice will issue a warning. Push the "Action" button on your Pocket PC, and the system will reroute you to your destination from your current position. Popular GPS solutions include options from Pharos (www.pharosgps.com), Navtech (www.navtech.com), and TomTom (www.tomtom.com).

Keyboards

Price: $70 to $100

A keyboard for your Pocket PC can be handy when you have to enter a lot of information and you have a place to set it up. As we've mentioned, the device's own text-entry methods, while impressive, still leave something to be desired. A real keyboard can be that something.

The Targus Universal Wireless PDA Keyboard uses the Pocket PC's infrared beaming port to communicate with the device, and it folds up for easy travel. The Compaq Portable Keyboard for the iPAQ also folds up but uses the communication port—you just snap your iPAQ down into it like a cradle and start typing. Think Outside (www.thinkoutside.com), selling under the Fellowes brand, has full-size keyboards that fold up, making a good compromise between keyboard typing speed and portability.

Memory cards

Price: $20 to $200

Memory cards come in SD, CF, and MMC (MultiMediaCard) card formats. MMC cards will fit in SD slots. The cheapest SD cards on the market right now hold 32MB of data, going up to 512MB (and 1GB versions should be available by the time you read this). The most expensive CF card now shipping can hold 6GB, putting your Pocket PC within striking range of a modest laptop in terms of available storage for programs, media, documents, and data.

continues on next page

In most cases, you simply stick the card in the slot, and boom, the device recognizes the card and makes it available to any program offering a storage card saving option (you may have do a soft reset—press the end of the stylus into the device's tiny reset hole). You can explore the card in File Explorer by tapping the Storage Card icon. Storage cards are especially great for storing music and video. Amazon.com will carry almost every type of Flash-based memory you could ever want.

Modems

Price: $50 to $100

Instead of a wireless card, you can stick with a good ol' modem for your Pocket PC. These are typically CF cards with an RJ-11 analog phone connector. Plug the card into your device and plug your phone cord into the connector, just like a regular modem. Then tap the Connectivity icon to set it up. Pharos (www.pharosgps.com) offers options in this category.

Screen protectors

Price: $20 a pack

Screen protectors are clear, thin sheets of plastic that you place over your screen to shield it from scratches, reduce glare, and improve handwriting recognition. Screen protectors are highly recommended as the best way to prolong the life of your screen. Boxwave (www.boxwave.com) has screen protectors that support a variety of PDAs.

Stylii

Price: $3 to $10

It's a good idea to have an extra stylus or two around for that day when—not if—you lose yours. You can choose from bright "fun" colors or get one that's also a real pen and a pencil or one with a penlight that can extend your device's battery by allowing you to turn the screen brightness way down. A great place to start looking is www.pdapanache.com.

Sync charger cables

Price: $20

A sync charger cable is an all-in-one cable that takes the place of your cradle and AC adapter for charging and synchronizing. Some even come with cigarette lighter adapters so you can charge your Pocket PC in the car! Boxwave (www.boxwave.com) offers a variety of sync 'n' charge cable and power solutions.

Wi-Fi cards

Price: $50 to $150

There are wireless networking cards for SD and CF slots available that can give your device access to the Internet through Wi-Fi networks and hot spots (see Chapter 10 for more). More practical, perhaps, if you have an iPAQ and a laptop, is to get a wireless PC card and an expansion pack that accepts PC cards. That way, you can use it to get wireless access on your laptop *or* your Pocket PC (just plug it into whichever machine you want to access the Internet with). Some CF Wi-Fi cards even include built-in memory. Sandisk (www.sandisk.com) and Socket Communications (www.socketcom.com) are good places to start looking.

Battery life extension

Check with your manufacturer to see whether
you can upgrade to better batteries or replace
worn out ones—or just buy an extra set for
emergencies. Also check out souped-up,
third-party chargers, such as the iGo
(www.igo.com) or one from Data-Nation
(www.data-nation.com).

INDEX

INDEX